This book belongs to

Jean Harding

HERBS for USE
and for
DELIGHT

HERBS for USE and for DELIGHT

An Anthology from *The Herbarist*

A Publication of

The Herb Society of America

SELECTED AND WITH AN INTRODUCTION

by Daniel J. Foley

Dover Publications, Inc., New York

Published in Canada by General Publishing Company, Ltd., 30 Lesmill Road, Don Mills, Toronto,
Ontario.
Published in the United Kingdom by Constable
and Company, Ltd., 10 Orange Street, London WC 2.

This Dover edition, first published in 1974, contains sixty-one selections from *The Herbarist,* A
publication of The Herb Society of America, published for the first time in collected form. The Introduction has been written by Daniel J. Foley especially for this edition.

International Standard Book Number: 0-486-23104-6
Library of Congress Catalog Card Number: 74-80287

Manufactured in the United States of America
Dover Publications, Inc.
180 Varick Street
New York, N. Y. 10014

Introduction

Herbs and the folklore surrounding them have been linked with mankind for millennia. Anthropologists, archaeologists and inquisitive amateur gardeners are still uncovering evidence of culinary and medicinal usage of herbs long before the time of Hippocrates and Theophrastus. Roots, stems, leaves, fruits, flowers and their fragrances were cherished for the specific virtues which they contained. A fresco painted in 1500 B.C. on the wall of a rest house near Knossos in Crete indicates that at an early date man also recognized the aesthetic appeal of these plants. One of the herbs depicted was a species of marjoram called the Dittany of Crete, which Vergil describes as the herb Venus used to heal the wounded Aeneas.

The virtues of herbs and their varied uses have been recorded since the days of the Greeks and the Romans, often in minute detail. Ancient and medieval manuscripts, many of which have been translated and published in recent years, are of more than antiquarian interest. Some of the information they contain is very curious; some is still pertinent. During the seventeenth, eighteenth and early nineteenth centuries, an impressive number of herbals, books of husbandry and treatises on gardening appeared. For those of little learning, there were books of "simples" replete with ancient and contemporary remedies for every conceivable ailment as well as hints on flavoring and preserving food, the making of dyes for clothing and a plethora of household hints. Well-being depended on a knowledge of herb lore.

A patch of herbs was grown near every abode, however small or wretched. At the manor house, the castle and the monastery, the herb garden was often elaborate, laid out in a formal manner with patterned beds, or knots, based on lacework designs. Sometimes it was a part of the kitchen garden. (Changing trends in the art of landscape gardening, particularly in the eighteenth century, had little or no effect on the traditional herb garden.) Housewives used its products to make sweet washing waters, perfumes, salves, ointments and potpourris. A small building on the grounds or a room in the house served as a still-room and the treasured still-room book contained the required recipes and formulas, many of which were regarded as family secrets. One recipe for a "sweet water" required that 33 herbs be steeped in white wine and brandy and then distilled. Such was the importance of herbs in bygone days.

With the expansion of the industrial revolution and the rise of modern medicine, the role of the housewife—mistress of herb lore—changed greatly. The evolution was comparatively slow at the beginning, but it gathered momentum as factories were built and cities and towns lured workers from rural areas. The cook stove gradually superseded the fireplace; the dye-pot was, for the most part, discarded. Grocers and spice dealers sold herbs, both fresh and dried, and gradually the herb patch in the dooryard and the knot garden became less important, except in remote rural communities where customs and folklore were deeply rooted. By the close of the Victorian era, herb lore had little meaning for the rising generation. In much of urban Europe and America, it became for many a body of knowledge as curious and remote as the antiquities of Egypt.

On a summer day in 1933, seven New England ladies met in the town of Wenham, Massachusetts and formed the Herb Society of America. They defined an herb as "a plant which may be used for physic, flavor or fragrance," and chose as a motto a phrase from the writings of John Parkinson, seventeenth-century herbalist, "For Use and for Delight." They were motivated by the belief that "much of the great volume of the world's knowledge about useful plants had been forgotten by the public and herbs had sunk to the level of a hobby among a few growers of old-time gardens. Consequently, one of the most intensely practical and rewarding branches of horticulture was being neglected, and its great potentialtities for pleasure and profit being missed."

This was a unique group of women, each with a special talent, but sharing a common interest. Mrs. Edward B. Cole, know affectionately in her home town of Wenham as "Granny Cole," had sparked the local historical society with her enthusiasm and directed the building of the Wenham Museum, which soon became famous for its doll collections, its special exhibits and its stimulating lectures. Mrs. Cole was a keen student of ethnology with an encyclopedic view of her subject that was colored not only by her scientific curiosity but also by her eagerness to teach and to share what she knew. Mrs. Albert C. Burrage, a woman of many talents, combined her taste and skill in the arts with her ability to organize and to publicize the work of the new Society. Mrs. Laurance A. Brown and Mrs. Edward L. Mitchell knew how to convey ideas and became keepers of records. Mrs. George C. Bratenahl, wife of the Dean of Washington Cathedral, possessed the talents of both artist and craftsman. Her crowning achievement was the establishment of the first nationally known American herb farm of the twentieth century at Bethesda, Maryland. Mrs. Ferris Greenslet, by nature a scholar and a collector, was an inveterate researcher who brought to light the extensive literature of herb lore and its practical application to everyday life. For Mrs. Charles L. Norton, the challenge was in the field of experimentation. She built a still-room and worked extensively in making herb dyes and other herbal by-products.

Mrs. Cole and her colleagues were able to realize their dream of revitalizing herb studies by establishing an herb garden, the first of many that the Society was to design and plant. From the grounds of the Wenham Museum, originally the home and wort-yard of Pastor Garrish in 1685, there sprouted, in a patch of herbs, a new field of adventure for modern gardeners and housewives that has resulted in hundreds of thousands of herb gardens and more than a hundred books and brochures on herb lore.

The Society has never had a drive for membership nor been interested in mere numbers, and has refused to allow itself to be used by those whose interest is mainly social and what we may call sentimental. The first group was slowly enlarged, by invitation, to include those seriously interested in the horticultural, botanical or utilitarian phases of herb growing. In its bylaws, it gauges the eligibility of a member according to results shown in work or research, or creditable accomplishment in the growing and use of herbs. This embraces a surprising variety of activities, as people have different slants on the subject. Some take a literary approach, the study of old herbals, the making of bibliographies and compilations; others, more practically inclined, undertake experiments with perfumes, cordials, dye-plants; still others become involved in the fundamental job of raising herbs out of the soil, developing new strains, collecting varieties, while keeping records on the action of fertilizers and comparing notes with other growers. The Society as such does not engage in commerce, although it is definitely interested in the possibilities of private and commercial herb growing as a national resource.

Dedicated amateurs who pursue a hobby with a purpose usually leave no stone unturned in their search for information. Their enthusiasm is only exceeded by their thoroughness as research becomes a consuming passion. This was essentially the pattern followed by the ladies who formed The Herb Society of America. They sought information here and abroad and tapped the resources of leading botanists and plantsmen. They collected seed and cuttings, raised and disseminated plants, planned and planted herb gardens and informed the general public through lectures and the publication of bulletins. No secrets were kept on the how and why of growing and using herbs; all knowledge and experience was shared. Within two years of the Society's founding, *The Herbarist,* an annual publication, was launched and it has become widely known for its first-rate research. More bulletins and pamphlets followed and still continue to be published by the Society (300 Massachusetts Avenue, Boston, Massachusetts 02115), which also mounts educational exhibits and displays at flower shows, aids professional research and has established a scholarship fund. All these activities have given The Herb Society of America and its publications a unique position in the gardeners' world.

Having carefully reread thirty-seven annual issues of *The Herbarist* containing more than 2,000 pages, it has been an exciting challenge to select the articles which appear in this anthology. I have endeavored to present a generous sampling of articles—many containing detailed information not usually found in popular books on the subject—which relate herb lore as well as the delights and pleasures of growing, using and enjoying the aromatic, culinary and medicinal herbs of our green world.

DANIEL J. FOLEY

Salem, Massachusetts
March, 1974

Contents

BURNET—A PENCIL DRAWING
    Louise Mansfield. (No. 3, 1937; p. 25)   2

NATURE'S BAGS OF SCENT
    Edgar Anderson. (No. 1, 1935; pp. 5, 6)   3

THE PRONUNCIATION OF *HERB*
    John S. Kenyon. (No. 19, 1953; pp. 7, 8)   5

THE MODERN HERB
    J. E. Connell. (No. 36, 1970; pp. 49–52)   7

ANGELICA ARCHANGELICA

      Mrs. Arthur B, Baer. (No. 9, 1943; pp. 13–17)   11

ANGELICA—AN ETCHING

      Caroline Weir Ely. (No. 9, 1943; p. 12)   12

ARTEMISIAS

      Mrs. Jay Clark, Jr. (No. 5, 1939; pp. 36–43)   17

SEVEN BASILS

      Helen Noyes Webster. (No. 2, 1936; pp. 34–41)   25

CHAMOMILE

      Albert F. Hill. (No. 8, 1942; pp. 8–16)   34

THOSE HERBS CALLED CHERVILS

      Helen Noyes Webster. (No. 13, 1947; pp. 5–12)   42

COMFREY—THE CINDERELLA OF PLANTS

      Maria Wilkes. (No. 33, 1967; pp. 47–50)   50

ORIGANUM DICTAMNUS L—AN ORIGINAL ETCHING

      Caroline Weir Ely. (No. 3, 1937; p. 2)   54

"RIGHTE DITTANY"

      Harriet Addams Brown. (No. 1, 1935; pp: 23–27)   55

DITTANY REDIVIVUS
> Anne Burrage. No. 2, 1936; pp. 58–60)   60

ON FENNEL—ONLY SLIGHTLY BOTANICAL
> Jessica Wood. (No. 23, 1957; pp. 31–34)   63

ALCHEMILLA—LADY'S MANTLE
> Hester M. Crawford. (No. 27, 1961; pp. 4–6)   67

LAVENDER—ORIGINAL ETCHING
> Caroline Weir Ely. (No. 6, 1940; p. 4)   70

IN QUEST OF LAVENDERS
> Edna K. Neugebauer. (No. 16, 1950; pp. 23–27)   71

LEMON VERBENA
> Mary Elizabeth Fitz-Gerald. (No. 8, 1942; pp. 36, 37)   76

LOVAGE
> (No. 10, 1944; pp. 14–16)   78

NOTES ON THE MARJORAMS
> Helen Noyes Webster. (No. 14, 1948; pp. 19–22)   81

HERB OF HONOR
> Helen S. Stephens. (No. 32, 1966; pp. 44, 45)   85

A STUDY OF MINTS

Western Pennsylvania Unit. (No. 29, 1963; pp. 65–67) 87

MINTS AND MICROSCOPES

Edgar Anderson. (No. 4, 1938; pp. 15, 16) 90

SOME COMMON MINTS AND THEIR HYBRIDS

Mable L. Ruttle. (No. 4, 1938; pp. 17–29) 92

CALENDULA OFFICINALIS

Marjorie Gibbon. (No. 7, 1941; pp. 5, 6) 105

POT MARIGOLD—CALENDULA OFFICINALIS

Caroline Weir Ely. (No. 7, 1941; p. 4) 106

THE WAY OF THE POET'S MARIGOLD

Dorothy Bovee Jones. (No. 28, 1962; pp. 53–59) 108

ROSEMARY—THE HERB OF REMEMBRANCE

Dorothy Bovee Jones. (No. 27, 1961; pp. 10–19) 115

VARIETY IN ROSEMARY

Edna K. Neugebauer. (No. 34, 1968; pp. 43–46) 125

IN PRAISE OF SAGE
Marjorie Warvelle Baer. (No. 30, 1964; pp. 34–38) 129

NOTES ON A FEW SAVORIES
Helen M. Fox. (No. 18, 1952; pp. 43–46) 134

THE TARRAGONS, CULTIVATED AND WILD
Edgar Anderson. (No. 2, 1936; pp. 9–11) 138

THYMUS
Helen S. Stephens. (No. 22, 1956; pp. 16–21) 141

THE THYMES
Elaine Sameth. (No. 37, 1971; pp. 47–50) 147

HERB GARDENS: 1960 NOTES ON DESIGNS
Fletcher Steele. (No. 26, 1960; pp. 14–18) 151

COLOR IN THE HERB GARDEN
Helen M. Fox. (No. 25, 1959; pp. 34–38) 156

HERBS IN THE ROCK GARDEN
Stephen F. Hamblin. (No. 24, 1958; pp. 40–44) 161

HERBS IN KNOTS AND LACES
Helen M. Fox. (No. 19, 1953; pp. 9–12)   **166**

HERB SYMBIOSIS—COMPANION PLANTS
Helen Philbrick. (No. 35, 1969; pp. 58–66)   **170**

THE SIGNIFICANCE OF BOTANICAL PESTICIDES
Steve Hart. (No. 37, 1971; pp. 51–55)   **179**

HERBS OF THE MEDITERRANEAN
Mary Wellman. (No. 30, 1964; pp. 21–24)   **184**

A LIST FOR AN OLD ENGLISH WORT GARDEN
Ellen Greenslet. (No. 1, 1935; pp. 16–22)   **187**

SOME HERBS FROM THE OLD WORLD
AND THE NEW
Alice T. Whitney. (No. 1, 1935; pp. 32–45)   **194**

THE TUSSIE MUSSIE, AN HERBAL BOUQUET
Edna K. Neugebauer. (No. 33, 1967;
pp. 67, 68)   **208**

POT-POURRI ALBUM
Mary E. Baer. (No. 20, 1954; pp. 20–26)   **210**

TASTES IN TEA

Edna Cashmore. (No. 20, 1954; pp. 27–35)   **217**

SOME NOTES UPON THE USE OF HERBS IN NORWEGIAN HOUSEHOLDS

Sigrid Undset. (No. 11, 1945; pp. 9–14)   **226**

DYEING WITH HERBS

Frances T. Norton. (No. 2, 1936; pp. 29–32)   **232**

INDIGO, THE TRUE BLUE

Martha Genung Stearns. (No. 5, 1939; pp. 6–12)   **236**

EARLY AMERICAN DYEING

E. McD. Schetky. (No. 21, 1955; pp. 16–24)   **243**

IN PRAISE OF HERBALS

Elizabeth Remsen Van Brunt. (No. 37, 1971; pp. 1–10)   **252**

FLOWERS AND PERFUME

Grace Chess Robinson. (No. 32, 1966; pp. 8–19)   **262**

THE 17TH CENTURY STILL ROOM

Adeline P. Cole. (No. 1, 1935; pp. 14, 15)   **274**

HERBS FOR MY LADY'S TOILET

      Mrs. A. L. P. Dennis. (No. 2, 1936; pp. 27, 28)   276

"RESEMBLING A CITRON PILL"

      Kay Betts. (No. 19, 1953; pp. 47–50)   278

SCENTED GERANIUMS

      Helen Van Pelt Wilson. (No. 13, 1947;
           pp. 17–27)   282

OUR OLDEST GARDEN ROSES

      Edwin DeT. Bechtel. (No. 16, 1950; pp. 6–17)   293

SPICE CARAVANS

      Foster Stearns. (No. 14, 1948; pp. 23–29)   305

SHIEN—SOME NOTEWORTHY EDIBLE HERBS
           OF CHINA

      Shiu-ying Hu. (No. 14, 1948; pp. 30–36)   312

WREATHS AND GARLANDS

      Theresa Cunningham. (No. 7, 1941; pp. 22–27)   319

HERBS for USE
and for
DELIGHT

BURNET — A PENCIL DRAWING BY LOUISE MANSFIELD
Owned by The Herb Society of America.

NATURE'S BAGS OF SCENT

EDGAR ANDERSON

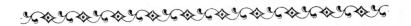

A SIMPLE hand lens, a folding pocket hand lens of glass and nickel, is a window into another world in which the obscure details of our naked-eye existence become magnified until they reveal their significance, variety and charm. Through a hand lens the felty surface of a mullen leaf becomes a silver forest of fantastic interlocking branches; the center of a violet is seen as an ornamented throne draped with richly-patterned velvet textiles of purple, white and gold. To the herbarist this charming world is more than a delight to the senses; it is of some practical importance in the production of scent and savor. Some of the aromatic substances to which our herbs owe their usefulness are carried deep inside the plant, but many are borne either on the surface or are even held above it in curious little globes or saucers. These scent-producing organs are known to botanists as "glands" or "glandular hairs." For the most part they take the form of smooth, secretory surfaces or of microscopic sacs.

In the rosemary the scent glands are most easily found on the green calyx just below the flower. They are thickly sprinkled over the surface, and through a hand lens shine like opalescent pearls against a background of green velvet. In wormseed the curious little glands which carry the essential principle of the herb are found deep within the flower itself. Each gland looks like a little foot attached at the ankle. The whole gland is quite transparent and within it can be seen a floating drop of a clear, golden oil. In hops the bitter principle is produced in fantastic, trumpet-shaped glands borne near the flower, particularly on the contorted, leaf-like structures which botanists have named "bractioles." When the hop flowers first

3

open the trumpets are empty, though they glisten brightly within. As the flowers mature the golden trumpets fill with the golden liquid, which darkens and hardens as it dries. When the hops are finally ready to be harvested, the trumpets have become cornucopias piled with a golden-brown exudate. They snap off from the plant at a brush of the hand; each one, to the naked eye, is a golden-brown grain of dust. It is hundreds of millions of these little trumpets which form the golden-brown "hop-meal" known to brewers and hop merchants.

If you are becoming an herbarist do buy a simple hand lens. One which magnifies eight to ten times is quite strong enough. Through it you will find a whole new, interesting world awaiting you. Through it you can amass for yourself another sort of herb lore. You will bring to light hidden beauties in the most humble garden herbs and understand the production of scent and savor with the precision of a master herbarist.

ARNOLD ARBORETUM

February 1935

THE PRONUNCIATION OF *HERB*

By JOHN S. KENYON

THE word *herb* belongs to a group of words, of which familiar examples may conveniently be considered in three groups: (1) heir, honest, honor, hour; (2) herb, homage, humble, humor, hostler, Humphrey; (3) host, heretic, horrible, hospital, hostel, hotel, human, humane, and some other words spelt with initial *h*. These words differ from all native English words beginning with *h* in that they were borrowed into English from Old French, and into Old French from popular, spoken Latin. In both popular Latin and Old French none of these words had any *h*-sound, though when written they often, though not always, continued to be spelt with a letter *h* by influence of ancient classic Latin, in which the *h* had been pronounced. Consequently, when these words were learned orally by English speakers, none of them had any *h*-sound.

Educated English people, however, in order to avoid the English dialectal tendency to "drop their *h*'s" in all native English words, and quite unaware of the history of these French words, were inclined to lean over backwards and so pronounce the *h* of the spelling, and thus by "spelling-pronunciation" most of these French words came to be pronounced in English with an initial *h*-sound. But, as usual in such language developments, they did not do a complete job of it. It was, however, so far carried out that the *h*-sound was added to the words of the third group in which the *h* was spelt (host, human, horrible, etc.) so that these words now all begin with the *h*-sound in standard usage. In two words of the same French origin, however, *able* (Old French hable, able) and *arbor,* "bower" (Old French herber, erber), in which English had lost the *h* spelling, there was no temptation to sound it, and so they have never gained the *h*-sound.

But in the second group of words (herb, humble, etc.) the addition of the *h*-sound was not completed, so that many cultivated speakers pronounced some words of the second group without the *h*-sound,

5

and others pronounced the same words with an *h*-sound. It is a matter of curious interest that the present hesitation by some speakers to pronounce *humble* without the *h*-sound probably goes back to Dickens's despicable character in "David Copperfield," Uriah Heep, who was always "so very 'umble." Though Dickens was ignorant of the history of the word, he succeeded, as he doubtless intended, in giving the pronunciation *'umble* a black eye with Englishmen, always fearful of wrongly dropping their *h*'s.

In the first group (heir, honest, honor, hour) popular practice has completely stood its ground in refusing to add an *h*-sound, so that today no cultivated speaker would venture to add an *h*-sound to these words, though the letter *h* is religiously written and printed in them, and, indeed, is useful in two of them.

The popular idea that words like *heir, honest, honor, hour* have lost their *h*-sound is the exact reverse of the fact: they have lost nothing, but have only failed to *gain* an *h*-sound which they never had in English; while words like *host, heretic, hospital, human,* etc., popularly supposed to have kept their *h*-sound, have only gained from the useless spelling with the letter *h* an *h*-sound which they originally had not had.

Now I shall be compelled to disappoint any who want to know which is "correct," *'erb* or *herb,* by declaring that all the foregoing facts in the history of these words have nothing to do with correctness. Correctness is, and always has been, solely a matter of general agreement in cultivated habits of speaking. If a very large number of cultivated speakers pronounce in a certain way, that way is "correct," even though it may have had its origin in ignorance or on a low cultural level. For such mistaken or lowly origin has started its climb to unquestioned good use in hundreds of habits of speech now impeccably emancipated from their shady past. The pronunciation of the word *herb* is a clear case of divided cultivated usage. Those who prefer *'erb* can rightly feel proud of preserving a well-founded tradition; those who prefer an unmistakably well-aspirated *Herb* can justly feel that they are at least not old-fashioned. But I hope that both parties agree in liking herbs.

The Modern Herb

J. E. CONNELL

The small herb garden was essential to its grower in pioneer days, but now, most people gather their herbs in supermarkets. Little bottles, their contents cleaned, dried, sifted, and sterilized, are lined up in rows and sell for prices the pioneers would not believe. These represent only a small proportion of our total consumption. The vast quantities of canned and frozen foods already contain carefully measured quantities of herbs. By far the greatest tonnage of our spices and herbs is used by food manufacturers.

In view of the fact that herbs will grow happily in our gardens, it is perhaps surprising that most commercial herbs in Canada and the United States are imported. The reason for this is basic economics. Our land is valuable and our costs are high. The yield of herbs per acre and the cost of production make most of them unattractive as cash crops. Less affluent nations can easily undercut our domestic costs. As a result the herbs we use resemble a United Nations roll call.

The leader in herb production no doubt is France where thyme, savory, marjoram, mint, rosemary, and others are major crops. Sage comes from Yugoslavia, Greece, Turkey, Spain or Albania. Mexico provides oregano and India, anise, cumin and fennel. One must not omit California, of course, where sweet basil thrives. In most of these countries herb growing is a local industry with many small producers. They, in turn, sell produce to agents who bring the crop to market. Marseilles is a major trading point for many herbs. In other countries, of course, such as Yugoslavia, the export of herbs is handled as a government monopoly.

Crops of herbs are field grown and sun dried. Much labour is expended in planting, harvesting and keeping the fields free of weeds. The dried material is graded and given a preliminary cleaning. Produce for export is packed in drums or, more often, compressed in bales overwrapped with burlap. Brokers in New

7

York, Montreal, San Francisco, and other cities act as prime importers and re-sell their product to commercial spice houses.

Very often herbs arriving on our shores leave much to be desired in cleanliness and quality. Further intensive processing is required by the spice merchant who must clean, sift, grind, and sterilize the product to suit his customers. A variety of equipment and techniques is necessary to purify herbs. Vibrating screens are employed to separate dust and coarse twigs. Gravity separators, which also work on a vibratory principle, will separate heavy objects, such as stones, clay lumps and extraneous metal. A fanning mill may also be used to separate leaves from heavier material. Herbs may be broken into particles or ground to a powder. Traditionally, herbs were hand rubbed through screens of the desired size. This has become very costly, and mechanical mills with coarse grinding plates are more often employed. Powdered herbs may be ground in hammer mills or grinders with fine abrasive plates. These grinders develop a considerable amount of heat from friction and the best results are obtained from mills with water cooled jackets. Normal growth conditions of herbs can give rise to bacteria populations and occasionally, insect infestation. Fumigation techniques with approved compounds are employed to eliminate these problems, usually prior to cleaning.

Prices of our herbs depend firstly on crop conditions in the producer country — the law of supply and demand — and secondly, on the amount of labour which must be expended in further processing. A crop failure can often send prices sky high. An example in 1970 is a serious failure of the celery seed crop in India. Current prices are five times their normal level.

Herbs have traditionally been used in whole or ground form for most food preparation and have required no further treatment. But in many modern foods their natural greenish colour and particulate form is no longer good enough. Meat processors shudder at the implications of green shades in their fresh sausage. Canners fear that herb particles will be regarded as contamination. Cheese makers like the flavor of caraway, but may consider the seeds unsightly. So the spice industry has been asked to provide the flavour without the substance, and this can be done. The flavour constituents of most spices and herbs are volatile. Modern engineering techniques have been adapted to separate the flavour constituents from the vegetable base.

Two processes may be involved, distillation or solvent extraction. The distillation technique is the older of the two and the more widely used. All of us are familiar with oil of cloves at the dentist's office. Similarly, herbs can be distilled to yield oils of sage or marjoram or dill. The crude herb is simply loaded into a large metal still pot, together with water. The pot is closed and heated to boiling. Steam emerges and is condensed. Along with the steam, little by little come the volatile flavour constituents. These are usually colourless and separate from the condensed steam as an oily liquid. In the trade, they are called essential oils.

In many applications the essential oils bear a very close resemblance to their parent material, and are used without further modification. It has been found, however, that some products, herbs in particular, lose character in the process. The reason for this is that not all the flavour will distill, for it is not all volatile. The grassy, woody, bitter notes are important too, and must be coaxed out of their shells by another method, solvent extraction. Herbs are steeped in a low boiling organic compound, such as hexane or acetone. These solvents dissolve all the flavour compounds, both volatile and non-volatile. It is then a relatively simple matter to filter out the spent herbs and evaporate the solvent. Left behind is a heavy, dark coloured material — the oleoresin. This contains a very complete flavour spectrum which closely resembles the original herb.

Both essential oils and oleoresins are very much stronger than the original herbs, sometimes being as much as 100 times more concentrated. This means that it would be very difficult to disperse minute amounts evenly in a food product. Normal practice is then to disperse the concentrates evenly over salt or sugar. The final product can be mixed to a strength equivalent to the original raw herb. Most food products contain salt or sugar in any event, and these "dry soluble" or extracted herbs disperse readily. Another advantage of this process is that flavour quality and strength can be standardized from year to year, eliminating variations which occur in field grown herbs. Since the flavour disperses evenly and completely through a food product, smaller quantities can be used to achieve the same flavour level. Often-times a good deal of the flavour in a natural herb remains unused for it never completely escapes from the vegetable fibers during cooking.

So whether they be whole or ground, essential oil or dry soluble, herbs continue to be used in foods. In fact, their consumption steadily rises. Populations have increased, but this is not the only reason. Our taste for fine food is improving. Travel has introduced people to new flavours, and immigration has brought new cultures to our midst. We have become more adventurous in our habits. We readily accept foods with high herb flavours, such as Pizza Pies, Dill Pickles, Herb Salads or Tarragon Vinegar. Un-doubtedly, modern food technologists and flavour chemists have stripped the herbs of some of their old mystery and glamour. No longer do herbs cure the ague or banish witches. But, a new witch-craft has taken over and the modern food technologist still relies heavily on herbs to perform his feats of magic. The herb gardens that the pioneer housewife planted may have withered and gone, but the flavour tradition she created blooms stronger than ever.

ANGELICA ARCHANGELICA

MRS. ARTHUR B. BAER

"Angelica, the happy counter bane
  Sent down from heaven by some celestial scout
  As well its name and nature both avow't."
                    Du Bartes: Sylvester's Translation, 1641.

IF Angelica were so virtuous what must Archangelica be? Why the plant first received these names is not altogether certain, but the popular explanation is that it was so called from its well known good qualities. Perhaps the latter name refers to St. Michael the Archangel, whose day falls on the Eighth of May (old style) when the flower would be in bloom and consequently was supposed to be a preservative against witchcraft.

Parkinson in his "Theatrum Botanicum" points out that all Christian nations call the plant by names signifying its angelic associations, and "likewise in their appelations hereof follow the Latine name as near as their Dialect will permit only in Sussex they call the wild kind Kex, and the weavers wind their yarne on the dead stalks." The Laplanders crowned their poets with it, believing that the odour inspired them, and they also thought that the use of it "strengthens life." They chew and smoke it in the same way as tobacco. The Letts endowed Angelica with magical powers, and the songs which are chanted by them when the herb is carried to market are very ancient.

The natural habitat of Angelica is Scotland, East Prussia, Iceland, Lapland and Syria. Before the war it was grown commercially in Germany (Thuringia and Saxony), in England, Poland, Russia, Belgium, Italy and France. It is cultivated extensively near Clermont-Ferrand in France for making liqueurs.

It is supposed to have come to this country in 1568. Angelica was mentioned as being in Adrian Van der Donck's garden

11

ANGELICA—An Etching *by Caroline Weir Ely*

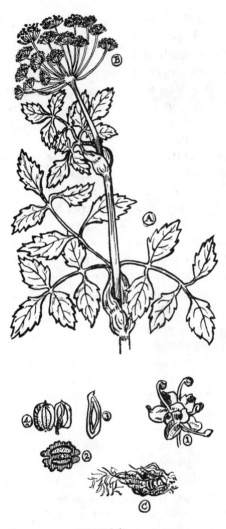

ANGELICA
(*Angelica Archangelica L.*)

A. Leafy shoot.
B. Inflorescence
C. Rhizome and roots
1. Flower.
2. Cross-Section of fruit
3. Mature carpel showing single seed
4. Mature fruits.

at Yonkers in 1653. This was perhaps the native Angelica Atropurpurea. Angelica seed listed as A. purpurea was offered for sale in the advertisements of the Boston Evening Post in 1771, and by Bertram in 1814.

Of all the Angelicas, and there are around fifty of them in the northern hemisphere, only two are likely subjects in the American herb garden: A. Archangelica, the cultivated Angelica, and A. atropurpurea, the wild American species sometimes known as Masterwort. They are lusty fellows, grown in the rich moist soil they love, spending a youthful year or so to develop into a rosette of leaves and a parsnip-like root, and then in a single season dramatically bursting up six to ten feet high to flower, set seed and die. Their leaves, rather like a cruder celery leaf, rise from bulbous bases so wide that they encircle the hollow stem. The flowers are small, but they are bunched in tight little pompoms and groups of these pompoms are compounded into a large sunburst. This whole inflorescence is technically known as an umbel of umbels, or a compound umbel, a dull enough name for such a fascinating structure, which in its main line resembles a bursting sky-rocket.

In flower, in leaf, and in general habit these two species of Angelica are very much alike and rather different from most of the other species of the genus. For one thing they are smooth-stemmed and smooth-leaved, as smooth as celery, while many of the other species are more or less hairy. The garden A. Archangelica differs from its American cousin A. atropurpurea in being a little less coarse, much less highly colored, and in having a more delicate aroma. The American species has a rank medicinal odour, the European a delicate and attractive one strongly reminiscent of Benedictine and similar liqueurs.

Angelica belongs to one of the most distinctive of the great plant families, the Umbelliferae, the "umbel bearers," as do also dill, borage, chervil, parsley and other lesser herbs. The leaves all possess the same pattern, being more or less cut as the case

may be. Through the whole family there runs a very similar
set of odors and flavours; the flowers are similar throughout
too, having a yellow-greenish color. The fruit, called seeds, are
6-7 mm. in diameter and greenish in color with five visible
striations.

Angelica is biennial only in the botanical sense of that term:
that is to say, it is neither annual nor perennial. The seedlings
make but little advance toward maturity within twelve months,
while old plants die off after seeding once, which may be at a
more remote period than in the second year of growth.   Only
very advanced seedlings flower in their second year, and the
third year commonly completes the full period of life. If the
flower heads are cut before seeding the plants can last many
years.

Angelica can be raised by seeding in the usual manner, but
germination is apt to be slow and irregular. It is best to store
the seeds as they ripen (in July and August), in moist sand
for several weeks before sowing. Seeds are sown in rows 11.8
inches apart with a distance of 24 to 28 inches between rows.
Sowing may also be accomplished through the use of small
pieces of root. Turning and layering the topsoil is the practice
used to prevent weed growth; the seeds are not damaged by
these procedures because they are deeply planted, 7 or 8 inches.
In order to produce a more aromatic root, the tops of the plant
are cut off to prevent formation of seed. Angelica grows best
in a moderate climate, in good soil, preferably with a deep layer
of moist clay. It likes, too, a partially shaded spot. It should
be planted on a fresh site every few years as it deteriorates
rapidly if grown in the same soil too long. It requires 8 to 11
pounds of seed per acre.

The harvesting season for roots is in the spring (April), or
fall (September or October), and seeds are also harvested in the
fall. After one year of growth the root is carefully harvested,
washed and dried by air. It is advised to keep roots ready for

sale in closed containers to protect them against loss of aroma and also against insects. The crop yield is from 900 to 1300 pounds per acre.

Essential oil is distributed throughout the whole plant, being found in the seeds, leaves, stems and roots. Commercially, the important parts are the roots, then seeds, and stems.

Angelica is largely used in the grocery trade and for medicine, and is popular as a flavouring for confectionery and liqueurs. The appreciation of its flavour was established in olden times when saccharin matter was extremely rare. Formerly the leaf-stalks were blanched and eaten like celery, but now they are candied. In the 16th, 17th and 18th centuries Angelica leaves were candied as well; the roots were made into preserves, and Angelica water was a favorite cordial. The flavor suggests that of juniper berries, and it is largely used with juniper berries or in partial substitution for them by gin distillers. The seeds especially, which are aromatic and bitterish in taste, are also employed in alcoholic distillates.

Medicinally speaking, the root, stalk, leaves and fruit possess carminative, stimulate, diaphoretic, tonic and expectorant properties, which are strongest in the fruit, though the whole plant has the same virtues. A remedy given in an old family herbal for hoarseness, sore throat or coughs is as follows: Boil down gently for 3 hours a handful of Angelica root in a quart of water, then strain it off and add to liquid narbonne honey (honey from thymes and mints) or best Virgin honey sufficient to make it into a balsam or syrup, add a few drops of nitre, and take.... several times a day.

Angelica may be cut into pieces and candied in sugar syrup for a confection. Another recipe is for Rhubarb and Angelica jam: Cut rhubarb into inch-length pieces; weigh and allow ¾ lb. sugar to each pound of rhubarb. Put in a kettle with sugar, a little lemon piece, and a few tender stalks of Angelica cut into small pieces. Cook down to a thick jam, stirring frequently. Put in glasses and seal.

ARTEMISIAS

MRS. JAY CLARK, JR.

IN the hunt for gray foliage plants of varying form and texture, a happy stumble brought me to this delightful family of many virtues and few faults, and around twenty have been gathered in, here and abroad. Of all the collection only three or four have not repaid interest and care. *Per se* they do not belong to the herb group, and yet it is one of the few plant families — I might say offhand the only one — which contributes members to the three divisional uses of the herbs: aromatic, culinary and medicinal. At first acquaintance I slipped on pronunciation, for with many gardeners it had been called ar-te-mee-sia, while it should be sounded as it is spelled, ar-te-mis-ia, a natural sequence from its supposed relation to the Greek goddess Artemis. The mistake is easily understood, as half the time the word is printed with a second *e* instead of the proper *i*. Legend and lore have no place here, in fact most of what we are told of the plant is factual and historical. From the carvings of the ruthless Assyrians, as interpreted by Dr. Campbell Thompson and given us in his monograph of their vegetable drugs, Artemisia's record goes back to 600 B. C. Figures of speech are always taken from familiar objects, and since Bible times wormwood has been the symbol of bitterness, for of all plants it possesses that characteristic. On the last night in Egypt, Moses had the escaping Children of Israel flavor their paschal lamb with bitter herbs, and later no matter how much they howled for the cucumbers and melons, leeks and onions and garlic they had left behind, wise Moses kept the cleansing bitterness in their diet, with his health and food laws, which even today are said to be the last word in science. From the Book of Exodus to the final Apocalypse, runs the mention of wormwood, in actuality and as the bitter symbol of futility, the purge of repentance, the curse of feckless judgment, until the frenzied star falls from Heaven upon a third of the rivers,

ARTEMISIA — PONTICA

blasting water and men from its bitterness. "And the name of the star is called Wormwood." This is the gentle plant we bring into our gardens of peace!

With rare unanimity authorities state that the artemisia of historic record was either *A. pontica,* called Roman wormwood, or *A. absinthium,* which we dub common wormwood, or both. *A. pontica* is found on either shore of the Mediterranean, is native of Southern Europe, indigenous to the Black Sea region, a difficult plant to keep in bounds. It spreads from underground runners into a lovely mass of fine feathery growth, stems not over a foot high, shrubby stalked with pale green leafage, gray underneath. It resembles *A. pedemontana,* the artemisia of Piedmont, Italy, but is twice as tall. The other probability of historic times is far better known. *A. absinthium* is an erect under-shrub, found wild in nearly every part of Europe, growing by the roadside and on heaps of old rubbish. The leaves and flowers are warm and bitter, with a strong smell; the roots are warm and aromatic, and it has always been a plant cultivated chiefly for medicinal purposes. What these are vary with the times. In the second century A. D., Dioscorides declares it to be a remedy against intoxication; Gerard in the sixteenth used it as a vermifuge, and the pharmacists recommended it for tonic properties, employing it as a stomachic. An infusion of the leaves, with the addition of a fixed alkali, is in a book of household remedies of 1854, as a powerful diuretic in cases of dropsy. Today its main uses are for the manufacture of the liqueur absinth, and various liniments. The cordial is concocted from wormwood and other flavoring ingredients as a powerful stimulant, but it has been suggested that the dangerous properties of absinth come not so much from *A. absinthium,* as from the mixture wrought into the infusion. In this country it has been put to a much tamer if more beneficent use, as an old-fashioned remedy for sprains, particularly in horses. At first it was a matter of an improvised poultice, then commercially it appeared under the name of Absorbine. Later for man's healing a more refined product appeared as Absorbine, Jr., and was long a remedy in our medicine cabinet before I had ever heard of the herb. After the war the plant was grown for this medicinal oil in large quantities in Michigan, but when the foreign imports returned in bulk, the crop was abandoned. That is the story of commercial drug growing both in this country and England: many of the plants grow wild on the Continent of Europe; the labor of harvesting them is undertaken for a small sum, and the distribution is well organized. So much for the medical artemisias.

In the aromatic division comes the plant of many names, *A. abrotanum,* Southernwood, affectionately called Old Man, Lad's Love, and regarded with a tender sentiment difficult to explain. It forms a low bush, with woody branches bearing very finely divided, pale milky green leaves that give off a strong scent when crushed. It is native to the South of Europe, Spain and Italy, and has been in England since 1548. The leaves have a fragrant, lemon-like odor, which is dependent, like all aromatics, on the volatile oil contained in the plant. The smell is supposed to be repellent to bees and moths, the reason the French call it *garde-robe* and put it among their woolens. I value it for its fragrance, a scent quite unlike that of any other herb, and for me one of the best. For those who like to run down *sobriquets,* the other names of Southernwood are Boy's Love, Maiden's Ruin; the French call it Bois de St. Jean and Citronelle, the Dutch name it Averonne and the Germans Stab-wurtz. A sweetmeat was made in England from the chopped fresh leaves of Southernwood mixed to a paste with sugar, recommended for sleeplessness, and in Italy it is employed as a culinary herb, to rub on lamb before cooking in the same manner as rosemary, as well as the young shoots used for flavoring cakes.

The artemisia devoted solely to kitchen rites is tarragon, a bewildering and temperamental member of the unpredictable family. While we are intimately acquainted with but one, there are numberless others, native of Europe, North Asia and North America, each quite different from the other. The classification most familiar is Besler's, who designates the cultivated tarragon as *Artemisia dracunculus var. sativa* and the wild species as *A. dracunculus var. inodora.* X. Marcel Boulestin, writing from London in 1930, says: "The true tarragon is difficult to obtain in this country, where nurserymen almost invariably send out in place of it a nauseous plant from North America, an understudy which is probably responsible for the neglect

ARTEMISIA — ABSINTHIUM

of the herb in English cooking." *A. dracunculus sativa* is commonly though inaccurately known as French tarragon, and is the salad herb, one of the few artemisias that is not bitter, though the taste is spicy with a tinge of camphor. It is a native of Central Asia and did not get to Europe before the sixteenth century, and as it does not seem to have set seed since that time, and is intolerant of wet cold winters, the necessary propagation by division makes tarragon an uncertain quantity. The culinary herb is *not* Russian tarragon, which does seed and is not worth using. Where does the name come from? The dragon-tail serpentine coils of the roots, or the legend that it sprang up along the serpent's track in the Garden of Eden. Take your choice.

In this same culinary division should be classed *A. vulgaris,* which is the Mugwort common on waste lands. It was once a substitute for hops in the manufacture of beer, and was also made into tea in England when the imported article cost seven shillings a pound. One writer, Dr. Fernie, avers that this was the plant first prepared as a drink by a French physician named Ordinaire at the close of the eighteenth century, a non-alcoholic tisane quite unlike the absinth of today. One more variety of the family has a mission which puts it in the medicinal section of the herbs, *A. Cina,* native of Russia, where the wild yield provides the world with the source of santonin, an anthelmintic against the round worm. Or in domestic circles, as I can testify, it is good for what ails the kittens!

The remainder of my collection is purely ornamental, having no utilitarian motive except sheer pleasure of form and gray softness. *A. tridentata* is the sage brush of our Western plains, fragrant after a shower, whose silvery velvet sheen is lovely in the extreme. Others equally happy in like quality are *A. albula; A. gnaphalodes; A. purshiana,* the cudweed; *A. ludoviciana,* white sage, and the European *A. maritima,* very like our beach wormwood, but taller. These are all of 2-3 feet growth. Lower plants of the same gray silver are *A. Stelleriana,* also called Old Woman and Dusty Miller, which grows on the stretches of the North Atlantic in pure sand, and is yours for the taking; *A. frigida,* fringed wormwood, whose silvery gray foliage is very finely cut, the woody stems holding it above the ground; *A. argentea,* whitest of all and delightful in sheen, the leaves fine

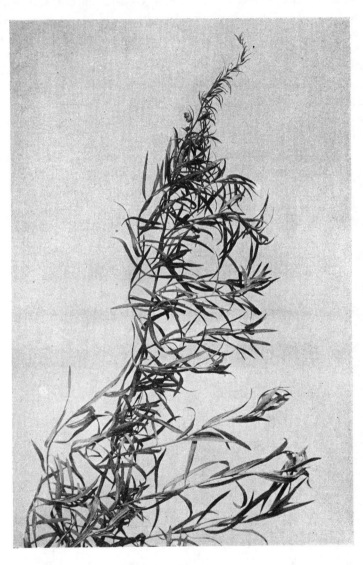

Artemisia — Dracunculus

threads of shining silk, and *A. spicata,* good for cutting and eighteen inches tall. The low ground huggers would have been suitable for a rock garden, had I possessed one, but they were quite happy in the sandy pockets of Artemisia Allée. Such were *A. Baumgartenii; A. glacialis; A. stellata,* finely cut foliage, fragrant, *not* to be confounded with *A. stelleriana; A. nana; A. granatensis; A. pedatifidia.* Then there are the annuals, *A. sacrorum* or Russian Wormwood, much used for moth repellent, and *A. sacrorum viridis,* Summer Fir, a bold, handsome thing of weed-like growth, and *A. annua* of no virtues I can discover! *A. lactiflora* should not go unmentioned, although it is a lottery — very lovely when the real Chinese plant is obtained; often, however, *A. vulgaris* is sent in its stead. All in all it is a fascinating family, whether it is approached through the door marked Herbs or merely the one that indicates Pleasure of Possession.

SEVEN BASILS

HELEN NOYES WEBSTER

I AM asked to write about the basils, seven of them, which were growing last summer in my garden, and which with careless familiarity I have always called by names gathered through the years from indifferent sources. And, as in search of a definite solution of uncertainties, I pursued my way through published accounts of past centuries, I found the same vagueness and confusion that, with accretions of folklore, legend and superstition, have seemingly been handed on from the old Greeks and Romans through Dioscorides, Theophrastus, and other transcribers down to the very latest of erudite garden treatises.

Now after many pleasant hours of browsing and elementary research I can truly say that I know little more than what these fragrant Ocimums in my own garden have, themselves, taught me. Spell it Ocymum if you will, but Theophrastus and others declare this to be a fodder plant, probably buckwheat, and not the herb Ocimum, so named from a Greek verb meaning " to be fragrant."

I am certain that this tropical group of plants with its comparatively few species, perhaps reducible to forty, and many horticultural and agricultural varieties and forms awaits the interest and modern revision of a systematic botanist far more competent than I. None of us who grow the tender things need to be reminded of their tropical origin. Annuals, with few exceptions, and easily raised from seed which ripens in the north none too well, the basils are mowed meekly down in their prime at the first dip of the mercury. Even heavy cloth covering will not save them for long if the days become cold. Paradoxically the seed of all our garden species sows itself if we leave the beds alone in the fall and spring. This is more easily said than done; for is there anything which can look as sorry and bedraggled as the first frozen basils when perhaps all around late thymes, hyssop and costmary are still blooming? But cover their demise with a heavy mulch of leaves and get your reward in very late spring when tiny purple and green leaved seedlings make their unexpected appearance. Of course the growing season may be long enough to give us ripened seeds to garner, packet, and label. But when you think that all is lost in premature frost, try mulching the frozen plants.

The East Indian basil, Tulasi, *Ocimum sanctum L.*, glues its falling seeds to the broad leaves below the flowering spike, spotting them as if with some fungus disease. The leaves fall and are wind-tossed away. I cannot find this fact recorded nor several other characteristics which make the Sacred Basil a good plant to grow in any kind of New England garden. It is a pretty, little, single-stemmed shrub, topped with three spikes of crowded soft purple flowers, the middle spike being always the longest. The whole plant is hairy, quite different in appearance from the basils of the O. Basilicum group, and has a curious resistance to frost which by all rights it should not exhibit. The Hoary Basil, *Ocimum canum*, although with whitish flowers, is so nearly like the Sacred Basil, *Ocimum sanctum*, that only as they grow together can I see any difference. The latter is taller, more shrubby, with lavender flowers, but both have the same fragrance of clove, lemon and cinnamon. O. canum Sims was first described in 1824 and pictured in *Curtis' Botanical Magazine*. The drawings here were made from plants raised from seed sent from China to the Directors of the Horticultural Society in England and grown in their Botanic Garden. It is closely related to *Ocimum Indicum*, a species frequently described in old herbals. Parkinson makes much of this Indian species, but it should not be confused with the species we know today as *Ocimum sanctum*. The latter is of East Indian origin, and grows in the Philippines, though Dr. Merrill says that " its appearance in these islands indicates only prehistoric introduction." Like other basils, both the Hoary and the Sacred Basil have been since early days of medicinal importance. Its precious sanctity assures entrance into the Hindu heaven and homes are guarded by the protective spirit of this herb. I once showed, to a missionary, who had known India for many years, these two species after they had reached midsummer height in my garden. " Yes," he said, touching first the leaves of Hoary Basil, and then Tulasi, " that is the most sacred plant in India." Some day I hope to grow, with these two basils, shrubs of the Tree Basil, *Ocimum gratissimum, Linn.*, which is said to be decidedly ornamental. The long heavy spikes of flowers are not unlike those of our wild Clethra. It is the " basilic en arbre " of the French kitchen garden.

Ocimum suave, Willd., the fever bush from Abyssinia, with its broad woolly dentate leaves and long spiked, close-set flowers, would fascinate me both by its beauty and long medicinal history in the welfare of the natives.

Concerning all the basils there is pleasant humor in the exuberance of exaltation or intolerance with which the ancient authors proclaim or denounce the virtues of this herb. The very earliest reference, to my knowledge, is where Chrysippus, about 250 B. C., declares that "Ocimum exists only to drive men insane." When Greeks heaped curses on its leaves, to most Romans it was the herb of love. " Even," says Cassianus, " the malignant quality of the herb is indicated by the fact that a she-goat that browses on everything, avoids Ocimum alone." And no ancient description is complete without direful warnings of its scorpion-breeding tendencies. But English literature teems with delightful allusions to basil. Read any of the Tusser editions of *Five Hundred Points of Husbandry* since 1557; turn to his directions for May and then go stroke your basil, as he bids, that " It may grow and multiply " the better for your sympathy.

Do we read with amusement of those superstitions which ring so true of belief? Do we remember how closely they are connected with all the herbs that have come from the Old World into the gardens of the New? Almost as precious as the Bible to the early settlers were their herbals of Tusser, Culpepper, and Coles, which contained all that was necessary for the housewife to know about the herbs, their uses and the art of simpling. Sweet basil is one of the herbs mentioned before 1806 in colonial garden records. Then we read of South American basils finding their way into European gardens.

Just when the mosquito bush, or wild basil, *Ocimum micranthum, Willd.*, was brought from Yucatan into Florida is uncertain, but it was so very long ago that Gray listed it in his " Synoptical Flora " as native. It seems likely that this basil is the same species as *Ocimum Campechia-*

num which Miller describes in his *Dictionary of Gardening* (1759) and calls the "Sweetest basil of Campeachy." Seeds were sent at about this time by Dr. Will Houston to England, and if we inquire as to the whereabouts of Campêche we learn that it is in Yucatan. There was probably a plant of *Ocimum micranthum,* or the Campêche basil, in my garden last summer; at least it seemed to have a well-labelled authentic counterpart among the pressed plants of the Gray Herbarium. This basil was very different from any others in my acquaintance. It is a low bushy plant, nearly smooth, with long petioles, ovate leaves, and white flowers, which, like the foliage, shows slight tinges of purple. I never had enough leaves for culinary experimentation, but, as Small's *Southern Flora* lists this basil as not uncommon in Florida hammocks, we may leave that to our southern members. The odor is flowerlike rather than spicy.

How valued an herb was basil is proved by the active exchange of its seeds between countries for many, many years. Then there was a long period of apparent apathy. War-torn states in the middle of the last century were not concerned with foreign plant introductions unless of importance as herbs of healing. Now once more there is interest in gardens of sentiment and fragrance. Lacking its basils, no herb garden is perfect. Ethiopia, Madagascar, Abyssinia, offer rich collecting grounds, and from these sources will come "age-old" forms of this historic genus as novelties to add interest to the gardens of America.

A unique species of Ocimum should in time find its way into our summer gardens. There is no more reason why the Saline Basil of Chile, Ocimum salinum, should not be one of our conservatory and garden habitants than heliotrope or fuchsia. The description of this plant in Molina's *Natural History of Chile,* as translated from the Italian by "An American Gentleman" in 1808, follows:

"In the Province of San Jago in Chile is found a species of wild basil, Ocimum Salinum, differing in its appearance from the common or garden species only in its stalk which is round and jointed, but in its smell and taste it resembles more the alga or seaweed than the basil. This plant continues to increase in growth from the first opening in spring to commencement of winter, and is every evening covered with saline globules that are hard and shiny and give it the appearance of being coated with dew. The husbandmen collect and make use of this salt instead of the common kind which it far exceeds in taste. Each plant produces daily about one half an ounce, a phenomenon the cause of which I am not able satisfactorily to explain as it grows in very fertile soil, exhibiting no appearance of salt, and is more than sixty miles from the sea."

Miller speaks of the "Studded Basil" as one of the varieties of "Great Basil," *Ocimum Basilicum*, and the ardor with which those seventeenth century horticulturists collected from every corner of the world arouses the surmise that this may be the Chilean Basil, although Miller does not speak of the salt.

To pass on to the well-known species and varieties of basils in the modern garden, we find, from *The Gardener's Dictionary*, written by Philip Miller, who was gardener to the Royal Society of Apothecaries in the garden of Chelsea (1768), that the growers of basil two centuries ago were assailed by the same perplexities as are our nurserymen of today. Note this comforting comment. Miller speaks of three " sortes of basils " growing naturally in India and Persia. " Of them there is a great variety which differs in size and shape and color of their leaves also in their odor, but as these differences are accidental so I have not enumerated them being convinced from repeated experiments that the seeds of one plant will produce many varieties."

Would that I had one of those prize packets! There may be some, however, who in their dealings with uncertain nurseries will remark caustically that it is not less so today. To read Miller's picturesque description of Great Basil's varieties is to be grateful that Linnæus was still in the throes of binomial nomenclature. His *Ocimum Basilicum*, sometimes called the "Great Clove-scented," is allowed five varieties, and we can almost see them growing:

1. Fringed-leaved basil, with the purple leaves
2. Green-fringed basil
3. Green basil, with studded leaves
4. Large-leaved basil

What more has Vilmorin to offer in his 1935 catalogue? He lists, under Basil, " Tall Green; Tall Violet; Delicate Green, suitable for stews; and Lettuce-leaved."

Before 1848, when De Candolle made his long list of Ocimum species and varieties from all over the world, the early herbalists seemed to content themselves with these three " Sortes," the Great Basil, the Medium

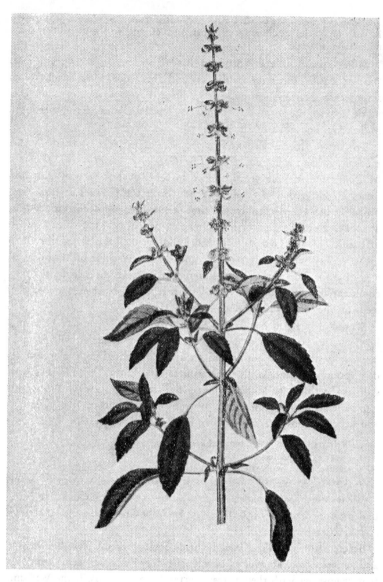

Ocimum canum (*Hoary Basil*)
From Curtis Botanical Magazine, *Volume* 51, 1824.

Basil, and the Lesser Basil, and this naïve classification is common in herbals up to the eighteenth century.

Exactly to what modern species some of these might be compared we can only conjecture. Certain it is that the Great Basil is *Ocimum Basilicum L.*, the kingly herb, royal enough to be carried by royal hands into royal chambers," and that no herb is more well defined in color, flavor, and habit. The yellow-green bushes a " cubit high " give welcome garden color for us between summer savory and wild marjoram. Its white flowers follow up in their opening the leafy stem for several weeks. This makes it one of my best bee plants. The leaves fold on their midribs in extremes of heat and cold, and their flavor is indispensable in cookery. The southern races know well the zest given by a few shreds of leaves or flowers sprinkled over fish, tomato, or spaghetti. When green, the leaves make a pleasing oil, and when dried are used as a snuff cure for nervous headaches. Like all other basils, it grows easily and quickly from seed sown when the earth is warm in well-nourished garden loam.

I greatly doubt if as such the seeds of Curly Basil may be bought in this country, but this basil is always appearing in our collections. It is probably a French agricultural variety of so-called Lettuce Leaf, but it is well worth growing under any name. The shrubs are coarser and over-top all my other basils. Its large wrinkled leaves and short spikes of crowded flowers make, when dried, the best herb pepper when in combination with costmary, savory, and marjoram. The fragrance may not be as pleasing but it is powerful and resinous.

This last form is sometimes spoken of as belonging to the " Medium Sorte " of basil. Perusal of old descriptions and study of woodcuts leave me nowhere as to its identity. I'm sure it must be among my garden basils, for after reading the list of varieties which Miller accords to Medium Basil I really don't see how we can miss it.

1. Common Basil with very dark green leaves and violet flowers.
2. Curled leaf Basil with short flower spikes.
3. Narrow leaf Basil smelling like Fennel.
4. Middle Basil with citron scent.
5. Basil with leaves of three colors.

What if imaginary aromatic differences are more marked than structural? What if next year each may shade off into something else — thus escaping binomial designation? I greet them every spring with friendly recognition, even as did the eighteenth century apothecaries' gardener.

Have I left purposely to the last the third " sorte," the little Lesser Basil? How easily we fall into the picturesque phraseology of those early herbalists!

Bush Basil, *Ocimum minimum, Linn.*, is as sharply defined a species as its taller cousin, Sweet Basil, and equally important in home, garden, and legend. Its small spicy bushes are so round and compact that they might have been treated by a topiarist. It was a favorite herb for pots with the English cottager who often gave it in compliment and well-wishing to a departing guest. The tiny green leaves are smooth and thick set on the many branches, and the white flowers are in leafy little spikes. Its two varieties I know as " Sweet Purple Bush," a name from our Southern gardens. They must be what Miller describes as " the smallest basil with black leaves and the smallest basil with variable leaves." The tiny purple flowers are always humming with honey bees which bend in their zeal the little six-inch bushes to the ground. Their fragrance combines all the odors of eastern spices. Do its leaves like those of Green Basil cure deafness when laid in the ears, make sweeter washing waters, or more potent medicinal oils? All this I do not know, but in sweet nosegays it excels.

And if of my basils I have talked too much and of more than the allotted seven, I offer no apology, but the assurance that if I am privileged to share any of them with my readers they will do likewise.

CHAMOMILE

ALBERT F. HILL

CHAMOMILE, or Camomile, is a very old inhabitant of our gardens, long esteemed for virtues both real and imagined. The literature of medical botany, folklore and horticulture, both past and present, is full of references to this herb and its many uses.

It is often difficult, however, to identify with accuracy the particular plant under discussion since the name "chamomile" has been used for a dozen or more species in some six genera. *Anthemis* and *Matricaria* are the principal genera concerned, with such familiar species as *Anthemis arvensis, A. Cotula, A. nobilis, A. tinctoria, Matricaria Chamomilla, M. glabrata, M. inodora* and *M. parthenioides.* Of these only two are of importance, the majority of references to chamomile applying either to *Anthemis nobilis* L. or to *Matricaria Chamomilla* L.

Confusion also exists in regard to these two species. Not only do writers fail to differentiate between them, or erroneously attribute characteristics of one species to the other, but the name "Common Chamomile" may be used for either species depending on the locality. In England, and usually in the United States, chamomile is *Anthemis* and Common Chamomile *A. nobilis;* in Europe chamomile is *Matricaria* and Common Chamomile is *M. Chamomilla.* It is impossible to state which interpretation is correct. In the first edition of Standardized Plant Names "Common Chamomile" was reserved for *Anthemis nobilis,* and *Matricaria Chamomilla* was called "False Chamomile." In the second edition of this work *Matricaria Chamomilla* is designated as "German Chamomile" while *Anthemis nobilis* becomes "Roman Chamomile." All this confusion is regrettable and unnecessary since the plants themselves are perfectly distinct and possess adequate scientific names of long standing.

MATRICARIA CHAMOMILLA *Linnaeus*

Reproduced from Hayne, Arzneigewächse 1 (1805) t. 3. *(Courtesy of the Botanical Museum of Harvard University.)*

ANTHEMIS NOBILIS *Linnaeus*

Reproduced from Hayne, Arzneigewächse 10 (1827) t. 47. *(Courtesy of the Botanical Museum of Harvard University.)*

Anthemis nobilis *Linnæus* Species Plantarum (1753) 984

Anthemis nobilis is a low growing, creeping or trailing perennial herb with a small much branched rhizome and numerous slightly hairy, prostrate, ascending or sometimes erect stems, which are freely branched and often root at the base. The whole plant is downy and pleasantly aromatic. The leaves are alternate, sessile, 1-2 inches long, blunt, very deeply 2-3-pinnate with numerous crowded short linear acute more or less hairy gray-green segments, so threadlike as to give the whole plant a feathery appearance. The few flower heads are solitary and terminal on long erect pubescent peduncles, which are woolly when young. The involucral scales are few in number occurring in 2 or 3 rows. They are adpressed, broadly oblong, blunt, with wide transparent membranous scarious lacerated borders and a slightly wooly mid-rib. The receptacle is solid, very conical, and bears between each floret, minute thin linear blunt often slightly hairy scarious chaffy scales, which are a little shorter than the disk flowers. The disk flowers are small, yellow, perfect, and very numerous, with a tubular corolla which is campanulate above, cylindrical and somewhat dilated at the persistent base, and bears a few oil glands on the outside. The ray flowers are fewer in number (12-20) and pistillate. The limb of the ligulate corolla is oval-oblong, 3-toothed at the apex and white. The branches of the stigma are recurved with brush-like ends. The fruit is a very small dry somewhat 3-angled smooth slightly compressed achene with three faint ridges on the inner face. There is no pappus, but the fruit is crowned by the persistent base of the corolla. The receptacle becomes more conical as the fruit matures. This species flowers in late summer.

Under cultivation, varieties are produced with double flowers in which all or nearly all of the tubular flowers have been converted into white ligulate flowers. These double flowers are larger, whiter and more showy, but cannot be grown from seed.

Anthemis nobilis is a common wild plant of western and

southern Europe, occurring from Portugal and Spain, through western and central France and Italy to Dalmatia and possibly to Germany and southern Russia. It is quite common in England, especially in the south, and extends to Ireland and to the western islands off Scotland. It is also a favorite garden plant. This species is frequently grown in the United States (it might well be called Garden Chamomile) and may occur as an escape from cultivation. This plant has been grown commercially in Belgium, England, France and Germany.

While it is impossible to identify with certainty the chamomile of Dioscorides and other classical and ancient authors, since there are so many plants with similar daisy-like inflorescences, it is possible to eliminate certain species from consideration. *Anthemis nobilis* could not have been known to the peoples of antiquity as it did not occur in the Italy of that period, in Greece or in Asia Minor. It does not seem to have been observed in Europe until after the Middle Ages when, according to Gesner, it was carried from Spain to Germany. That it was not an ancient German plant is borne out by the fact that there are no names for it in Old German. The first references to this species are to be found in the Anglo-Saxon herbals and Middle English medical books where it is known under a number of names, chief of which is *maythen*. This old Saxon name for chamomile continued to be used in England for hundreds of years. We may safely assume that *Anthemis nobilis* was first used and cultivated in England. It must have been grown for centuries prior to the end of the 16th Century for at that time it was a common weed near London, and the double variety was also known. It had also become established on the continent for Camerarius noted its abundance near Rome in 1598 and gave it the name Roman Chamomile.

Anthemis nobilis has enjoyed an amazing reputation as a domestic medicinal plant and was extensively used in early days. There were almost no human ailments which chamomile was not supposed to alleviate or cure, and it was also valued as the "plant's physician," in the belief that its presence in a garden tended to keep all the other plants in a healthy condition. While most of the supposed virtues have proved to be non-existent in the light of modern medical science, Anthemis is still a valuable medicinal plant, particularly in England where it is known as Roman Chamomile. Both the dried flower heads and an essential oil which is distilled from the flowers (or from the whole plant) are utilized.

The Roman chamomile flowers used in medicine are always the double flowers obtained from cultivated plants, although these contain a smaller amount of the medicinal principles. One of the constituents is an aromatic bitter which makes the flowers valuable as a stimulant, carminative and tonic, at least in moderate doses. In large doses they are emetic. They may be used as an antiperiodic or as a useful stomachic in the treatment of dyspepsia and flatulence. For many years they were used for poultices and fomentations.

The oil, which was known as early as 1677, has similar properties. Valuable for its stimulant antispasmodic and carminative action, it is much used as a tonic and bitter stomachic. It is often added to purgative pills to prevent griping. The oil is bright blue in color when first distilled, but becomes yellow or brown on exposure to the air.

The medicinal value of *Anthemis nobilis* is not the only reason why this species has been a favorite garden plant for so many years. The creeping habit of the plant makes it a valuable substitute for grass as a ground cover. On dry banks and in arid places generally it soon forms a flat compact mat. Chamomile lawns have long been a familiar feature of the English landscape, the moist climate keeping the plants bright green, thick and vigorous. Such lawns have not succeeded as well in the drier climate of the United States. In Elizabethan gardens this chamomile was much used on banks and for turf seats, while in modern gardens it is utilized for walks, paths, the interspaces between the knots of formal gardens and similar places. English gardeners are coming to feel that Anthemis tends to exhaust the soil of its nutrient material, a far cry from the old belief that it was the plant's doctor. Fragrant when crushed and uninjured by trampling feet (a characteristic long recognized) or the passing of a lawn mower, this plant should be more widely used. The intriguing name "Whig Plant" was given to this species during the American Revolution because, like the Whigs, it throve better for being trampled on and kept prostrate.

Matricaria Chamomilla *Linnæus* Species Plantarum (1753) 891

Matricaria Chamomilla is an annual herb with an erect solid smooth shining strongly striate pale green stem, one to two feet in height and much branched, with long slender branches. The leaves are numerous, alternate, sessile with a dilated base partly surrounding the stem, oblong-oval, obtuse, 2-3-pinnate with narrow setaceous acute curved spreading smooth bright green segments. The flower heads are numerous, terminating the slender glabrous branches and forming a more or less corymbose inflorescence. They are small, about 5/8 of an inch in diameter. The flat involucre consists of a single row (sometimes 2 or 3 rows) of from 10-30 very small equal linear blunt smooth imbricated scales with scarious brownish ends and transparent margins. The receptacle, at first broadly ovoid and solid, becomes elongated, conical, ovoid and hollow. It is smooth and lacks scales. The disk flowers are perfect, very small and numerous with a pale greenish yellow, deeply 5-toothed tubular corolla which has a few oil glands on the outside. The anthers have a large terminal appendage. The ray flowers are rather numerous (15-25), crowded, overlapping and pistillate. The limb of the corolla is barely 1/4 of an inch long, oval-oblong, faintly and bluntly 2-3-lobed at the apex, white, involute and erect in the bud, spreading in the flower and afterwards quickly deflexed. The styles are spreading.

The fruit is a very small oblong-ovoid smooth pale gray achene, somewhat curved, with five faint ribs on the concave side and crowned with a slightly raised border. There is no pappus. This species flowers in July and August. There are no double varieties.

The principal differences between *Matricaria Chamomilla* and *Anthemis nobilis* may be summarized as follows: smaller size, annual rather than perennial habit, coarser leaves, somewhat corymbose rather than solitary flower heads, elongated and hollow rather than conical and solid receptacles, and the absence of scales between the florets.

Matricaria Chamomilla is a Eurasian species found throughout Europe from the Mediterranean region north to England and southern Scandinavia and eastward to the Ural Mountains. In Asia it is native in the Caucasus, Asia Minor, Persia, Afghanistan and northern India. It occurs as a weed in China, Australia and the United States where it is occasional on ballast ground and in other waste places. Because of its habitat it might well be designated Wild Chamomile.

This species was known to the Greeks and Romans and may have been the chamomile to which Dioscorides and other writers of antiquity refer, although this is open to question. It has been used by the German people from earliest time, as is evidenced by the fact that it was once considered sacred to Balder, the Sun God, and by the numerous names for the plant in Old German. *Matricaria Chamomilla* is extensively cultivated in Europe, and has a place in all peasant gardens. It is grown on a commercial scale in Hungary, Belgium, Russia, Poland and Germany. Our word *Chamomile* and the specific epithet *Chamomilla* are derived from the Greek words *chamai* (on the ground) and *melon* (apple). This is most appropriate since the plant is low and pleasantly aromatic throughout with an odor suggestive of ripe apples.

Matricaria Chamomilla finds its chief use in medicine. Always preferred on the continent of Europe, this German or

Hungarian Chamomile, of the drug trade has now almost completely supplanted *Anthemis nobilis* for such purposes in the United States, and is the only chamomile recognized as official in this country at the present time. Its properties are similar to those of Anthemis. A hot infusion of the dried flower heads is used as a carminative, tonic and gastric stimulant. It is particularly valuable in cases involving poor digestion, convalescence or general debility.

One of the most interesting uses of Matricaria is as the source of a herb tea or tisane. The French, who are perhaps the greatest connoisseurs and certainly the greatest users of these aromatic beverages, include chamomile as one of the six most favored herbs. These tisanes play an important part in French daily life, as well as constituting the first cure for ailments not serious enough to require the services of a doctor. The increasing number of devotees of herb teas in this country find themselves agreeing with the French that Matricaria yields a much more pleasant and soothing beverage than does Anthemis, and one highly to be recommended as a nightcap.

In Spain, Matricaria flowers are used to flavor one of the lightest of their sherries, which is known by the Spanish name for chamomile, *Manzanilla*. Experiments are now being carried on with these flowers as a possible flavoring ingredient of domestic Vermouth.

An extract of Matricaria flowers is much used in beauty parlors as a wash for blonde or light red hair. The tonic properties of the chamomile are beneficial and the dark amber liquid seems to bring out the natural color of the hair. The flowers of *Anthemis nobilis* are sometimes utilized for this purpose but the light amber extract obtained from these is not considered as efficacious.

The essential oil extracted from *Matricaria Chamomilla* flowers is reported to be a solvent for platinum chloride and is used in the glass and porcelain industries in the process of coating containers with platinum. This oil also finds a use in the perfume industry as a blend in some of the oriental compounds, often in combination with pachouli, lavender and oak moss.

References to the use of Matricaria as a ground cover are apt to be confusing. It is obvious that this annual species is not suitable for a permanent cover, such as lawns, path, etc. It does, however, form satisfactory mats for sunny, gravelly banks and may even be cut back with a lawn mower, but such use is only temporary.

Research Department of
The Botanical Museum of
Harvard University.

THOSE HERBS CALLED CHERVILS

By HELEN NOYES WEBSTER

A casual history of these herbs runs through literature from the age of the earliest herbals and mediaeval treatises to modern manuals and vegetable garden books. The antiquity of their group names is significant. *Scandix* originated with Theophrastus (300 B.C.), *Chaerophyllum, Myrrhis, Sison* (*Cryptotaenia*) are traced to first-century Dioscorides, and *Caucalis* to *Hippocrates* (400 B.C.).

As compared with other herbs of ancient fame, descriptions of chervils are brief and singularly free from folklore, magic and imaginary medical virtues. They are prosaically treated and no romance attends their culture. Indeed, one writer disdains their very existence, remarking that this is "only a small genus of mostly small plants common throughout Europe."

Black's Gardening Dictionary of the last century records two species of chervils, and proffers advice "to the unwary amateur to whom these plants may sometimes be offered by dishonest plant salesmen."

Happily, however, today's awakened interest in herb-gardening and appreciation of the delicate herb blending so long an art in French cookery, admits at least our garden or salad chervil, *Anthriscus cerefolium,* to its rightful place among the aristocrats of seasonings.

And for those who garden in books, Eleanour Rohde writes of sweet chervil, *Myrrhis odorata,* her "love among the tender herbs," and calls it "the handsomest plant of the border with its great fern-like leaves and sweetness." Well I know that those of us who have watched the frilled leaves of *cefeuil* take on their crimson hues as nights grow cooler would not count our gardens happily complete without these little plants.

The meaning of the common name, chervil, is lost in the

42

ages. Pliny may have had something to do with it, and there is some connotation with the characteristic curled or much divided foliage. *Anthriscus* from the Greek for flower and fence, alludes perhaps to this chervil's hedge-loving habit, and *cerefolium* is, of course, "leaf of Ceres."

Under *Chaerophyllum,* which refers to the fragrant "joy-giving leaves," and three other closely allied genera, more than forty species have been described by European herbalists, naturalists and bontanists. Their botanical nomenclature is replete with confusing synonomy, and around them is centered a bewildering array of folk names. Regardless of authority, at least fifteen are called chervils with some descriptive adjective. *Scandix, Myrrhis, Selinum, Cerefolium,* in addition to *Anthriscus* and *Chaerophyllum* have been used synonymously from earliest times in herbal and even modern literature.

Resemblances and differences in these herbs are quaintly based upon their much divided foliage, the sharp elongated fruits, often enlarged edible roots, and the sweet anisate odor and taste which to greater or less degree pervade the whole plant. Inflorescence, if we except the showy white clusters of sweet chervil, is pale and in the typical loose umbels of the parsley family, *Umbelliferae.* They resemble and are often confused with the parsleys, where the variation in foliage between the curled and the plain leaved forms is like that in the varieties of garden chervil, *Anthriscus cerefolium.*

Wherever we may chance upon them it is true that modern descriptions of the chervils—indigenous or European—have not added much to the observations of the early herbalists.

Camarius wrote about the "wild chervil with edible tuberous roots" (*Chaerophyllum bulbosum*) in 1588. Salmon's English Herbal of 1710 describes and pictures three other species; and as we compare their counterparts on the modern herbarium sheets, the woodcuts in these herbals are delightfully true.

Needle chervil, *Scandix Pecten-Veneris,* was seldom omitted from any list these old authors compiled. According to 16th century Gerarde, "it hath no such pleasant smell as chervil, but it hath long seeds like needles or like the great teeth of a combe whereof it took its name," and likewise came *Scandix*, "to sting."

Toothpick chervil with "leaves like turnips" was well known to the ancients, and a favorite reproduction in their tomes. To quote Salmon, "It hath leaves like wilde carrots and hard quills whereon the seeds do grow which are good to cleanse the teeth and gums."

The salad or garden chervil, with which we are most familiar, survived many names until Linnaeus gave it the present accepted cognomen, *Anthriscus cerefolium*. The same plant was known to the ancient Greeks as *Chaerophyllum*, and was eaten as a pot-herb by the Romans. It has been described as *Selinum* and now and again we see it referred to as *Myrrhis*. There is, however, no doubt that this chervil was the *Cerefolium* listed in the famous capitulaire of St. Gall monastery, 9th century, when Charlemagne was king.

Curiously, the herb was cultivated in Brazil in 1647, but no mention was made of its use in America until a century later. It escaped from the gardens into which it had been introduced and is now found growing wild in damp shady spots to its liking. For many years I had known only *cefeuil frisé*, this chervil's delicate little variety with the curled leaves, which I had grown with intermittent success in my Lexington garden.

Acquaintance with real aromatic chervil came about thus. A friend, rummaging through her closet shelves, handed down to me a thick packet of seeds marked "cefeuil," which she had bought in France. Chervil seed was a rarity not easily obtained, for few gardens grew the herb, and as a dried product it was seldom sold or imported. As the seed was not fresh, I sowed it doubtfully thinking of previous disappointments when seed bought through nursery catalogues either never came up, or yielded only a few delicate little plants of slight savor, though a lovely garnish for the salad bowl.

Therefore I was wholly unprepared for the bed of sturdy, dark green, intensely aromatic plants which that seed produced. The herb looked more like Italian parsley which was beginning to find its way into our market gardens, and it was so called even by the learned. But seeds, flowers and the definite anisate aroma soon belied that diagnosis.

I gave over the patch to a Girl Scout who cut and dried the herb most intelligently. She sold it all in bulk to a New York herbalist who was enthusiastic over its success in her herb blends. Since then I have seen true *Anthriscus cerefolium* growing like a weed in the cool shade of a cedar hedge.

If fresh and viable, the seed of garden chervil will be ready to harvest in six to eight weeks from time of sowing. Good garden soil more neutral than alkaline is safest. Chervil will not thrive in open sunny places, but if allowed to self-sow in cool ground, seedings are often found green under the first snowfall.

Harvesting should be done in June at the height of the herb's succulence, and careful drying, not over ninety degrees, will give an aromatic product of the desirable green color.

Chervil, fresh or dried, is at its best when used in blends with other herbs, an art which the American cook is learning to appreciate. It is the most significant of herbs in the epicurean *"Omelette aux fines herbes."* Chopping it into cream cheese or into the butter substitutes of today's rationing with basil, tarragon and chives is a very special way with cook and hostess.

Evelyn (1699) insists that "the tender tips of chervil should never be wanting in our sallets being exceeding wholesome and cheering of the spirits."

Another chervil, commonly described in books on vegetable gardening, is the bulbous-rooted chervil, *Chaerophyllum bul-*

bosum. In this species the roots alone are used. They are dark-skinned and of a flavor between a potato and a chestnut.

A United States agricultural report of 1836 tells of seed sent to this country by a Consul stationed at Munich. He writes, "The great value of this vegetable to American gardens is not wholly its deliciousness to the epicure, but the earliness of its maturity thus supplying the place of potatoes." This must have been the chervil so popular in Holland at that time and where it was said, "without chervil as a seasoner the Dutch serve scarcely a soup or a sallet."

Sweet chervil, also known as "Sweet Cicely," is *Myrrhis Odorata* (L.), "that herbe of very good and pleasant smell and taste like unto chervil which hath caused it to be called 'The Great Sweet Chervil.'" The plant has a plenitude of common names, alluding mostly to the flavor and fragrance of root and leaves,—thus myrrh and anise myrrh.

It prefers shade, or better, the sifting sunlight of shrub borders. Once established in good composted soil, this perennial herb will live for years, shedding its long black shining seeds soon after flowering in June.

As these take a full year's resting period before germination I like to propagate the plant by root division in very early spring before the first leaf unfolds from the deeply buried crown. There must be an "eye" on every piece broken from the thick, fleshy clump of roots. Seedlings transplant successfully only when one little triangular leaf appears and the diminutive tap root is not broken in the process.

Perhaps we have been thinking of sweet chervil too long as a garden ornamental to realize its full value as a flavoring herb of worth. In herb blends and alone, the young green leaves fresh or dried can be used as are those of salad chervil.

Gerarde makes note of the robust roots of sweet chervil. "They are most excellent in a salad if they be boiled and afterwards dressed as the cunning cook knoweth better than myself, notwithstanding I used to eate them with oil and vinegar, being first boiled which is very good for old people that are dull and without courage."

Cutting back the first growth of the great fern-like leaves sends up a fresh succulent supply which only the heaviest frosts can vanquish, and all summer the sugary leaves and juicy stems are garden nibbles for the children who call this herb their "candy plant."

In my garden, or rather in various shaded spots of the yard where they have seeded themselves, are two lovely wild sweet chervils or "Cicelys." Their generic name, *Washingtonia,* honors George Washington for reasons I do not know, although *Osmorhiza* (scented root) is a much more significant synonym. Both are natives of our rich woodlands and not uncommon. Roots of *Washingtonia longistylis,* the smooth-leaved species, are pungently fragrant and aromatic. They are eagerly sought by our foreign population from Mediterranean shores, and eaten as are those of the other chervils, both boiled and raw. Less pleasant in taste but with decorative, softly incised foliage, the woolly sweet cicely *Washingtonia Claytoni* is equally interesting.

Other wild chervils have come through the years from their homes in the old world to our shores. They are truly beautiful plants, none grossly coarse, all much alike in their soft compounded foliage, more or less aromatic and with the mericarp fruit of their family.

Of ten or more European species of *Anthriscus* described by Hegi in "Flora von Mittel Europa" (1906-1931) only two species, according to Britton and Brown, have appeared in America. Both are called "wild chervils." *Anthriscus sylvestris* (L.) *Hoffm.* has been found "as a waif" on Staten Island and "in ballast around seaports." *Anthriscus vulgaris Pers.* with its curious spiny fruits is known as "burr chervil." It was recorded from Nova Scotia, but since has probably spread southward along the coast. *Caucalis Anthriscus* (L.) Huds.

sometimes called "rough cicely" and "scabby head" from its
bristly fruits, is hemlock chervil. It is another adventive from
Europe which has spread to the midwest.

Thirty or more species, all natives of warmer parts of the
world, are included in the genus *Chaerophyllum*. Aside from
C. bulbosum (L.) of the vegetable garden, only two have been
naturalized in America. Teinturier's chervil, *C. Teinturieri,*
Hook. is unusual in that unlike most of these moisture and
shade-loving herbs it prefers sun and the dry sandy soil of
more southern states. Spreading chervil, *C. procumbens* (L.)
Crantz., is now found in many states and it is not unlikely
that our country folk have learned to make use of this wild
aromatic.

In his book on edible wild plants Professor Fernald refers
to a wild chervil, *Cryptotaenia canadensis*. His mention of
this herb led me to the pages of Peter Kalm's Travels into
America, 1749. There I found the herb under its old name,
Sison, meaning running brook, an indication of the herb's
predilection for wet places. To quote exactly the words of that
indomitable traveller, "It (*Sison canadensis*) abounds in the
woods of all North America. The French call it *"cefeuil
sauvage,"* and make use of it in the spring in green soups like
chervil . . . It is another wild cicely, and universally praised
here as a wholesome antiscorbutic plant, and is one of the best
that can be used in the spring."

Although never belittled by the hunter of wild foods, the
chervils may be lightly dismissed by authorities as of slight
economic importance. Yet it has interested me that in my
search for authoritative data I find no reference to any poisonous
or deleterious species. It is quite true that in this era of
prodigious plant travel, more chervils may have been introduced and their species as yet unrecorded. But time alone can
tell whether these little-known herbs will eventually. find themselves esteemed habitants of our gardens.

SELECTED BIBLIOGRAPHY OF REFERENCES CONSULTED

Matthiolus: De Plantis Epitome, ed. Camerarius, 158ᶜ
Salmon: The English Herbal, 1710.
Gerarde: Herbal, ed. Johnson, 1633.
Miller: The Gardener's Dictionary, abridged edition, 1735-1740.
Kalm: Travels into North America, 1749.
Stone: The Flora of Chester County (Pa.), with special reference
       to Flora Cestrica by Dr. Wm. Darlington, 1945.
McMahon: American Gardening, 1806.
Burr: Field and Garden Vegetables, 1863.
Sturtevant: Notes on Edible Plants, ed. Hedrick.
Henderson: Handbook of Plants, 1890.
Bailey: Standard Cyclopedia of Horticulture, revised edition, 1935.
Bailey: Principles of Vegetable Gardening, 18th edition, 1941.
Fernald and Kinsey: Edible Wild Plants of Eastern North America,
       1943.
Gray: Manual of Botany, 7th edition, ed. Robinson and Fernald.
Britton and Brown: Illustrated Flora of the U. S. and Canada,
       2nd edition, 1913.
Hegi: Die Flora von Mittel Europa, several volumes, 1906 through
       1931.

Additional information was obtained from specimens in the
Gray Herbarium, Harvard University.

Comfrey — The Cinderella of Plants

MARIA WILKES

Through the years comfrey has achieved a place in the sun to make life infinitely more desirable, healthy, and yes, even more beautiful for animals and humans. Comfrey was first grown as a crop for feeding pigs and horses. In the 1880-1890 period, England was producing yields of between 80 to 100 tons an acre of the so-called common comfrey, which is a native of Britain and Europe, including Russia. It was a natural hybrid between *Symphytum asperimum* and *Symphytum officinale*.

This comfrey was sent to Henry Doubleday at Coggeshall by one of the British or Scottish successors to Joseph Bush, Head Gardener to Catherine the Great of Russia, who had laid out and planted the grounds at St. Petersburg Palace (now a Park of Rest and Culture in Leningrad). This led to what is now called an F1 hybrid. In the cross, however, the small triangles that fit together over the stamens around the base of the pistil failed to open to allow the entry of bees to pollinate the flowers, unlike the wild species. This meant that the seed was and still is scarce and the seed that is disseminated only produces similar varieties with the same problem. The first cross vigor was lost.

Now there is a series of mixtures which, by constant selection and removal of undesirable variations have become strains, of which there are a great number. None of these have produced the 100 tons to the acre in Britain of the early days, like the plants Henry Doubleday sent Kew, as published in their Annual Report for 1879 and illustrated on Plate 6466 of *Curtis' Magazine* for that year as *Symphytum peregrinum*.

Another of the early published reports in 1882 by Rev. E. Highton of Bude, England, told of the great fodder value of comfrey for pigs and horses. With an analytical eye and love of farm animals, British livestock men kept on developing many clones and strains. They discovered that comfrey had a singular medicinal substance, Allantoin, which had been discovered by

Photograph by HELEN D. CARSWELL

Comfrey (Symphytum officinale) in garden of Edna Neugebauer

Vauquelin and Buniva in 1800 and synthesized by Grimaux from urea and glyoxylic acid in 1876. Allantoin is also found in tobacco seeds, sugar beets, wheat sprouts and about 0.8% in comfrey. Like other alkaloids of the purine series, it influences diuresis, muscle action and the central nervous system.

Comfrey was found to be high in both calcium and phosphate and very high in potash with some iron and manganese and a trace of cobalt. The nutritional value of comfrey leads in protein, fibre, carbohydrates and moisture over soya bean, groundnut-meal, cotton-cake and Lucerne meal in dry form analysis. No crop is so high in protein in relation to fibre.

Comfrey is a coarse perennial herb up to 5 feet in height, leafy, branching, with hairy stems and leaves. The lower leaves are generally larger than the upper ones. The fleshy root is extensive and generally adapted to moist, cool places. Cultivated comfrey is often referred to as Russian or Quaker comfrey *Symphytum officinalis* (Common), *Symphytum tuberosum* (tuberous) and *Symphytum uliginosum*. *Symphytum asperum* (Lepechin) or *aspertimum* (Donn) has been collected in the Lower Mainland of British Columbia as an introduced escape. The flowers range from whitish, yellowish or dull purple to magenta. The plant is propagated by root cuttings or root "off-sets" and crown cuttings, or crown "off-sets."

It was found that people could greatly benefit by adopting this valuable herbal plant for human use and, gradually, the many benefits discovered have piled one upon the other, so that a large tome would be necessary to cover the story, for it has been said that comfrey was used by the Herbalists for 2,000 years. In the summer of 1959, Mr. F. Newman Turner, who was consultant to the Society of Medical Herbalists in England, discovered Vitamin B-12 in comfrey. Later experimentation led to the further belief that comfrey is possibly the only plant to extract Vitamin B-12 from the soil.

The Henry Doubleday Research Association of Bocking, Braintree, Essex, England, under the guidance of Mr. Lawrence D. Hills, sends comfrey in various forms to asthmatics in the tropics. Also a comfrey vinegar is manufactured, as well as salves and creams for healing wounds. From New Zealand we may obtain a line of healthful comfrey products as well as toiletries of great promise. In our health resorts we find it in the magic green drinks served morning and mid-afternoon, in creamy comfrey soups and cocktails. Comfrey may be used with vegetables.

Comfrey is of simple culture, in good soil, with fertilization to keep it growing and producing foliage (all the year in Southern California). One phase which appeals to the writer is the use of comfrey's flowers, which are edible. The blooms develop at the top of the stems with umbels of small bell-like flowers. These flowers contain a certain amount of honey, and if served on salads with parsley, on open-faced sandwiches or floating in soups, comfrey adds another facet to the enjoyment of nature's products supplied for our benefit.

In picking the leaves to use fresh, cut them down to the base, collecting them from the second row up, which leaves the basal leaves to absorb the soil splatter and the possibility of slugs or snails. Wash the leaves, cut them in strips and place in an enamel or glass saucepan, cover tightly and put over a low flame for a very few minutes. Do not boil. There should be enough moisture to let them cook enough without burning. However, it might be necessary to add a tablespoon of water before putting on the fire. Keep any liquor which may remain for gravies or soups. Season with herbal salt and any dressing preferred. The flavor of comfrey is a blend of endive and asparagus.

Although comfrey is known to perform better in richer soils, it also has the capacity of improving poor soil. In England, it has been found to be a splendid aid in growing better potatoes. The Russians have grown it for composting as well as for their daily uses for men and animals. It may be planted in spring or autumn, but for ordinary garden use it may be obtained in containers.

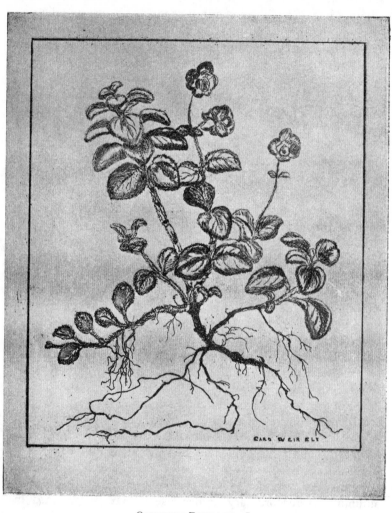

ORIGANUM DICTAMNUS L
An original etching by Caroline Weir Ely

This plant was propagated in Wenham, Massachusetts, from the root
brought from Crete in 1936.

The Partridge Fresco. From Pavilion of "Caravanserai," Frontispiece of
"Palace of Minos." Vol. II, Part 1, Sir Arthur Evans. By permission
of the Macmillan Co., Publishers.

"RIGHTE DITTANY"

HARRIET ADDAMS BROWN

ONE of the most interesting phases of herb growing is the struggle
to secure for our modern gardens authentic species of the herbs mentioned in the old records. These may be found listed under many
different names and wander from genus to genus to the complete
mystification of the unwary.

"Dictamnus" or "Dittany" is one of the oldest of these medical
herbs of mystery. Headed by Hippocrates himself, and including
among the more familiar names Apuleius, Theophrastus, Dioscorides,
Pliny, Plutarch, Cicero and Virgil, the long list of ancient sages who
discussed the provenance and virtues of this Cretan Herb, reads like
the catalogue of a classical library of the Golden Age.

Theophrastus (Sir A. Hort's translation) has perhaps the most
comprehensive description. "Dittany is peculiar to Crete. This plant
is marvellous in virtue and is useful for many purposes. . . . Its leaf
is like Penny-royal, to which it also bears some resemblance in taste,

but the twigs are slenderer. They use the leaves, not the twigs nor the fruit. . . . The leaf is useful . . . above all against difficult labour in women. . . . It is given as a draught in water. It is a scarce plant, for the region which bears it is not extensive, and the goats graze it down because they are fond of it. The story of the arrows is said to be true—that if goats eat it when they have been shot it rids them of the arrow. This, then, is Dittany and such its properties. The virtue of Dittany is perceived directly it is taken into the mouth, for a small piece has a warming effect."

Virgil's description is the most vivid in the famous passage which tells of Venus helping to heal the wound of Æneas:

> "A branch of healing Dittany she brought
> Which in the Cretan fields with care she sought.
> Rough is the stem, which woolly leaves surround.
> The leaves with flowers, the flowers with purple crowned.
> Well known to goats; a sure relief
> To draw the pointed steel and ease the grief."
>
> *Æneid, Bk. XII.* (DRYDEN)

The classical belief in the medicinal properties of Dittany continued for generations, but while the old writers seem to have agreed as to the appearance and properties of the plant, by the first quarter of the 16th century a note of botanical confusion creeps into the records.

Caspar Bauhin, in his *Theatri Botanici*, Basle, 1523, at the end of a long list of Dictamnums, adds, *"D. Albus Vulgo, Sive Fraxinella."*

In 1548 William Turner writes: "Dictamnus groweth in Cady and hath rounde, thick, rough leaves. I have not seen it growing but dry oft. It may be had in Venice and in Antwerp. Some abuse for this 'Fracinella.' Dictamnus may be named in English 'Righte Dittany.'" Twenty years later he triumphantly writes: "I have seen Dittany growing in England in Maister Riches garden naturally, but it groweth nowhere else that I know saving only in Candy."

He also states that "Lepidum is called in English 'Dittani,' but foolishly and unlearnedly. In Duche 'Pepperkrout,' that is, 'Pepperwort,' because it is so exceedynge hote, which name were more fitter in English for this herb than the name of 'Dittani.' That the name

Photograph of Origanum Dictamnus L. from the Gray Herbarium of Harvard University, courtesy of Mr. C. A. Wetherby, Curator.

of 'Dittani' might abyde proper unto ye 'Righte Dittano' which begynneth now to be set and sowen in England."

The *Hortus Kewensis* confirms Turner, and lists "Dittany of Crete" as "cultivated in 1551 by Mr. John Riche." The *Hortus* also records it as "Cretan Marjoram," "cultivated by Mr. John Gerard."

In 1764 Linneus, in his *Genera Plantarum*, referring to Bauhin, removed Dittany from the genus "Dictamnum" to the genus "Origanum," and we may find our herb from that time on listed as *Origanum Dictamnus, L.*

Thanks, however, to the researches of the distinguished archæologist, Sir Arthur Evans, whose excavations in Crete have turned fairy tale to fact, "Righte Dittany" has received still further proof of identity and we can stand firm against the usurping claims made by the bastard dittany, *Dictamnus Fraxinella*, to the heritage of centuries of lore and legend which rightfully belongs to *Origanum Dictamnus*.

Sir Arthur Evans has unearthed a fresco in Crete, near the ancient town of Knossos. Once it decorated the walls of what he has named "The Caravanserai," an ancient rest house of the middle Minoan period, that unbelievable era of civilization of 1500 B.C. It is a frieze of birds, perched on bushes and plants. One of these plant forms so closely resembles *Dictamnus* as described by the ancient writers, and is so similar to the plant now growing on the rocky Cretan cliffs, that we may feel quite confident that here is what must be the earliest extant picture of this "literary celebrity" among herbs, famous down the ages as the "Marvellous healing herb of Crete," and still called "Diktamno" by the Cretan peasants. Sir Arthur describes the living plant which he found in the crevices of the rocks as having "Round leaves like Penny-royal . . . lilac-veined and covered with soft, downy hairs, answering Virgil's description. The flower which emerges from a cluster of overlapping bracts is labiate, and is also of a delicate purple hue." [1]

---

[1] From *Palace of Minos at Knossos,* Vol. II, Part 1. By permission of the Macmillan Co., Publishers.

Both this description and the fresco itself are corroborated by the unique specimen of *Origanum Dictamnus* now in the Gray Herbarium of Harvard University, which was collected in 1846 by Theodor Von Heldreich, Director of the Botanic Garden at Athens. Except for comparative scale, which was an unimportant point with early decorators, the shape of the leaves and the habit of growth of the painted plant leave little doubt but that in these prehistoric fragments we have a vindication of the identity of Dittany and a record which gives us an unbroken plant pedigree for over three thousand years.

The restoration of this historic plant to common knowledge and its propagation on these alien shores would be an interesting and worth-while project for those members of the Herb Society who "delight in looking backward."

Bibliography

A. Musa: *Apuleius Barbarus.*
Meursius: *Creta*, Lib. II, p. 109.
Caspar Bauhin: *Theatri Botanici*, Basle, 1523.
William Turner: *The Names of Herbs*, 1548.
                Herball, 1568.
William Coles: *Adam in Eden*, 1657.
Gerard: *Herball.*
Joannes Raius: *Plantarum Historiam.*
John Quincy, M.D.: *A Compleat English Dispensatory*, 1749.
Woodville: *Medical Botany Supplement*, 1779.
Kniphof: *Botanica in Originali*, 1758.
Zorn: *Icones Pl. Med.*, 1779.
Curtis: *Botanical Magazine*, 1795, Vol. IX.
Sir Arthur Evans: *Palace of Minos*, Vol. II, Part 1.

DITTANY REDIVIVUS

ANNE BURRAGE

IN the 1935 issue of THE HERBARIST, at the end of an article on Origanum Dictamnus L., the author suggested, as a worthwhile project, the introduction to American gardens of this historic herb. It can now be announced with pride that the "sacred healing herb of Crete" has arrived in this country. The following excerpt from a letter from Mrs. Ellery Sedgwick tells the story: —

"When I left for a cruise in the Adriatic last summer I was asked to try and procure seeds of the true Dittany. This little herb is not known in this country and grows only on the hills in Crete. I laid my plans early and spoke to the Greek interpreter on our ship and also to the lady who helps run the cruise. After visiting the excavations and the Museum we arrived at Candia, the port of Knossos, at high noon — and alas, all the shops were closed for the inevitable siesta. Our Greek in-

60

terpreter failed me in this crisis. Keeping the boatload of impatient people waiting, I bribed a man to see what he could do. Soon he arrived with a bunch of herbs, but I was sure they did not answer the description of the true Dittany. We put off for the ship and on getting aboard, to my joy, Mrs. Anderson presented me with a pot in which grew a little herb which I felt convinced was the Origanum Dictamnus. She had visited a Cretan woman who had been her cook in New York and had now returned to Candia to live. Knowing the " ropes " this woman had procured in one of the provisions stores the only plant of Dittany which they had and which is used on the Island in flavoring drinks.

" The herb was some five inches high and had five or six little purple labiate flowers with protruding stamens at the end of its branches, and resembles exactly the pictures of the specimens of Dittany at the Gray Herbarium of Harvard.

" This little plant travelled on top of a basket from Patmos to Halicarnassus and from Rhodes to Malta, and other ports, and through France on the train. When the flowers fell the bracts became very prominent at the ends of the branches. Nothing could discourage it and it put forth tiny round leaflets when I watered it, which I was told to do every two or three days. The sea voyage and neglect when at home had no effect on its vitality. It seemed to me to have the endurance and persistence of an age-long struggle for existence and its insignificant appearance belied its survival through some three thousand years.

" May it keep these persistent qualities among our richly cultivated and easily discouraged plant life."

.   .   .

Those of us who love herbs are deeply indebted to our good friend for her contribution of such an historic and legendary plant to our gardens, and it is hoped that, when another season has passed, there may be sufficient cuttings for further propagation.

An additional note of interest has come in a letter from Mrs. G. C. F. Bratenahl of Washington, D. C., who writes: —

Shortly after hearing about this precious plant of the "Righte Dittany," the lost Origanum Dictamnus of Crete (see Mrs. Laurence A. Brown's article, HERBARIST 1935) I came across an article by Eleanour Sinclair Rohde entitled:

"A Collection of Marjorams." (Published in *My Garden,* an English monthly, November 1934 issue.) After speaking of the more familiar varieties of this delightful herb family—those plants that look so "homely and comfortable" in any garden—Miss Rohde writes of Origanum Dictamnus, the "Dittany of Crete" . . . sub-shrubby with downy foliage and pink flowers in August and September. This marjoram, which attains nearly a foot, needs a very warm spot. In Victorian times "Dittany of Crete" was almost as favourite a window plant with cottagers as musk. It is an excellent plant for a cold greenhouse, provided the temperature in winter does not fall below 45 degrees. The compost should be two parts fibrous loam and one part silver sand and leaf mould. During the winter the plants need the minimum of water and as much sunlight as possible. O. Dictamnus can be easily increased by cuttings taken in the spring and struck in sandy soil under a bell glass in the greenhouse. . . ."

Who is familiar with another marjoram that Miss Rohde also includes in her "Collection"? *Origanum microphyllum:* "Marjoram Gentle." It is not listed in Bailey's *Hortus,* Mrs. M. Grieve's *Herbal,* nor does Mrs. Webster mention it. Parkinson describes it with "heads hoary and soft" and Miss Rohde tells us that it has a far sweeter scent than even Sweet Marjoram. "Few aromatic plants have such an exquisite scent. Sweeter and yet also spicier than lavender with just a trace of heliotrope. It needs a light soil and a very sunny sheltered spot." *QUERY:* Could this be, by any happy chance, that "intensely pungent dried marjoram, also from Crete" which accompanied the "lost Dittany" on its long brave journey?

ON FENNEL — ONLY SLIGHTLY BOTANICAL

By Jessica Wood

It is pleasant to be reminded of the long continuity of the human race by the names of time-honoured herbs whose ancient leaves have acquired a human meaning through their association with man in all ages. Their names are legion.

But it is the great perennial umbellate, Fennel, with which I am here concerned, within whose hollow stalk Prometheus brought fire from heaven, that most precious gift to man. It has, however, historical signficance from its connection with one of the most incredible battles of all time.

In a recent paper I mentioned that the Greek word *Marathon* means fennel, and that the celebrated battle of Marathon, 490 B.C., was fought on a field of fennel; and added that statues of the Athenian athlete Pheidippides who ran the 150 miles to Sparta for aid against the Persians always show him holding a sprig of this herb.

The first statement provoked some doubt in the minds of a couple of readers. However, any complete lexicon of the Greek language will verify the meaning. For instance, in Liddell-Scott, under Marathon we find: a demus on the east coast of Attica, probably so-called from its being overgrown with fennel (marathon). The old Century Dictionary and Cyclopedia under Marathonian gives detailed information regarding the Latin word *marathrum* meaning fennel and its derivation from the Greek marathon.

I note that Strabo in his Geography alludes to horse fennel by its

Latin name *hippo-marathi,* the entire word plainly from the Greek. Mrs. Helen Morgenthau Fox, in her "Gardening with Herbs for Flavor and Fragrance," says that the ancients rarely specify the fennels by name, though the herb is mentioned by Theophrastus, Hippocrates, Dioscorides and Pliny.

The Greek geographer Strabo[1] indirectly clarifies this matter. Describing Iberia (Spain), he tells us of a road that runs through "what is in the Latin called Fennel Plain because it produces so much fennel." Here the translator supplies a footnote: "Literally, the Greek is 'Plain of Marathon.' Strabo avoids translating 'Fenicularius,' the term actually used by the Romans, into Greek."

A much earlier translation[2] renders the passage in this wise: ". . . the plain called in the Latin tongue the plain of Marathon, on account of the fennel growing there." This is perhaps an oblique and withal a perverse mode of research to prove that the famous Plain of Marathon in Attica was in reality a great field of fennel.

The stirring poem "Pheidippides" by Robert Browning refers to the "Fennel-field."

In his Persian Wars Herodotus tells us that, according to the courier's own account, he fell in with the god Pan on his journey, but there is no mention of fennel. However, Browning makes use of this incident narrated by the Greek historian and makes Pan give him a sprig of the herb. The poet further indulges his poetic license when he identifies Pheidippides (Phidippides, Philippides) with the herald who was no doubt sent from the Fennel-field to Athens with news of victory over the Persians, but whose name is *not* preserved in history.[3]

Apropos of this, note the quotation below.[4] This query was proposed by an English army man right after the modern Olympic of 1908: "Now that the Marathon race is over and the story of Pheidippides is no longer required as a romantic setting, might I ask the authority for the legend in question? We are told by Herodotus, Pausanius and Cornelius Nepos that Pheidippides ran from Athens to Sparta to summon the Lacedaemonian troops to the help of the Athenian and Plataean forces against Darius and reached the latter place in two days. But I can find no verification of his 26-mile run from Marathon to Athens after his return from Lacedaemon." The editor admits that there seems to be no substantiation of the legend.

One wonders how far Browning's poem may have been responsible. It was published in the First Series of his Dramatic Lyrics in 1878-9, and could well have lent some enthusiasm toward the inauguration of the marathon race at the first modern Olympic in 1896. In fact, it is surprising how many authorities seem to have derived the bulk of their findings from this poem and treat the whole thing as authentic.

There are other errors. One recent reference book[5] astounds us by insisting that the Spartans were present at this engagement, when all the world knows that they were conspicuous by their absence.

A lately published encyclopedia, Collier's, 1950, asserts that the marathon race was instituted at the *ancient* Olympic festivals to commemorate the feat of Pheidippides who ran from Marathon to Sparta. "Needless to say," writes H. D. F. Kitto in "The Greeks," a Pelican book, "the marathon race was never heard of until modern times"; and he states further that "the Greeks would have regarded it as a monstrosity." To be sure, foot-races were run at Greek festivals, the length varying from 200 yards to three miles, according to one chronicler. But the first so-called marathon race was run at Athens in Greece at the new Olympic games when they were set up there in 1896. The distance covered since 1908 has been standardized at 26 miles and 385 yards, approximating the length of the longer road from Marathon to Athens. The name marathon quickly entered the language and it now stands for any type of endurance test.

We are told that the earliest mention of Marathon occurs in Homer,[6] long before the decisive battle: "She (Athena) . . . came to Marathon and Wide-wayed Athens."

From the foregoing, one might conclude that the writer is one who delights in the role of a breaker of images or in attacking cherished beliefs. On the contrary, I heartily concur in the opinion so gracefully expressed by Eleanor Farjeon:[7] "Tales, incidents and legends which, if they are not as true as the facts, may still have a still greater power than these in waking imagination. . . . And if the legends are not the very tree of history, they are the birds that sing in the tree, and will go on building their nests there, year after year, till the tree itself is dead."

REFERENCES

1. *Strabo* — Howard J. Jones trans. Vol. II, p. 95. Putnam's Sons

2. *Hamilton and Falconer,* Vol. I, p. 240. Bell and Sons, London

3. See *The New Century Dictionary and Cyclopedia,* 1954

4. *Popular Fallacies Explained and Corrected,* edited by A. S. E. Ackermann, Lippincott, 1924

5. *Why You Say It,* Webb B. Garrison. Abingdon Press, 1955

6. *The Odyssey* — George Herbert Palmer, VII, 80. Houghton

7. *Preface to Mighty Men,* Eleanor Farjeon. Appleton-Century-Crofts

---

(EDITOR'S NOTE — Foeniculum: According to Sophocles and others, Prometheus brought down the spark of fire from heaven "hidden in a stalk of fennel." The plant referred to is not the ordinary Foeniculum, but the Giant Fennel, Ferula communis, of which we read: "The hollow of the stem is occupied by pith, which, being dried, takes fire like a match (i.e., a slow-match), without injuring the outer portion; and the stem is therefore much used for carrying fire from place to place. . . . This custom is of high antiquity." Tournefort.)

ALCHEMILLA — LADY'S MANTLE

HESTER M. CRAWFORD

"Of all our natives," says Mr. Abbot with an amiable degree of enthusiasm, "this is the most elegant plant."

James Sowerby. English Botany 1794

THUS does the old Botanist describe this fascinating herb, which in medieval days was considered a panacea for almost any illness. It takes its name from the Arabic word Alkemelych (alchemy).

The name, Lady's Mantle, indicates its association with the Virgin Mary. Synonymous are Lion's Foot, Bear's Foot, Nine Hooks, Stellaria, Leontopodium, Pes Leones, Pat a Leonis and Sanicula major; in French, it is Pied de Leon; in German, Frauenmantle; in Irish, falaing Muire; to list only a few. The many local names in many countries indicate its importance and usefulness as a medicinal herb.

Alchemilla vulgaris, the variety we commonly grow in our herb gardens, is a lovely, lacy, spreading perennial. The leaves are rounded, and very precisely accordion-plaited, as a lady's cloak or mantle might be, with the always present dewdrop which gives the whole plant a sparkle all its own. The greenish-yellow "flowers" (there are no petals) are so tiny, they seem like a small yellow cloud above the leaves, or a bit of lace to trim the mantle. The fine hairs covering most of the plant, stems and young leaves, give a softness of texture which is most enchanting. Alchemilla will spread over several square feet, in time. It can be divided, and has even self-sown in my garden.

Botanically, this plant is of the genus Alchemilla, the order Rosaceae. Most Alchemilla are natives of the Andes, only a few being found in Europe, North America, and Northern and Western

67

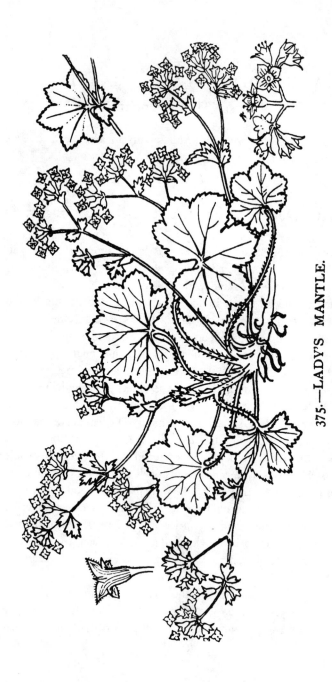

375.—LADY'S MANTLE.
ALCHEMILLA VULGARIS.

Photo by Paul E. Genereux

From *The Handbook of Plant & Floral Ornament* by R. G. Hatton

Asia. These are definitely plants of northern and colder areas. I have found references to seventy-nine varieties, but only three grow wild in England: *A. vulgaris,* or Common Lady's Mantle; *A. arvensis,* Field Lady's Mantle, or Parsley Piert; and *A. alpina,* found only in mountainous regions. Several varieties found in Europe have been naturalized in North America.

The virtues of Alchemilla are many. Some old writers attributed its wonder-working powers to the whole plant, others held that the alchemical virtues were imparted to the dewdrops found in the plaits and cups of the leaves.

Gathered in June and July, when the leaves and flowers are at their best, the entire plant was used and dried. The roots, when used, are better fresh. The plant has astringent and styptic properties because of the tannin it contains. It was, therefore, used to "stay bleeding" of all kinds, to heal wounds, to allay vomiting, for bruises, and for countless other cures.

In our herb gardens, Lady's Mantle gives us another exquisite plant in shades of yellow-green. This is a plant which has inspired beautiful designs in painting, botanical illustrations, embroidery, and tapestry. As we contemplate it on a warm sunny day, we see yet another form and pattern for our enjoyment.

BIBLIOGRAPHY

The Herbal, by John Gerarde, 1633.
Theatrum Botanicum, by John Parkinson, 1640.
The British Herbal, by John Hill, 1756.
English Botany, by James Sowerby, Vol. III, 1794.
The British Flora, by William J. Hooker, 1833.
Index Londinensis, Prepared by O. Stapf, 1929.
A Modern Herbal, by Grieve and Leyel, 1931.
The Standard Cyclopedia of Horticulture, by L. H. Bailey, 1939.
Gray's Manual of Botany, 8th edition, 1950.
The English Flora, by Geoffrey Grigson, 1955.

LAVENDER

Original etching by Caroline Weir Ely

IN QUEST OF LAVENDERS

By EDNA K. NEUGEBAUER

I SUPPOSE every herb lover has at some time set out on the adventure of collecting—Herbs for glamorizing foods, Herbs for pot pourris, scent-bags, incense, Herbs for teas, for home remedies, Herbs for a historical garden; or, as I have been doing, a collection of the species of a single herb.

First the idea comes, through reading, a chance remark or a failure to secure a plant. Then determination. If no one has collected the Lavenders, why don't I do it myself?

When I set out on my search for lavenders I already had six or seven in my garden: *officinalis (vera), the* lavender, a pink and a purple form of *officinalis, stoechas,* Dwarf Munstead, the green and the grey dentate. Then I read that a University botanical garden listed and grew others, and after several letters of inquiry I finally received a helpful list of nurseries. More correspondence, and price lists came. Then during the spring of 1948, packages arrived from Massachusetts, Maryland, Ohio, Oregon, and the northern part of my own State. The feathery *L. multifida* was in bloom when I opened its package, and has been ever since. *L. pinnata's* wedge-shaped heavy leaves have proved my special favorite. Of course there were duplicates and some misnamed, but not many. When this nursery list was exhausted, I seemed to be at the end of the trail.

So many lovely lavenders are described in the English herb books that I next tried herb gardens in England, and early in the spring of 1949 I received two shipments of cuttings. Here I learned about the necessity of securing a permit to import and the long, long lapse of time from the arrival of the card saying the plants had been shipped to their appearance, fumigated, unhappy and gray. The journey was just too much. Though I

71

LAVENDERS — LEAVES

STOECHAS

OFFICINALIS

DENTATA
(GREEN)

DENTATA
CANDICANS
(GRAY)

MULTIFIDA

PINNATA

PINNATA BUCHI

CANARIENSIS

set them carefully in sand and covered them with glass, they met a speedy end. However, the loss was not total. I have had a continuing correspondence with two English herb authorities connected with the herb gardens.

In the late spring of 1949 six packets of seeds came with *Hortus Botanicus, Coimbra, Portugal* stamped on two, and *Ain Seba, Morocco* written on two others. These packets bore species names I had never seen before: *mairei, canariensis, pubescens,* as well as the already known *pinnata* and *latifolia.* Three of these varieties have already bloomed. They seem to mature much more quickly than the *officinalis.* Midsummer brought another lot of seeds, but as yet there are no results to report.

Such a collection as I have been making has been possible through the suggestions of the writers of our herb books; Botanical Gardens (even foreign ones will assist) ; the Plant Introduction Service of the U. S. Department of Agriculture; persons who read and answer those letters to the Editor in magazines (I sent letters of inquiry to both an American and an English garden journal) ; a commercial grower of lavender; a chemist in the perfume industry; with final identification by a plant taxonomist.

Naturally I wished to learn more about these unusual lavenders, where they came from, how they grew. Though the chapters on lavender in our herb books are delightful, they deal mainly with the English lavender (*officinalis*), in its many forms, dwarf to tall, and varying colors from white through pink and lavender to deep purple. There are two reasons why most listings end here. First, the other species are much less hardy to frost, and second, they are less fragrant or lack fragrance entirely. What then do they have? Variety and often extreme delicacy of leaf, and unusual form in the flower spike.

In attempting to learn of these rare forms I consulted both the Index Kewensis and Index Londinensis, a new and educational venture for me. The number of species of Lavendula listed was astounding, but I learned little about the plant except the land to which it was native and when and by whom it was first found and recorded. For the Indexes are to plant life what the Reader's Guide is to general information, an index to other material; and very few of the books and magazines referred to are readily available.

Not till last November did I secure a copy of the most authoritative study made on the species Lavendula, by Miss Chaytor working with herbarium specimens at Kew Gardens and reported in the Journal of the Linnaean Society in 1937. According to this study there are twenty-eight distinct species of *Lavandula,* and of these *officinalis* in all its forms is only one. These species are grouped into five general classifications. Most are native to the lands bordering the Mediterranean Sea, one of Somaliland in East Africa, two of India. Of the twenty-eight species I have only eleven, of which six have been definitely identified. There should still be a good deal of letter-writing ahead of me.

Lavandula officinalis (vera) is undoubtedly the most widely dispersed, being grown commercially in England, France and other European countries, in Kenya and South Africa, Tasmania, and near Olympia, Washington. And, I suppose, in home gardens the world over in every climate that is at all favorable, one can find the loved English lavender. There are closely related species, with broader leaves, downy leaves, and with green leaves. It is valued, of course, for its fragrant lavender flowers, appearing in July and August.

For interest of bloom the species closely related to *L. stoechas* come first. In both *L. stoechas* and *L. pedunculata,* its bigger sister, the flowers are extremely small and a black purple with yellow centers, often arranged in four neat rows along the chubby spike. Each spike is tipped by spectacular bracts of lavender-purple, from a third to a fourth the length of the entire spike. The leaves of both are very small and in shape like those of *officinalis;* the growth is shrubby and twiggy. Though

the growth is much more generous and the foliage quite different, being neatly notched along its margin, *L. dentata* has a
similar spike and bracts though the color is paler in bract and
bloom. There are both a green and a gray leaved variety, the
leaves of the latter being larger and somewhat felt-like. This
group blooms in winter.

The third and largest section of the *Lavendula* species contains several that have dainty, fern-like or lacy leaves such as
multifida, pinnata, canariensis and *pubescens*. These also are
winter bloomers so far as I have had experience with them.
The stems are long, the spikes long and slender, sometimes
broader at the base and tapering to a point. Some varieties
even have branched spikes, a central one with two others coming
out near the base and at an angle. Though the species in this
section that I have grown are of the divided leaf-form there are
others with entire leaves, one almost round, others broadening
at the center and narrow at the tip. So far as I have had experience with this group there is practically no fragrance, and they
are very tender to the cold.

As yet I have been unable to secure any species of the other
two sections, one of which is the India lavender. But I do not
doubt that I shall eventually find them all.

However, I do not want that time to come too soon. If and
when I secure the twenty-eighth lavender, an interesting adventure will have come to an end. No more letters with foreign
stamps, no seed packets from friend or alien *Hortus Botanicus,*
no boxes to be opened in expectation, no flats of seedlings or
tiny pots to tend, no buds to watch day after day for their
flowering, no friendly letters of suggestion and encouragement,
no final identification to be recorded. But it would seem that
my quest will continue for some years.

LEMON VERBENA

LIPPIA CITRIODORA, Lemon Verbena is a native of Chile and Peru, grown in warm climates in the open, and indoors farther north, mainly for its delightful lemon fragrance. The three whorled leaves are narrow and rough, with the mid-summer flowers white or pale colored, borne in pyramidal panicles. Lippia was named for Francois Joseph Lipp, naturalist of Vienna, and contemporary of Linneus, and botanically the species resembles Lantana, another member of the Verbenaceae, rather than Verbena itself. Confusion comes from the plant's appearance under the scientific names of *Aloysia citriodoro; Verbena triphylla; Lippia triphylla; Lippia citriodora,* and a common title *Yerba Louisa,* of Mexican tradition. When Emperor Maximilian and Empress Carlotta began their tragic adventure in Mexico in 1864, they enlarged the splendid urban gardens of the Montezuma palace. It was not considered kingly to cultivate plants for utility or profit, so the gardens were made to abound in fragrant herbs. Among others was the delicious lemony plant, and these imperial exiles named it Yerba Louisa after Carlotta's mother, wife of the Belgian king Leopold.

The term Verbena Oil is often heard, with the conclusion that Lippia citriodora is used in its manufacture, but the U. S. Department of Agriculture has this to say:

> "Inasmuch as its price is out of proportion to its value, the oil is not an article of commerce. For most purposes, it can be replaced by the much cheaper Lemon Grass Oil, which for this very reason is known as East Indian Verbena Oil. Inasmuch as genuine Verbena Oil is but rarely to be had, statements concerning it must be taken with some reserve."

Although seeds were imported from Europe before the war started, propagation of the Lemon Verbena is mostly done by taking cuttings of new growth. Early in the Fall bring in the plants and for a while give very little water while they go through a rest period. In February shake off the dust and trim the weaker growth, pot in fresh soil and place in the sunlight, watering freely. New growth springs up in the course of a few weeks and these new shoots can be used nicely for slips.

If possible it is good practise to keep the old plants growing from year to year, as each season adds to the strength of fragrance as with Rosemary. In Tennessee the plants are left in the ground with success, further north, they may survive in the cold frame if cut to the ground. The safest way is to house them during the winter. Increased growing of Lemon Verbena, Lippia citriodora, will assure householders of the pungent, clean scent so desirable in the linen closet and pot-pourri.

Experiments in the cultivation of Lemon Grass in this country have been undertaken by Dr. A. A. Bourne, Chief of Agricultural Research of the United States Sugar Corporation. In 1937-38 some 240 acres were planted on sandy soil not suited for sugar cane. The crop was processed for oil, and studies made as to the usage of the spent grass. This was found to be suitable feed for beef cattle when supplemented with small quantities of protein. Due to the utilization of this by-product, foreign competition (327,661 pounds of Lemon Grass oil from British India imported in 1938) can be fairly met.

Mary Elizabeth Fitz-Gerald
St. Louis. Mo.

Ligusticum Levisticum.

Published by Phillips, & London, Nov. 1st 1806.

"Lovage"

From Woodville's "Medical Botany."—1832 Vol. I. Page 140.

LOVAGE

LOVAGE (*levisticum officinales*) is an old-timer among the herbs, which has been sadly neglected in the past generation or two. Too few people are aware of its virtues and it deserves to be revived as one of our familiar culinary herbs. It is distinguished by its strong celery flavor and aroma, and was used as a celery substitute by our forefathers, being easy to grow, and adaptable to almost any soil, though its favorite environment is a rather moist heavy soil with a good deal of shade. Here it will grow to a height of seven or eight feet and send up a flower stalk another foot. The umbellacious seed-head stands far above the main plant; if the seed is not to be used, the stalk can be cut out early and a greater growth of leaf induced; but its aromatic seeds attract birds, especially goldfinches, which should endear it to the garden lover. It is tall enough to make a handsome background plant in the border.

Lovage, or wild celery, appears in the list of household herbs in Walafrid Strabo's Little Garden, and it grew in the Herbularius or medicinal herb garden of the famous Abbey of St. Gall, which takes it back to the 8th century. In old New England the root used to be candied in sugar syrup in the same way as sweet-flag root, as a candy and a breath purifier, and was called Smallage by our grandmothers. It was very largely grown for sale at the Shaker colonies. A lovage leaf will alleviate the pain from a bee-sting if crushed and rubbed on. The aromatic celery-like leaves are very good in salads, and there are few soups or stews in which an onion is considered essential, where a few lovage leaves would not be equally welcome.

The plant may be left in the clump indefinitely, after it is established in some damp corner near a pool or garden faucet; but a quicker method of increase than growing from seed is to divide the clumps every two or three years.   The seed when maturing is subject to attack from carrot fly and aphids, if the birds don't get it.

Lovage is known to modern commerce as a source of oil for flavoring tobaccos and for perfumes, and the root in medicinal preparations.   But one wonders why it has disappeared so generally from the herb patch where thyme, sage and parsley are still known and used.

NOTES ON THE MARJORAMS
By HELEN NOYES WEBSTER

WILD Marjoram, *Origanum vulgare,* has taken possession of
our herb gardens, and the variations of this species are many.
Herb gardeners are puzzled, and the nurserymen admit the
nomenclatorial confusion which exists in their catalogued offer-
ings. They find botanical lists redundant with synonyms which
make accurate explanations about the culinary and horticultural
uses of these herbs difficult. We also notice the name "origano"
being used with increasing frequency by those who print very
special recipes for the gourmet. The varieties vary so mark-
edly in habit, inflorescence and aromatic qualities that we are
tempted to consider here several separate species. However,
close botanical scrutiny reveals even to the layman certain characteristics common to them all, and upon these characteristics
their nomenclature is based.

The true *Origanum vulgare* is a Linnean species, introduced
very early into Colonial gardens, from which it has spread into
pasture lands and along the roadsides of New England. Flowers
and leaves are strongly aromatic when crushed or dried, and
the colonists used the leaves for tea; but as a flavor herb wild
marjoram does not compare favorably with the delicate annual
sweet marjoram, *Marjorana hortense.* Glands filled with the
strong essential oil can be seen if the leaves are held to the light
or examined with a lens. Distilled, this oil has a strong caustic
reaction which has been used for centuries in the farrier's lini-
ment. A fresh leaf, crushed into the cavity of an aching tooth,
is a well known counteractent of pain. Not unworthy of comment, too, is the soil-binding value of wild marjoram and its
varieties, for its invincible, ramifying roots, usurping as they are
in the small herb garden, can be useful to hold shifting sand

81

and gravel slopes. And when thymes and salvias are fading, marjoram's colorful, fragrant flowers offer welcome nectar to the honey bee.

Typically, this herb is a robust plant with two-foot reddish, woody stems which rise from creeping perennial roots. The entire plant is hairy with thickly set small ovate entire leaves. Like many species of the family of Labiates to which the Marjorams belong, the so-called "flower color" is in the bracts, those small leaflike structures which subtend the flowers. In *Origanum vulgare* these bracts are closely imbricated in red, rose or greenish spikelets. The delicate paler small flowers wither or fall soon after pollination, but the colorful bracted spikes linger through December, in some varieties growing redder with the cold. Frequently these reddish hues are carried down into the stem leaves, which makes wild marjoram popular for winter bouquets. Inflorescence is that of a typical corymb with flower clusters more or less compact.

Soil conditions and sunlight are responsible for habit and color variations in *Origanum vulgare*. In loam and shade the herb is less woody, and throughout less colorful and fragrant. Bloom is paler or even white, and the lax sprawling stem and the bracts are green.

These white-flowered forms may account for confusion with pot marjoram, *M. onites*. I have never seen the latter species growing, but the Gray Herbarium specimen in the collection of Old World marjorams shows a sturdy, bushy plant of perhaps two feet with hoary foliage and pale flowers. Their green bracted spikelets are four-sided, tomentose and much longer than those of the knotted or sweet marjoram, *M. hortense*. They are crowded into a densely corymbose cluster so large that it gives the impression of throughout inflorescence.

Neither of these similar species is hardy in the north, but both are native perennnials of Mediterranean lands. Nor have these choice aromatics ever been found in the wild. Up to date we have no record of pot marjoram outside any garden nor has any authentic specimen been sent to the herbarium of the Herb Society of America.   Seed obtained from sources here and abroad are likely to produce plants of wild marjoram, *O. vulgaris* and its varieties.

Three entirely different collections of Origanums were sent this summer for identification to the Bailey Hortorum at Cornell.   One was a bushy white-flowered variety, extremely aromatic, with green woody stems and bracted spikes somewhat resembling those of sweet marjoram.   Dr. Bailey referred this herb to the European species *O. virens,* or as synonymous with *O. vulgare var. virens;* and such was its determination by Dr. Lyman Smith, now of the Smithsonian Institution.   Its origin seems to be from Italian and Greek gardens and it is one of those herbs popularly called "origano."

I have a beautiful rose-colored marjoram, blooming about midsummer in my garden, which I sent to Dr. Bailey for identification, for I felt sure that here was perhaps the famous winter marjoram *O. heracleoticum* described by English writers.   My marjoram is not as robust as the typical species and the foliage is paler green with soft, thin leaves.   The inflorescence is in delicate flat-topped corymbs with tiny bracted spikelets rose gray in color.   Of course it was diagnosed as "just another variety of wild marjoram, *O. vulgare."*   It seems to be distinctly a garden form which has not yet escaped and is frequently seen.

But I must confess that were it not so charming, growing out into the sun from the hemlocks and regal lilies, I should have grown impatient long ago with its all-possessing roots.   However, the latter fortunately travel so near the surface that the deeply rooted bulbs of the lilies do not suffer, and when their dried stems and leaves are past, I have the rose and gray of this lovely herb until snow buries all.

The third specimen which I sent to Cornell was one I found

rising through the tall weeds of a sunny, neglected herb garden. It was a strong woody herb, most colorful with the longest spikes of deep red bracts that I had ever seen. The air around was filled with the fragrance of its purple flowers and the humming ecstacy of honey bees hovering over their rich nectar. The herb bore such a close resemblance to *O. vulgare var. prismaticum* that I was nonplussed over the ultimatum from authority that it was only an undesignated variety of wild marjoram. Still, in that intriguing collection of marjorams from the Old World in the cases of the Gray Herbarium is its counterpart in white flowers, labeled *O. vulgare var. prismaticum,* collected from a wall in China many years ago.

Just which herb is rightly called "Origano" is still, for me at least, a matter of conjecture. Several species are so called, as is also the commercial mixture of dried leaves which is made up from whatever marjorams, wild or cultivated, are used in the cookery of the region where they grow.

Herb of Honor

HELEN S. STEPHENS

Favorite herb! How can one possibly make that decision with the lovely thymes, the rosemary which grows to such beauty here on the Pacific Coast, and all the others around in such profusion? However, if the choice must be made by me, it will have to be the aptly named sweet marjoram. *Origanum marjoram* or *marjoram hortensis* is in truth sweet — sweet in appearance and having the sweetest fragrance. It belongs to the family labiatae and is native to the Mediterranean region, like so many of our herbs.

In the cooler regions, it must be treated as an annual, but in its native area and here near the Pacific Ocean, it is perennial. It comes very easily from seed and germinates in about two weeks. It does not take kindly to dividing, but may be propagated by layering. The little plants grow twelve to fifteen inches high with a square, brownish main stem and wiry side branches covered with charming gray-green, velvety, small leaves, rounded at the tips.

The blossoms consist of tiny green, knobby growths, sometimes called "knots" — hence the name "knotted marjoram" which it is so often called. The knots are square and consist of minute leaves folded one against another with the tiniest of white flowers coming out from between them. The flowers are unimportant and it really doesn't matter whether or not they are fragrant because the leaves give off such sweetness.

Lore

In the early Greek and Roman days sweet marjoram was used to crown young married couples. It was called the symbol of honor and also was said to possess the gift of banishing sadness. I'm sure that was true, because no one could inhale its fragrance without pleasure and touch its soft velvety leaves without being comforted.

Uses

The oil from the plant is very fragrant and is used in perfumes and for perfuming soaps. The leaves, fresh or dried, are used for seasoning roasts, stews and sausage and are said to aid digestion. A few cuttings tied into a small bunch may be used for basting meats when barbecuing.

In the Landscape

It is such a charming small plant that it may be used in many ways and in almost any spot in the garden. In one place in my garden it is used as a tiny hedge bordering both sides of a path. It is kept trimmed to about six inches and although the stems look a little grey and woody when first sheared, it is soon covered all over with fresh green velvet leaves. After all, it has a right to grey stems as this same little hedge is now in its fourth year!

Fragrance

I have left the fragrance until last, as to me its loveliness almost defies description. Some call it spicy, some mention pine or heliotrope. To me, it is the fragrance of the woods where I walked as a child, which no doubt explains my love affair with it.

A Study of Mints

Compiled by the Horticultural Committee
Western Pennsylvania Unit
The Herb Society of America

Mrs. Samuel Duerr, Chairman   Mrs. Everett Partridge
Mrs. Edward P. Mellon II   Mrs. Frank B. Varga
Mr. Wilbur K. Monks   Mrs. George L. West

This able committee has undertaken studies of some of the common families of herbs, the species of which are difficult to distinguish. We feel that this study is botanically accurate and helpful. Others, of equal exactitude, will be published as they become available.

Family: Labiatae   Genus: Mentha

SPECIES	COMMON NAME	HABITS OF GROWTH
M. SPICATA L. (M. spicata var. viridis) (formerly M. viridis L.)	SPEARMINT, Lamb Mint, Pea mint, Greenmint, Roman mint, Garden mint, Spire mint, Brown mint.	Smooth, reddish stems, often light green at tip, usually branched. Erect, 2' high.
var. crispata	Curly Leafed Spearmint, Curly Mint	Hairy stems, long and weak, 2' high. Sprawls in late summer.
M. LONGIFOLIA L. (Hudson) (same as M. silvestris L.) (formerly M. spicata var. longifolia)	HORSEMINT, Hairy mint, White Wooly mint.	Stems tall (3' or more) and pubescent.
M. ROTUNDIFOLIA L. (Huds) VAR. BOWLES (formerly M. spicata var. rotundifolia)	APPLEMINT, Round leaf mint, wooly mint.	Erect, 2' or more. Entire plant covered with a thick soft pubescence which gives it a grey appearance.
var. varigata Hor.	PINEAPPLE MINT, apple mint	Similar to above but more slender and about 10" high.
M. PIPERITA L. var. officinalis	PEPPERMINT White peppermint (Mitcham)	Smooth, slender stems, light green with reddish undertone; erect, branched; to 3' high.
var. vulgaris	Black peppermint	Taller, thicker stems of bronze purple blended with green.
var. crispula	Crisp leaved peppermint	Reddish purple stems
M. ARVENSIS L.	CORN MINT, Field Mint	More or less erect, branched, 1-2'
var. piperascens	Japanese Mint	Stems taller, stiff and erect
var. Canadensis	American wild mint	
M. GENTILIS L.	Red mint, Ginger mint, Runaway robin	Stems slender, erect, branching, dark purplish-red, about 2' high.
var. varigata	AMERICAN APPLE MINT, Golden mint.	Low growing, spreading, creeping.
M. AQUATICA L. VAR. CRISPA BENTHAM (formerly M. crispa L.)	WATER MINT, Curled mint, Balm mint, Cross mint.	Hairy stems are weak, tending to sprawl. Much branched.
M. CITRATA EHRHART (formerly M. piperita citrata)	CITRUS MINT, Bergamot mint, orange mint, lemon mint.	Decumbent or partially so at maturity. Very leafy, branching, reddish stems. Possibly glabrous form of M. aquatica.
var. Eau de Cologne or Chartreuse		Overground runners, metallic purple.
M. REQUIENI BENTHAM	CORSICAN MINT, Spanish Mint	Prostrate creeper, 1/2" high
M. PULEGIUM L.	ENGLISH PENNYROYAL, Pudding grass	Prostrate creeper, mat-forming. Much branched, red maroon stems.

FRAGRANCE, TASTE	LEAVES	FLOWER
Very aromatic; all culinary menthas can be used for sauces, jellies, and candied leaves.	Oblong or ovate-lanceolate, acute, irregularly toothed, glabrous, sessile, heavily veined; light green.	July-August, pale violet (grey look). Long narrow continuous spikes, terminal and in upper axils. Central spike often exceeds others in length.
Very aromatic; all culinary menthas can be used for sauces, jellies, and candied leaves.	Broad, dull; crinkly, with heavily veined undersurface.	July-August, pale purple in slender terminal spikes.
Very aromatic; all culinary menthas can be used for sauces, jellies, and candied leaves.	Almost stemless. Vary from ovate or lanceolate to oblong; acute, sharply serrate; glabrous above, underside heavily pubescent. Pinnately veined.	July-August, pale purple in short compact slender terminal spikes, but varies considerably.
Delicate, apple-like	Round to elliptical, nearly sessile, rugose and net-veined, crenate-dentate, pubescent.	Pink-white, reddish to lilac in long slender spikes, terminal and in upper axils.
Pineapple when young, more minty when old.	Leaves smaller, with irregular white and cream patches; some shoots fully albino.	Greyish-white, August.
Sensation of coolness in mouth because of menthol content; finest oil.	Elliptical to lanceolate, 1"-3" long. Rather long stalked, nearly glabrous, serrate, acute. Light green.	July-August, pale violet in dense clusters on long slender interrupted spikes, axillary and terminal. Spikes at tips of side branches often longer than center.
More oil and stronger, but not as fine quality.	Dark green tinged with purple	Reddish purple terminal spikes
	Bronze-purple unless in shade, twirled.	Mauve terminal spikes
Strong odor and taste	Ovate, oblong, or lanceolate; serrate, petioled, more or less hairy (varies).	July-August, pale lilac, on upper leaf axils only.
Grown in Japan for its high menthol production.	Sharply serrate, deep green; leaves larger, narrow, pointed.	Pale mauve in axillary whorls.
	Leaves more lanceolate but varies	Lilac white or white, July-Sept.
	Ovate, coarsely and sharply serrate, short-stalked, dark green	Pale purple in whorls on leaf axils.
Fruity, refreshing	Smooth green leaves streaked with yellow-cream.	Pale purple in whorls on leaf axils.
Pungent, piny-resinous	Round-ovate, short-petioled, lacerate-dentate; curved and twisting, glabrous or slightly pubescent.	August-September, pale purple slender elongate terminal clusters.
Lemony, but first whiff like lavender	Oval or ovate, slender-petioled, serrate, glabrous. Dull dark green edged with purple.	Lavender purple flowers in axillary whorls and short dense ovoid spikes, July-September.
Delightful, fruity	Roundish to cordate, green with hint of bronze to bronze-purple, according to location.	Lilac, rounded terminal spikes.
Strong mint odor	Roundish, 1/8" across	Pale, purple flowers borne in few-flowered verticils in axils.
Strong, bitter aroma and taste; somewhat toxic, use with caution.	3/4" maximum length, round to oval; petioled, entire or somewhat crennate	Flowering stems sometimes ascend 18" from mat of leaves, with bluish interrupted whorls in leaf axils.

MINTS AND MICROSCOPES

A foreword to the article by Mabel Ruttle

EDGAR ANDERSON

IT IS difficult to grow mints without losing faith in botanists. No amateur expects to be able to name all the plants of his garden, accurately and well, but he does expect that a professional botanist should be able to do so. Yet if he submits his mint collection for determination the results are almost inevitably disappointing. If the work is done honestly some of the mints will be left quite unlabelled and other names will be followed by a questionmark. Our amateur will be even more disturbed if he consults a second botanist and then finds, as he certainly will, that the two sets of names do not agree.

Yet there is here no real need for losing faith in botanists or in botany. Rather there is needed a better understanding about the whole business of plant naming. Strange as it may seem, the naming of plants is not a finished process, done once and for all time. It is rather a series of approximations which come closer and closer to the truth as botany progresses. Some groups of plants are relatively simple to provide with names, as for instance, the maples of New England. Sugar Maple, Red Maple, Mountain Maple, and Striped Maple; each one is distinct in leaf and twig and bark. But there are groups of plants which are far from this simplicity and the mints of Central Europe are such a group.

Had man taken no interest in mints they would have been somewhat difficult to classify; his love for them has tangled the original snarl. For centuries he has been digging them up and carrying them from place to place, growing them in his gardens and letting them run wild again. Strange, garden-bred hybrids which would never have occurred in nature have been spread wide by his efforts.

But man always learns at last to deal with the complexities he creates and the mints are no exception. Within the last two decades botanists have hit upon a strange new way of untangling the relationships of certain groups of plants. Root tips are imbedded in tiny chunks of paraffin and sliced thinner than the thinnest tissue paper, for examination under the microscope. From such material we learn the number of hereditary units or chromosomes which characterize each variety and form. The information as to chromosome number may be very helpful in understanding the relations between the various species of a genus. Some are simple and have only two sets of chromosomes. Such species in the genus Mentha are M. *rotundifolia* and M. *longifolia,* each of which has two sets of 12 chromosomes. Other species and varieties have four sets, as for instance, M. *spicata.* There is good reason to believe that the species and varieties with the higher numbers have come from the fusion of two or more simple ones. This new technique is still more or less in the experimental stage, but it has already advanced to the point where it may be very helpful in interpreting a difficult genus.

Dr. Mabel Ruttle (Mrs. Nebel) has been one of the pioneers in this technique and fortunately for us she turned her attention to the wild and cultivated mints. She collected and studied them as they grew wild in Europe and America. She cultivated them in her experimental garden, and many of them she submitted to detailed microscopic examination. Her work is so new that as yet even few professional botanists are aware of it. The Herb Society of America is fortunate to be able to present a discussion of our garden mints which is of practical value to the herb gardener and which at the same time is a report from the advancing front of science.

SOME COMMON MINTS AND THEIR HYBRIDS

MABEL L. RUTTLE

A GENUS such as Mentha may be regarded systematically as consisting of a very large number of small species (Trautmann, 1925, in Javorka, Magyar Flora lists 210 small species) or as consisting of a small number of inclusive species, each consisting of several subspecies and numerous varieties (Briquet, 1891, 1896; Topitz, 1913; Schinz and Keller, 1914; Hegi, 1914; Fraser, 1926, and others). If, as in this genus, the species and varieties hybridize freely in nature, a wild population is obtained with a large number of intergrading forms.

In 1928 I attempted to check with the aid of cytology, embryology, and genetics the validity of these systems of classification in Mentha. For this purpose I collected mints from different botanical gardens in Germany, Switzerland and England and in the field in the neighborhood of Berlin and Freiburg, Germany, and along the coast near Dartmouth, England. Part of this collection was brought to Geneva, N. Y., in 1929. Here the collection was further augmented by the addition of mints collected around Geneva and received from various sources. Self- and open-pollinated progenies of the species and progenies of the fertile crosses between the species have been grown. The chromosome number has been counted in root tips of the principal species and in some hybrids; the shape and size of the embryo sacs have been measured and compared.

The following plants have been studied in some detail: 1. Corsican Mint (*Mentha Requienii* Benth.), a good species, very uniform progeny; 2. Pennyroyal (*M. Pulegium* L.), a good species with diploid and tetraploid forms and hybrids between the two; 3. Woolly Mint (*M. rotundifolia* (L.) Huds.); 4. European Horse Mint (*M. longifolia* (L.) Huds.); 5. Water Mint (*M. aquatica* L.); 6. Field Mint (*M. arvensis* L.). Numbers 3, 4, 5, and 6 are all good

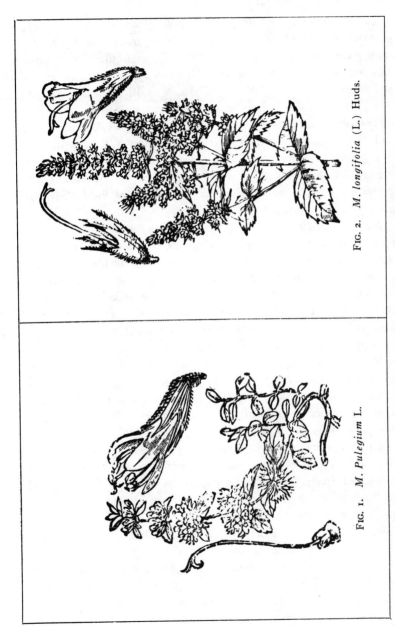

FIG. 2. *M. longifolia* (L.) Huds.

FIG. 1. *M. Pulegium* L.

Figs. 1-6 from *Illustrations of the British Flora*, L. Reeve & Co., pp. 195-197

species but they all hybridize readily; 7. Spearmint (M. *spicata*), probably of hybrid origin, offspring very variable. It hybridizes readily with numbers 3, 4, 5, and 6; 8. Egyptian Mint (M. *Niliaca* Jacq. em. Briq.), a hybrid between M. *rotundifolia* and M. *longifolia* and between M. *rotundifolia* and M. *spicata;* 9. Peppermint (M. *piperita* (L.) Huds.), a hybrid between M. *aquatica* and M. *spicata* or more probably between M. *aquatica* and the hybrid between M. *spicata* and M. *rotundifolia;* 10. American Wild Mint (M. *arvensis* var. *canadensis* (L.) Briq.), probably a good species, often considered a variety of Field Mint; and 11. Japanese Peppermint (M. *arvensis* var. *piperascens* Briq.), usually considered a variety of Field Mint but more probably a distinct species.

Mentha Requienii Benth. (Corsican Mint) is a small creeping mint native to Corsica and Sardinia. The refreshing minty odor of the leaves is attractive. It forms a soft green fragrant mat in the rock garden near a tiny stream where it is covered with soft purplish flowers. It is rather delicate and is mostly winter-killed at Geneva. Its seeds are fertile and the progeny very uniform. The chromosome number in the body cells is 18 (fig. 8), which sets it apart from the other species of the group.

Mentha Pulegium L. (Pennyroyal) is also an odd member of the genus *Mentha* and quite unrelated to the other species (fig. 1). I found it growing abundantly all along the coast at Dartmouth apparently escaped from cultivation. The material I used for study was growing in the Botanical Garden, Berlin-Dahlem. There were two forms growing together and not separable by appearance only; one had 20 ± chromosomes, one 40 ± chromosomes. The two forms hybridized freely, producing a population with 30 chromosomes. Seedlings of these varied greatly in size, shape and vigor. Some dwarf forms of these seedlings were more suitable for the rock garden than is typical M. *Pulegium.* This species like M. *Requienii* does not hybridize with other mints.

The large interrelated group of mints found throughout Europe, Asia Minor and North Africa has been divided by Briquet (1891, 1895), Hegi (1914) and others into five main species (figs. 2, 3, 4, 5, and 6): *Mentha rotundifolia* (L.) Huds. (Woolly Mint); M. *longi-*

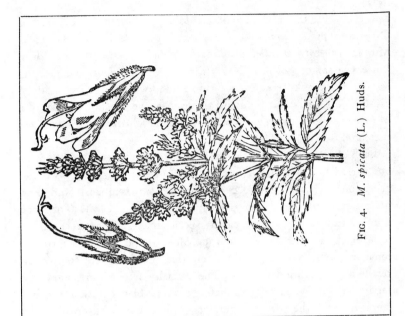

Fig. 4. *M. spicata* (L.) Huds.

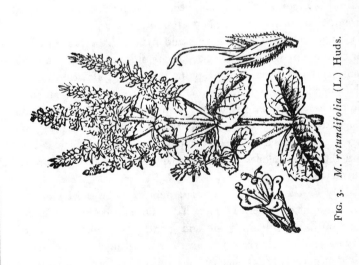

Fig. 3. *M. rotundifolia* (L.) Huds.

folia (L.) Huds. (European Horse Mint); *M. spicata* (L.) Huds. (Spearmint); *M. aquatica* L. (Water Mint) and *M. arvensis* L. (Field Mint). *M. rotundifolia, M. longifolia* and *M. spicata* bear their flowers in spikes and have leaves with no or very short petioles. In *M. aquatica* the flowers form a terminal head with one or two axillary clusters just below the head and the leaves have distinct petioles. In *M. arvensis* the flowers are borne in axillary clusters, the leaves are petiolate.

Each of these five species consists of several subspecies and numerous varieties. Each of the five hybridizes freely in nature with the other four. These hybrids occur naturally, some frequently and some quite rarely, and have been given specific names (fig. 7). The large number of varieties of the parent species makes for an even larger number of varieties of each hybrid. Most of the hybrids are sterile, some are partially fertile and set few seed and others are completely fertile and set abundant seed. The partially fertile and completely fertile hybrids when self-pollinated produce plants with a random segregation of the parent characters. These may back-cross to the parents and cross with each other and with other species producing still other types, so that it soon becomes impossible to tell the exact parentage of many of the plants found in nature.

Certain clones of these species and hybrids have proved of value for their essential oils. These have been cultivated in the old civilizations, certainly in ancient Egypt, and have followed migrations. Thus, in addition to natural varieties there are horticultural varieties, the production of single clones. If these were apples they would be designated by such names as McIntosh or Cortland, but being mints, they are designated by specific and varietal names which cover not only the special clones of commercial value but a large number of other clones.

Many of these species, varieties, hybrids and special clones have been brought to America. They have run wild both by seed and by clone until every little brook and glen has its mint variety, often varying just a little from that in the next glen. It also seems probable that natural crosses have occurred between these European mints and the native American mint.

Fig. 6. *M. arvensis* L.

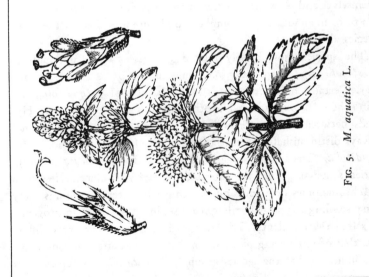

Fig. 5. *M. aquatica* L.

M. rotundifolia (fig. 2), *M. longifolia* (fig. 3) and their hybrid *M. Niliaca* Jacq. em. Briq. (Egyptian Mint) proved easy to collect in Black Forest rambles. The branches of *M. rotundifolia* tend to stand at rather large angles to the main stem giving the plant a somewhat rigid appearance. The hairs on the backs of the deeply-veined, rounded leaves are long and branched, giving the character-istic woolly covering. In *M. longifolia* the angle of branching is more acute, the leaves longer, the hairs thick but unbranched.

The chromosome number in body cells of both *M. rotundifolia* and *M. longifolia* is 24 (figs. 10 and 9). Progenies from self-pollinated seed of both species are fairly true to type. The two species hybridize freely and produce the fertile hybrid *M. Niliaca,* also with 24 chromo-somes (fig. 13). Segregation occurs in hybrid seedling populations according to Mendelian principles, crosses occur within the segregants and back-crosses to the parents with the result that *niliaca* types may be collected, in the wild, varying all the way from plants closely resembling *M. rotundifolia* to plants closely resembling *M. longifolia.* Now when one considers that both *M. rotundifolia* and *M. longifolia* are composed of numerous varieties which cross freely between themselves and between varieties of the opposing species, one can be-gin to form an idea of the complicated picture presented by these two species alone.

The species most closely related to these two is undoubtedly *M. spicata* (fig. 4) with a chromosome number of 48 ± (figs. 11 and 12). Certain characters of *M. spicata* resemble *M. rotundifolia,* cer-tain others *M. longifolia,* while others are different from either. Hy-brids between *M. spicata* and *M. rotundifolia* occur and are not always distinguishable from those between *M. longifolia* and *M. ro-tundifolia.* The chromosome number in different *spicata* seedlings varied somewhat from the expected, plants with more or less than 48 chromosomes occurring quite frequently. Sterile seedlings, very hairy seedlings, typical fertile *spicata* seedlings occurred in progenies of selfed *spicata* plants. The odor of different plants is very differ-ent, that of some being pleasant, that of others quite obnoxious. All this indicates that the species group *M. spicata* possibly represents a segregant of a hybrid between *M. rotundifolia* and *M. longifolia* in which the chromosome number has doubled but is for some reason not quite balanced.

Spearmint of commerce, commonly called "M. spicata," has 36 chromosomes. The leaf venation resembles M. rotundifolia, the clone is quite sterile and rarely or never sets seeds. It possibly represents a hybrid between a particular M. spicata and M. rotundifolia or M. Niliaca.

M. aquatica (Water Mint) is a large vigorous mint found in low places throughout Germany (fig. 5). I collected it also along the coast near Dartmouth, England. The flowers are borne in heads, with perhaps one or two axillary clusters, the leaves have long petioles, the odor is indifferent. The chromosome number is 96 (fig. 14).

In spite of the great difference in chromosome number I was able to hybridize M. aquatica and the other mint species in the 12-ploid series. These hybrids were in all cases sterile. Hybrids of M. spicata x M. aquatica are regarded as M. piperita (L.) Huds. This name has been applied in particular to the commercially grown " Mitcham peppermint,"[1] but it is also applied to the large group of other hybrids of similar parentage just as the name "M. spicata" has been applied both to commercial spearmint and to the large and variable spicata group.

The hybrids between M. spicata and M. aquatica which I have made and grown are distinctly poor in both quantity and quality of oil. Apparently the parents must be more carefully selected in order to produce typical peppermint or it is possible that peppermint is the product of a cross between one of the numerous varieties of M. Niliaca (M. spicata x M. rotundifolia) and M. aquatica. This possibility is also indicated by the chromosome number (fig. 16).

Besides Mitcham peppermint there are several other varieties grown which yield a good quality of peppermint oil. It is possible that the early colonists brought some of these to America as well as Mitcham peppermint. They have apparently escaped from cultivation, occasionally have set seed and so account for the various peppermints found growing wild in the various glens. Although Mitcham pep-

---

[1] For commercial spearmint and peppermint see Fig. 3 and Fig. 2. U. S. Dept. of Agric. *Farmers' Bulletin* No. 1555.

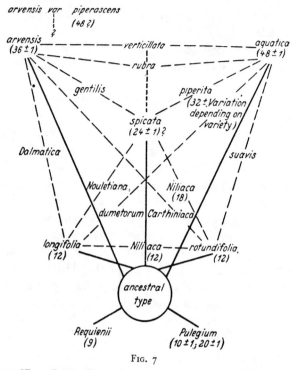

FIG. 7

[From Ruttle, Gartenbauwissenschaft 4, Diag. 1. p. 463]

This figure shows the five interrelated species and their hybrids indicated by the broken lines. Heavy black lines indicate the "supposed origin" of the species. As indicated M. Requienii and M. Pulegium show different lines of origin. The position of the species on the chart is arbitrary except as influenced by external morphology and chromosome number. The chromosome numbers given are half the number in the somatic cells and are consequently half the number given for the species in the text and in figs. 8-16.

permint is usually completely sterile it may on rare occasions produce anthers with apparently viable pollen and may through very occasional seeds in the course of years have yielded occasional progeny. M. *piperita* var. *citrata* Briq. (Bergamot Mint) represents a possible segregant more like the *aquatica* parent, or possibly even a mutant of M. *aquatica* itself.

The hybrid between M. *aquatica* and M. *rotundifolia* produced interesting offspring, the odor of which is distinctly pleasing. Some readers may care to grow this in their gardens.

M. arvensis (Field Mint) is commonly found along every little brook in south Germany. It is a small low-growing creeping mint with considerable variation in plant type and a most vile odor. The chromosome number is 72 (fig. 15).

The American Wild Mint, *M. arvensis* var. *canadensis* (L.) Briq. has the axillary flowers of *M. arvensis*. The habit of growth is quite different, however, and the odor is much more pleasant. This plant is often listed as a valid species under the name *M. canadensis* L. which may be more correct. The number of its chromosomes and its crossing relationships with the other species should be first determined.

Japanese Peppermint, *M. arvensis* var. *piperascens* Briq., is a tall vigorous plant very different from the small creeping field mint of the German brooks. Its self-pollinated progeny is variable as regards odor, vigor, leaf shape and resistance to mildew. Its chromosome number approaches 96. This evidently should be regarded as a distinct species. This mint is valuable commercially because of its high oil yield and the high menthol content of its oil. The roots are, however, winter-killed in New York and Michigan. To produce a plant with a good oil yield and high menthol content but with more vigorous roots this plant was crossed with *M. aquatica*, *M. arvensis* (European), *M. rotundifolia*, *M. longifolia* and *M. spicata*.

The progeny of the cross with *M. arvensis* (Field Mint) were distinctly bad in odor, the cross with *M. longifolia* was not particularly promising. The cross *M. spicata* x *M. arvensis* var. *piperascens* yielded several vigorous progeny. One plant in particular stands tall and straight, has dark red stems with long purplish spikes of flowers, large for a mint. The odor is also quite pleasant and rich in menthol. It blooms late and should, I think, be a pleasant addition to an herb garden. Another plant from a similar cross but using a different *spicata* parent has white stems and less beautiful flower spikes but a somewhat more pleasant odor. Both of these plants have distinctly vigorous rootstocks and can be grown on high land.

Among the plants of the cross *M. aquatica* x *M. arvensis* var. *piperascens* are plants with less vigorous roots than *M. aquatica* but more vigorous than *M. arvensis* var. *piperascens*. The menthol content is

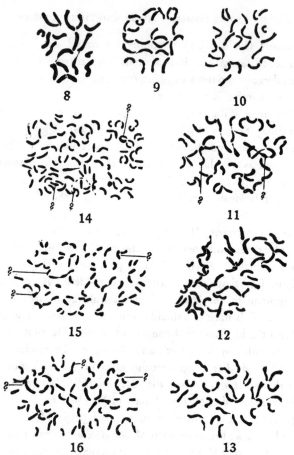

From Ruttle. *Gartenbauwissenschaft* 4, *figs.* 54-62

The number of chromosomes* in body cells of the different Mentha species. Interrogation marks indicate points at which the interpretation is somewhat doubtful.

Fig. 8. *M. Requienii.* Metaphase† showing 18 chromosomes.

Fig. 9. *M. longifolia.* Metaphase showing 24 chromosomes.

Fig. 10. *M. rotundifolia.* Metaphase showing 24 chromosomes.

Fig. 11. *M. spicata,* seedling. Metaphase showing 48± 2 chromosomes.

Fig. 12. *M. spicata?* Hairy type growing in *M. spicata* plot, Berlin-Dahlem. Metaphase showing 48 chromosomes.

Fig. 13. *M. Niliaca* var. *Lamarckii.* Metaphase showing 36 chromosomes.

Fig. 14. *M. aquatica.* Metaphase showing 96 chromosomes, 91 from one section and 5 from the adjoining.

Fig. 15. *M. arvensis.* Seedling. Seed obtained from Czechoslovakia. Metaphase showing 72 chromosomes.

Fig. 16. *M. piperita* "Mitcham," from the Karl Pabst Seed Co., Erfurt. Metaphase showing 65-69 chromosomes depending on whether certain chromosomes are one long or two shorter chromosomes.

* Chromosome. Formed bodies in the cell nucleus, made of protoplasm, bearers of hereditary units, constant in number and shape for each species, visible during nuclear division and easy to count at the stage of division called metaphase.

† Metaphase. The stage of nuclear division during which the chromosomes are arranged on a central cell plate and during which the chromosomes divide and the halves begin to migrate to opposite ends of the cell.

at least as high as in the parent Japanese peppermint. These plants are not so ornamental as those of the cross M. *spicata* x M. *arvensis* var. *piperascens* but if one likes the odor of menthol one will like to have a little of this mint in the garden.

Certain varieties of mint in addition to the ones described have been grown in gardens and given common names. Variegation is a common mutation in mint seedlings. I obtained numerous variegated seedlings of M. *arvensis*. The pretty variegated woolly mint commonly grown in gardens and called Pineapple Mint is undoubtedly a variegated mutant of M. *rotundifolia;* the Golden Apple Mint a variegated mutant of M. *gentilis*, the hybrid between M. *spicata* and M. *arvensis*. One suspects that in this case the M. *arvensis* may possibly have been M. *arvensis* var. *canadensis*. A count of the chromosomes might yield some evidence.

Crispa-leaved types also represent a common mutation in the mints, a mutation common to all species and many of the hybrids. Of the 2,000 seedlings grown at the Station many were crispa-leaved. The degree of crinkling varied greatly, sometimes the edges were simply deeply notched, sometimes they were deeply lacerated. Leaf size, plant type, hairiness and odor were very variable. Two types are commonly grown in gardens, a broad-leaved smooth *Niliaca* type usually sterile and one plant of which had 36 chromosomes, and a crispa-leaved *spicata* type usually quite fertile but having exceedingly variable progeny and having in one plant examined 48 chromosomes.

The evidence furnished by genetics and by a determination of the chromosome number has accordingly established the mint species whose chromosome numbers are some multiple of 12 as being a closely related group. At the same time Japanese peppermint (M. *arvensis* var. *piperascens*) should possibly be regarded as a distinct species. M. *spicata* represents a hybrid in which the chromosome number has doubled but in which certain chromosome groups are unbalanced. Spearmint of commerce is possibly a hybrid between particular *spicata* and *rotundifolia* or *niliaca* parents.

The amount of work so far done on this genus has shown mere indications of what may be done towards a further systematic understanding and classification and also towards a selection of plants

for breeding for the production of plants with a higher yield of oil,
with better quality of oil, with higher resistance to certain diseases,
and with more vigorous rootstocks adapted to different soils. Moreover, what has been done in this genus has not yet been begun in
America in the majority of the herb plants, the perfume producing
plants and the drug plants.

BIBLIOGRAPHY

BRIQUET, JOHN.

   1891. *Les Labiées des Alpes maritimes.* Mat. p. servir a l'hist.
   d. l. flore des Alp. mar. (Burnat).

   1895. *Labiatæ.* In Engler u. Prantl, Natürl. Pflanzenfam. 4,
   181-384.

FRASER, JOHN. 1926. *Menthæ Britannicæ.* Report of the Bot. Exchange Club for 1926, 213-247.

HEGI, S. 1914. *Illustrierte Flora von Mitteleuropa.* Pub. by J. F.
Lehmans, München, Mentha 5 (4) 2335-2357.

RUTTLE, MABEL L.

   1931. *Cytological and embryological studies on the genus
   Mentha.* Gartenbauwissenschaft 4: 428-469.

   1932. *Chromosome number, embryology and inheritance in the
   genus Lycopus.* Gartenbauwissenschaft 7: 154-178.

   1930. *The bearing of cytological studies on breeding possibilities
   in the genus Mentha.* Amer. Ass. Hort. Soc. 1931: 335-336.

   1932. *Interspecific hybridization in the genus Mentha.* Proc.
   6th Int. Cong. Genetics, vol. 2: 311-312.

SCHINZ, H., U. R. KELLER. 1914. *Flora der Schweiz.* Publ. by Rau-
steen, Zurich: Mentha, part 2: 241-250.

SCHNARF, K. 1917. *Beiträge zur Kenntnis der Samenentwicklung
der Labiaten.* Denkschr. Akad. Wiss. Wien. 94, 211-275.

SOUÈGES, R. *Recherches sur l'embryogénie des Labiées.* Bull. Soc.
bot. France. 68: 441-464.

TOPITZ, ANTON. 1913. *Beiträge zur Kenntnis der Menthenflora von
Mitteleuropa.* Beihefte Bot. Zbl. 30: 138-264.

TRAUTMANN, R. 1925. *In Javorka:* Magyar Flora III, Mentha: 905-
970.

CALENDULA OFFICINALIS

(A note on the frontispiece)

MARJORIE GIBBON

CALENDULA, " the little hour glass," has its official name from the Greek Kalends, " because it is to be seen in floure in the Kalends almost of every monthe," and it is undoubtedly one of the earliest plants known to the medicine man. Originating in the Canary Islands and along the Mediterranean shores, the Calendulas spread generally over Europe and across to England. Many names, grave and gay, were acquired as it journeyed over the world. In Italy it became *Fioridi ogni mese;* in Holland, Dodoens wrote of it as " St. Johan's Blum " and added that it was " unknown in shoppes as many good herbes be." The French are concerned to call it *" Soucis,"* while Germans term it grimly *" Todtenblumen."* In England, its name had a more cheerful significance—"Husbandman's Dyall," "Sunnes Bride," " Golds," a lovely name, and after being ascribed to the Virgin Mary, " Mary's Gold," until finally combining the lowly with the high, we call it the Pot Marigold, a homely, friendly flower as it brightens a corner of the modern herb garden.

The plant soon strayed from the " Apothecarie's " to the " Dame's Garden." The temptation is irresistible to suggest a Marigold Meal for a compleat and courageous hostess. The dinner begins with mutton broth, and " none," says Gerard, " are well made without Marigold petals, and Marigold buns with golden yellow butter." Next, the main dish of " good fat beef, garnished with a few Marygold flowers . . . and serve up with sippets." The proper vegetable to go with this will be the " buds before they be floured. Boiled and eaten with butter . . . they are exceeding pleasant." Then a salad decorated with the blossoms, " for Marigolds *should* be present at the last rites of the crab that meets its end in a salad, for all to gaze upon and not to eat." Accompany this with a Farmhouse Marigold

POT MARIGOLD — CALENDULA OFFICINALIS
Original etching by Caroline Weir Ely

Cheese. " Mix the new milk of seven cows with the cream from the milk of seven more cows. . . . Add to this three or four handfuls of Marigolds bruised a little. . . ." Top off with a " Tart of Marygold, Primrose or Cowslips " and wash down with Marigold wine, " very golden and pleasant."

If this dinner of herbs fails to induce the proverbial contentment, why, *similia, similibus curantur* — just take a potion of the petals pounded in vinegar for " they strengthen the heart exceedingly and are very expulsive."

Superstition has given place to science, salves in commonplace containers have replaced plaisters and unguents in gally-pots; electuaries and potions are simply doses, and possets merely drinks of a sort, but the Calendula, " vivid, pungent, strong," continues today for the benefit of the " compleat woman " or her man its healing functions. In the flourishing herb shops in England an infusion of Calendula is sold as an internal medicament for varicose veins and measles, and it is also used in many ointments and washes for skin affections. In America, its use is confined to cerates and lotions, chiefly for its styptic qualities.

Yet, most of all, we prize it, not " for Ladies' Closets and their Stillalories," but for its charming contrast with the many grays in our herb gardens, and to cut and bring indoors to brighten a dreary day with its golden sunshine and so best to " cheer the heart."

The Way of the Poet's Marigold

DOROTHY BOVEE JONES
Bethlehem, Pa.

The pot marigold is the single, annual calendula which is the ancestor of all the double ruffled giant calendulas which grow in many gardens. It is a modest plant, dear to herb growers because of its long history of culinary and medicinal use, because it is in bloom all summer, and because of its many literary associations. It is the only calendula which belongs in the herb garden.

Its name, *calendula officinalis,* signifies that it is in bloom every month in the year, coming as it does from calends, the name of the first day of the month in the Roman calendar. *Officinalis* after the name of a plant signifies that it has been used for medicine.

In the gentler climates of its native lands, continual blossoming would be possible, but in my Pennsylvania garden, the seeds must be started indoors to have plants blooming by the first of June. It is in flower until December first, because the first frosts will not discourage it, and when the sun comes out, after a freezing night, a bud or two will usually open, providing one of the last bits of color in the herb garden.

For many centuries its habit of closing at sunset, and opening dripping with dew in the morning, has endeared the pot marigold to poets. Hyll says " This flower of certain is called the husbandsman's dyall, for that the same too aptly declareth the hours of the morning and evening, by the opening and shutting of it; also named the sunn's flower, for that after the rising of the sun until noon, the flower openeth larger and larger, but after the noontime unto the setting of the sun, the flower closeth more and more, and after setting, is wholly shut up together."

King Charles, during his royal meditation in "A Walk in a Garden on the Isle of Wight" says

> " The marigold observes the sun
> More than my subjects me have done."
>
> (1592-1664)

"A Wife," in 1613, says of her husband " His wit, like the marigold, openeth with the sun."

Nicholas Breton, an obscure Elizabethan writer, says in " Six of the Clock " — " It is now the sixth hour; the sweet time of the morning; and the sun at every window calls sleepers from their beds. The marigold begins to open her eyes, and the dew on the ground doth sweeten the air."

In " Dombey and Son," Dickens mentions the small front gardens that had " the unaccountable habit of producing nothing but marigolds."

Observant Shakespeare mentions them several times. Perdita, in "A Winter's Tale" (Act 4, Sc. 4), speaks of

> " The marigold that goes to bed with the sun
> And with him rises weeping: these are flowers
> Of middle summer, and I think they are given
> To men of middle age."

In the " Dawn Song " of " Cymbeline "

> " And winking Mary-buds begin to ope their golden eyes;
> With everything that pretty is, — My lady sweet, arise! "

From " Lucrece " —

> " Her eyes like marigolds had sheathed their light
> And canopied in darkness sweetly lay
> That they might open to adorn the day."

Because of its great popularity in England, it is easy to think of the pot marigold as an English flower; it is, however, a native of the countries that border the Mediterranean from the Canary Islands to Persia.

The pot marigold was used in ancient Rome as a substitute for the more expensive saffron, in coloring soups, syrups

Photograph by the author (at 4.30 p.m.)

POT MARIGOLD (*Calendula officinalis*)

" But, maiden, see the day is waxen old
And 'gins to shut in with the marigold."

Brown's "Pastorals" (1615)
Book 1, Song 5.

and conserves. Yellow was the symbol of luxury. Medicinally, it was used in many ways.

It seems likely that the plant followed the same trade
routes as saffron in its journey to the far east. In China, it
was used as a dye, and in India, the Buddhists held the flower
sacred to the goddess Dwiga, whose emblem is adorned with
the flowers. Her followers wore garlands of marigolds at
her festivals. In Greece, the marigold was a funeral offering.
In " Pericles," Marina, strewing flowers on her nurse's
grave, said

> " The purple violets and marigolds
>   Shall as a carpet hang upon thy grave
>   While summer days do last."

In " Two Noble Kinsmen " (Shakespeare and John Fletcher)
there is a line about "marigolds on death beds blowing."

In Mexico, too, the marigold is the flower of death, and is
never used on festive occasions. There is a tradition that it
sprang from the ground stained with the blood of the natives
who died at the hands of the Spanish invaders.

The marigold also reached Scandinavia, because Bergius,
in his " Materia Medica," published in Stockholm in 1778,
mentions its therapeutic uses.

In France, the poet Rapin tells of the mythological origin
of the marigold. Of all the gods that dwelt on Mt. Olympus,
Apollo was the most attractive, and nymphs and shep-
herdesses vied with each other to gain his attention. Among
the attendants of his sister Diana were four little wood
nymphs; every one of them was in love with the beautiful
sun-god. When Diana found them quarreling, she was
greatly displeased, and turned them all into " gold-flowers."
Ever since, yellow has been the color that represents
jealousy. In Chaucer's " The Knight's Tale " the Queen
refers to " Jalousye, that wered of yelewe gooldes a gerland,
and a cokkaw sittinge on hir hand."

The common French name of the marigold is " souci du

jardin," derived from solsequieum, sun-follower. In Provence, it is known as gauche-fer, meaning left-hand iron, because the brilliant yellow disk resembles the polished shield
worn by warriors on the left arm.

In England, however, the marigold was most highly
prized, and it is in England that a considerable literature
concerning its uses is still extant. The plant almost surely
travelled north with the Roman armies, and became naturalized in Britain in early times. It is not known just when the
name " pot marigold " came into use. In Saxon England, the
name of the flower was " gowles," the general term for
daisy. From this, it was an easy step to " golds," because of
its color, so highly esteemed. It has also been known as
death-flower, cowbloom, gouls, goulans, king-cups, butterwort, bull flower, care, water dragon, drunkard, publican
and sinner, yolk of egg, shining herb.

In the early days of Christianity, when many pagan rites
were transferred to the worship of God and the Christian
saints, it was usual to give the name of the Virgin to anything
that was beautiful. The " golde " was one of the most desired of flowers, and in time became the " Mary-golde." In
an old church calendar, it is named as the flower for Lady-
Day, March 25th, when the feast of the Annunciation of the
Virgin is celebrated. A 14th century manuscript says

> " Golde is bitter in savor
> Fayre ———— is his flour
> Ye golde flour is good to seen."

The Saxon rules for harvesting the yellow petals of the
flower, the only part of the plant ever used, are explicit.
They must be picked only when the moon is at the sign of
the Virgin, and not when Jupiter is in the ascendant, for then
the herb loses its virtue. The harvester must be "out of
deadly sin " and must say three Pater-Nosters and three
Aves. Among its many virtues, it gave the wearer a vision
of anyone who had robbed him.

In England, the plant earned a good reputation for curing all kinds of skin diseases, jaundice, headache, toothache and inflamed eyes. It was used as a tea made of the fresh flowers. The dried petals, mixed with powdered root of madonna lilies, were used as a plaster for felons. The petals mixed with honey were taken to cure " trembling of the heart."

The flowers have long been used as a hemostatic, and, looking far ahead in history from those early times, we find that they were used in our Civil War. During the first World War, Miss Gertrude Jekyll, the noted English gardener, gave the use of a large field of her estate in Sussex for the cultivation of marigolds; untold bushels were shipped from there to the first-aid stations in France to be used as dressings for the wounded.

The marigold crossed the Atlantic with the first settlers, and appeared in John Josselyn's famous list of " New England Rarities," published in 1672 in Boston. He reported that marigolds were " thriving " in the New World.

In addition to its uses in medicine, the marigold is one of the few herb flowers ever to have wide use as a pot herb. Either fresh or dried, the petals were used to color butter and cheese, to make marigold custards, yellow with the chopped petals. John Gay, a Devonshire poet (1685-1732), wrote in " The Shepherd's Week ":

> " Fair is the Gillyflower, of gardens sweet,
>   Fair is the Marigold, for pottage meet."

Macaulay, in his " History of England," observes that " People of the 15th century brewed gooseberry wine and cured marigolds."

Everyone did not agree with its " meetness " for pottage, however, for Charles Lamb, in his essay on " Christ's Hospital," mentions the boiled beef that was served on Thursdays, " with detestable marigolds floating in the pail to poison the broth."

Sylvester's " Du Bartas " — seventh day of the first week — has the following:

" Cans't thou the secret sympathy behold
Betwixt the bright sun and the marigold
And not consider that we must no less
Follow in life the Son of Righteousness? "

Today, the marigold is more popular as an ornament of
the herb garden than as a medicine or a condiment. However, tincture of calendula is still available to pharmacists,
and is an ingredient in calendula ointment, a healing salve
that is still used, as it was in our forefathers' day, in country
districts in the United States.

Dried flower heads and powdered petals are still to be
found in herb shops, as is marigold honey. The marigold is
not a popular seasoning herb today, but a culinary adventure
awaits the cook who will take the trouble to learn to use it
skilfully. In Holland, the pulverized herb gives an indefinable flavor to soups and stews, and the Dutch will often
place one petal in a pudding, with extraordinary results.
The French and English use marigold petals to color and
flavor drinks, and cheese is still colored with the powder.
For someone who is fond of saffron, the powder may be
added to bread and cakes with similar results, and a soupçon
in chicken broth is enjoyed by those who like the exotic,
somewhat acrid flavor.

Partial Bibliography

Genlis, Stephanie de Saint Aubin. *La Botanique.* London, 1811.
Gunn, John C., M.D. *New Domestic Physician.* Moore, Wilstach, Keys
    and Co., Cincinnati, 1861.
Rohde, Eleanour Sinclair. *The Story of the Garden.* (Medici Society)
    " Printed in England," 1932.
    Shakespeare's Wild Flowers. " Printed in Great Britain," 1935.
    Herbs and Herb Gardening. " Printed in Great Britain," 1936.
Wheelwright, Edith Grey. *The Physick Garden.* Jonathan Cape, 30
    Bedford Square, London, 1934.
Carter, Annie Burnham. *In an Herb Garden.* Rutgers University
    Press, New Brunswick, N. J., 1947.
Leyel, Mrs. C. F. *Cinquefoil.* Faber and Faber, 24 Russell Square,
    London. N.D.

ROSEMARY — THE HERB OF REMEMBRANCE

Dorothy Bovee Jones

THE Andalusian poet Juan Ramon Jiminez, winner of a Nobel prize for Literature in 1956, wrote

" The flute and the drum announce the festival of spring:
Long live the roses, the roses of love!
Let the green of the meadows enter with sun!
Come to the fields for rosemary, come, come,
    for rosemary and for love!"

Thus, the great herb rosemary, emblem of love, symbol of remembrance, has cast its ancient spell upon a modern poet.

Rosemary, *Rosmarinus officinalis,* is a native of the shores of the Mediterranean, France and Spain. When, drenched with dew, the sun sparkles on its flowers and leaves, it well deserves its name " dew of the sea." In southern France, the perfume from the great gnarled woody rosemary plants, clinging to the rocky headlands above the Mediterranean, makes one want to linger and breathe deeply. Sir Francis Bacon said that when the wind was right, the fragrance from the rosemary reached ships twenty miles at sea.

For over two thousand years, this plant has been treasured for its heady fragrance, for its medicinal virtues, real and imaginary, for its culinary uses, for its symbolism in folklore, and for its poetic associations.

Egyptians grew the plant in their wall gardens, and the Arabs, in Algeria and Morocco, used it as a clipped border for their rose gardens. The Romans used it as a clipped hedge around their formal

Photograph by the Author

A SPRIG OF ROSEMARY

gardens. In his "Natural History," Pliny says, "The garden avenue is bordered with box, and where it is decayed, with rosemary, for the box, wherever it is sheltered with buildings, grows plentifully, but where it lies open and exposed to the weather and sprays from the sea, it quite withers up." Rosemary was in its element in these exposed positions.

Wreaths of rosemary adorned the heads of youths and maidens in festivals in Rome, where it acquired the name "coronarius." Describing the beautiful centaur-female Hylonome, Ovid says, "Hylonome, of those half-beasts the fairest in all the woods;

And she was dainty, if such creatures could be,

Combing her hair, or mane, twining the locks with rosemary."

Rosemary was a favorite strewing herb in ancient Greece, where it was thought to be a powerful disinfectant, in an age when sanitation was unknown. In Greece, virgins were adorned with rosemary before the sacrifice at the altar; later it was burned as incense in place of a living sacrifice.

Rosemary travelled north to Britain with the Roman armies. During the Dark Ages, it was treasured and sheltered in monastery gardens. Growing useful herbs was more than an interest for the cloistered monks; it was a way of life. But for their care, many herbs would have been lost. Forbidden to eat meat, committed to manual labor, growing herbs and studying their uses gave purpose to their lives, and enabled them to help the poor and sick who lived outside the monastery walls.

The travels of rosemary north of the Alps were aided, possibly, by the great Charlemagne himself; certainly by his son, "Louis the Pious", who succeeded Charlemagne in 814. Having long known his father's interest in useful herbs, one of King Louis' first acts was to order rosemary planted in the royal garden, presumably at Aix-la-Chapelle, Charlemagne's favorite residence, and the site of Louis' coronation.

Louis the Pious lived in close association with the monks and monasteries, and in every known account of plants grown in monastery gardens, rosemary nears the top of the list. The liqueur,

Chartreuse, made by the Carthusian monks since 1607, by a still-secret formula, is thought to contain rosemary.

The 13th century trading companies promoted an exchange of plants, also: the Hanseatic League, a union of countries around the Baltic which furthered German trade; the Easterlings, a guild of German merchants in London; and the Russian and Turkish trading companies which had an important effect upon British trade with those empires. Crusaders, returning from the Holy Land, brought rosemary with them, and ordinary travellers carried it also.

Childlike beliefs in the magical, almost holy properties of this herb have existed for so many centuries that it is easy to understand why it has travelled all over the world. Who, for instance, when going on a journey, would leave at home a plant whose powdered flowers bound in a linen cloth on the right arm make a man light and merry? a plant which would cure a cough if an infusion of its leaves in white wine were drunk? or a branch of which, placed under a bed, would ward off evil spirits and bad dreams? It was believed that a chaplet of rosemary leaves would comfort the brain, improve the memory and strengthen the heart.

The following quotation from "Don Quixote", who had lost half his left ear in an encounter with the Biscayan, shows the plant to have had a good reputation in Spain. "One of the goatherds had a remedy that would quickly cure him; . . . fetching a few rosemary leaves, which grew in plenty thereabout, he bruised them, and mixed a little salt among them, and having applied the medicine to his ear, he bound it up, assuring him that he needed no other remedy, which in a little time proved very true."

In the handwriting of Queen Elizabeth of Hungary, there may be seen today, in a library, formerly the Imperial Library of Vienna, a manuscript dated 1235. It contains the formula for the famous "Hungary water," a distillation of rosemary, lavender and myrtle. The Queen was paralyzed, and tradition says that this recipe was invented by a hermit especially for her. Rubbed with it every day, it did indeed effect a cure. The preparation became well-known, especially in southern France, in the neighborhood of Montpellier, where it was widely used. The Queen's formula for "Hungary water"; is as follows:

> " 1 gallon brandy or clean spirits
> 1 handful of rosemary
> 1 handful lavender
> 1 handful myrtle

"Handfuls are measured by cutting branches of the herbs twelve inches long. A handful is the number of such branches that can be held in the hand. After measuring, the branches should be cut up into one-inch pieces, and put to infuse in the brandy. You will then have the finest 'Hungary water' that can be made."

In France, rosemary was burned with juniper berries to prevent contagion in hospitals and churches. Because it smelled like incense, the old French name for it was " incensier."

Rosemary was used to embalm the dead. In his "Histoire Naturelle", Valmont Bomare (1731-1807) reported that when coffins were opened after several years, branches of rosemary that had been placed in the hands of the dead were found to have grown so that they covered the corpse.

An authentic use of rosemary in France today, around the perfume-manufacturing city of Grasse, is the distillation of rosemary oil.

While rosemary has been used by the people of many lands, the records and references are most complete in England.

Rosemary was naturalized in Britain before the Conquest, but it was re-introduced by the Normans in 1066, brought with them from their continental gardens. The Saxons were more expert as herbalists than the Normans, but under the rule of the latter, much of the old Saxon literature fell into ill-repute and was destroyed. Only four Saxon herbal manuscripts survive. The oldest of these was the Leech Book of Bald, written in 900 A.D. This is a treatise on the medicinal uses of herbs, and it is said to be, by those who have seen it, in the British Museum, a beautiful example of Saxon work, looking as fresh and clean as if it had just come from the hand of

Cild, the scribe. This old manuscript has a peculiar importance as in it are found accounts of herb lore and folk medicine which go back to an age of even greater antiquity than that in which the book was written.

It was not only among apothecaries and herbalists that rosemary held its reputation. Roger Hackett, a celebrated Doctor of Divinity, said, in a sermon entitled "The Marriage Present", published in 1607, "Speaking of the powers of rosemary, it overtoppeth all the flowers in the garden, boasting man's rule. It helpeth the brain, strengtheneth the memory, and is very medicinable for the head. Another property of rosemary is that it affects the heart. Let this rosmarinus, this flower of men, ensigne of your wisdom, love and loyalty be carried not only in your hands, but in your hearts and heads."

Newton, in his "Herbal to the Bible" of 1587, says, "The smell of this plant quickly comforteth the brain, memory and inward senses, refresheth all the vital powers, and not a little recreateth and cheereth both the heart and mind of man."

The most famous rosemary plant that ever travelled to Britain was one sent from France, in the second decade of the 14th century, by the Countess of Hainault to her daughter Queen Philippa of England. The Countess' letter to her daughter, preserved in the British Museum, is a poetic treatise on the virtues of rosemary. It is important because it describes one belief that has never been recorded in any earlier manuscript, that "a rosemary bush passeth not commonly in hight the hight of Criste while he was man on earth," and that after it reaches the age of Christ when he was crucified, at 33 years, it grows only in breadth. This letter records, also, many surviving beliefs about rosemary that have never been found in any earlier source.

In England, it took hundreds of years for the rosemary plant to make the short journey from the palace garden of the nobility to the country cottage of the peasant. By the 17th century, however, the plant was commonplace. In "The Schoolmistress" by Shenstone (about 1735) there are these lines:

" And here trim rosemarine, that whilom crowned
The daintiest garden of the proudest peer;
Ere, driven from its envied site, it found
A sacred shelter for its branches here."

Always and everywhere, rosemary appears as the herb of remembrance. Its vitality, its evergreen foliage, the folk belief that it strengthened the memory, all combined to give it this universal significance. Sir Thomas More, owner of the fabulous 16th century garden in Chelsea, wrote, " As for rosemary, I let it run all over my garden walls, not only because my bees love it, but because 'tis the herb sacred to remembrance."

The following lines are from a song popular in Elizabeth's reign, called " A Handful of Pleasant Delights " (1566):

"Rosemarie is for remembrance betweene us daie and night;
Wishing I might always have you present in my sight."

Tied up with remembrance was its use at weddings and funerals. Ophelia said to Laertes, " There's rosemary, that's for remembrance; pray, love, remember."

Herrick said,   " Grown for two ends;
It matters not at all
Be't for my bridal or my burial."

Writing of a bride who died of the plague on her wedding day in 1603, Decker says "Here is a strange altercation, for the rosemary that was washed with sweet water to set out the bridal is now washed with tears to furnish the burial."

When Juliet's nurse finds her dead, in " Romeo and Juliet," Friar Laurence says, "Dry up your tears, and stick your rosemary on this fair corse; and, as the custom is, bear her to the church." They all go forth, casting rosemary on her.

Sprigs of rosemary, usually gilded, were distributed to wedding guests, though Robert Hackett, in a sermon in 1607, admonished against this practice. "Smell sweet of ye flowers in your native sweetness; be not gilded with the idle arts of man."

In a play of 1617, "A Fairy Quarrel," one courtier inquires, "Your master is to be married today?" Another replies, "Else all this rosemary is lost."

When Anne of Cleves arrived in Greenwich for her wedding to Henry the Eighth, she wore in her hair a coronet of gold and precious stones, set full of branches of rosemary. A sprig of rosemary in a bride's bouquet was an omen of a happy marriage.

In "Knight of the Burning Pestle," by Beaumont and Fletcher (1611), a host gives directions for the marriage feast of his daughter: "I will have in only a couple of neighbors and their wives, and will have a capon in stewed broth and a good piece of beef stuck with rosemary."

The herb has been as much a part of Christmas celebrations as bay, mistletoe and holly. Walter Scott, in "Marmion," describes a Christmas feast:

> "Then was brought the lusty brawn
> By the old blue-coated serving-man,
> Then the grim boar's head frowned on high
> Crested with bays and rosemary."

The boar's head with rosemary was an ancient tradition, probably Norse.

Christmas legends cluster around this herb. When the Holy Family sought shelter on the Flight into Egypt, the bushes, through which they passed, crackled, and made their presence heard. Only the rosemary stretched out its branches in silence and let them pass safely through. Another familiar legend is that the Virgin threw her cloak on a rosemary bush and the flowers, white before, turned blue in her honor. When Mary hung the Christ-child's clothing on a rosemary bush, she found she had hung them on a sunbeam, and thereafter, the plant was endowed with miraculous powers.

Rosemary must have come to the New World by various routes. One wonders how it made the journey to Guatemala. In a study of the native gardens of Santa Lucia, one of the plants was rosemary.

In the North, rosemary came in 1606, with Captain John Mason, founder of the state of New Hampshire, thus becoming one of the earliest gardening links with England. In Josselyn's list of 1672, he reported that "rosemary does not thrive" and that it is "no plant for this country." That is readily understood, if the plants were left outdoors at the mercy of a New England winter. People must have learned to care for it, however, for the plant continued to spread, and an example of its migration exists in a remarkable festival which takes place every year in St. Louis. Dr. Edgar Anderson says that this celebration is definitely a pre-Christian survival from the German duchy of Swaben, a province in the Middle Ages. Descendants of these early Swabians emigrated to St. Louis, bringing with them their old traditions, inherited from their pre-Christian ancestors. It is as rowdy a celebration as one could ever attend; a little boy and a little girl are crowned king and queen, the girl wears a crown of rosemary leaves. The herb is identified with a virgin, a woman, a queen.

Tracing the history of present-day usage of rosemary in this country, it is likely to lead us back across the centuries to the same early uses in Europe and Asia.

In the rituals of the Greek Orthodox Church in Bethlehem, Pa., and other cities where this denomination exists, rosemary is an important herb today. The traditional services originated in 318 A.D., with the discovery of the Holy Cross by St. Helen. At the foot of the Cross grew a basil plant, and from that time to the present, basil has been the holy herb of this church. Basil being an annual, however, there are many months in the year when fresh basil cannot be obtained. Thus rosemary, which is always green, takes its place. In the St. Nicholas congregation, many parishioners own a potted rosemary plant, so that fresh branches are always available for the use of the priest. With a cross wrapped in rosemary, he brushes the holy water on whatever is to be blessed, be it a new home, a new baby, a new sheep, or even a new well. The water of a new well is never used until the priest has blessed it with holy water.

Rosemary is always used, even when basil is in season, to decorate the ikons in the church.

What of this historic herb today? In the mild climate of its native countries, rosemary is a perennial, as it is also in California, in parts of the state of Washington, in some of our southern states, and in England. It thrives in a cool climate tempered with salt winds from the sea, and in such places attains a great size. The roots are said to be the tender part of the plant, and if they can be kept from freezing, it will survive the winter.

With some protection, rosemary can be kept outdoors through a sub-zero Pennsylvania winter. In a deep pit, covered with glass, the plants come through the winter in fine condition; planted with the protection of a house, or even an unheated garden-house on the north, the other three sides, surrounded with a frame of glass and plastic, rosemary seems as happy as in the south of France. These plants bloom most of the winter, and when the frame is lifted, for air and watering, on a warm, sunny day, the trapped fragrance is overpowering. Sometimes a plant growing against a warm southern wall will survive, even blossoming in March, but it is never as green and beautiful the following summer as one that has enjoyed real protection.

To herb-growers everywhere, much of the old magic still clings to rosemary. Sprigs of it are still tucked into letters, for, as Thomas More said, "A sprig of it hath a dumb language." It goes into nosegays, it is slipped into bridal bouquets, and branches of it are laid lovingly in the hands of the dead. It decorates the house at Christmas, and its pungent fragrance and rich green foliage are enjoyed at all seasons of the year. It remains a culinary herb of great distinction.

Across the world, wherever it grows, a sprig of rosemary is never just a fragrant green herb, but a bit of human history in one's hands.

Variety in Rosemary

EDNA K. NEUGEBAUER

Rosemary belongs in every herb garden, no matter how difficult it may be to maintain in the north, as potted plants taken in during the winter, or as new plants each year. Although there is only one species of rosemary, *Rosamarinus officinalis* (translation: dew of the sea, medicinal) the gardener finds many interesting varieties, with differences in leaf, flower, color, size, or manner of growth. Few of these are listed or described in manuals or herb books, two only at all widely.

Rosmarinus officinalis, with no variety name, is the one always listed from the time of Dioscorides to the present. It is a shrub to six feet in height, growing out of doors in Southern California, with lavender-blue flowers, not at all showy. The leaves, according to Hortus, are revolute, dark and shining above, white tomentose beneath; the flowers are in short axillary racemes. This is true of all varieties, though the size may vary.

The other rosemary usually listed is *Rosmarinus officinalis prostratus*, also called dwarf, creeping, or trailing rosemary. Here in Southern California it grows from eight to twelve inches tall, but spreads for a much greater distance over the ground. Its flowers are a true blue, its foliage quite fine and dense. It is recommended by a local landscape architect for uses in an outdoor planter box, to cover a bank, along paths or steps where its crushed foliage will give a pleasing aroma, at corners of walks, under low windows, or against a foundation wall. The late Eleanor Chalfin had an article in The New York Garden Journal in 1961 telling how she had developed an interesting bonsai from this smallest growing rosemary. This variety is called a "toughie" here in Southern California, but all references to it in books or articles written in the north say it is the tenderest rosemary and the first to suffer from frost.

There are several varieties listed by color, as *Rosmarinus officinalis albus*, a shrub to about three feet with showy white flowers. Another is *R. o. roseus*, pink rosemary, growing four to five feet, with very inconspicuous flowers, much resembling those of the species in color. The only way to consider them as pink is to hold a spray near one really blue. It, more than any other variety I have come across, tends to have gilded leaves occasionally. As there is a variety called gilded or golden, which I have never secured, I wonder if this could be it.

The largest growing variety, six feet tall, is *R. o. Tuscan Blue*, which I have never found listed, though Miss Rohde writes in her "Herbs and Herb Gardening" of such a rosemary growing "at Mount Triano, above Florence — with larger flowers and leaves, both bigger and bluer than the type." As Florence is in Tuscany and the description well fits this variety, I surmise the two are the same. Besides being tall it has a wide spread and is attractive the year round, whether in bloom or not.

In her "The Years in My Herb Garden," Helen Morgenthau Fox lists and describes *Rosmarinus officinalis angustissimus*, Benenden Blue, a plant of which she sent for our Southern California Unit's Herb Garden at the Arboretum in Arcadia and which I later grew from a cutting for my own garden. I consider it the most striking of the tall varieties. Here it grows five and a half feet tall and is much broader, making a lovely green mound the year round. Its leaves, as its name implies, are very slender and its lovely blue flowers, in late winter, are the largest and deepest blue of any variety. This variety received an award of merit from the Royal Horticultural Society in 1933, more than twenty years before it came to California.

Another, my latest addition, came as *R. o. ingrami*, later identified as *R. o. Collingwood Ingram*. This name, and Benenden Blue given the previous variety, recalled some correspondence years ago when I was seeking lavenders. I looked up those old letters and found that Collingwood Ingram's home in England was named Benenden. In reply to the letter I sent off at once asking about these rosemaries, he replied that he had found his Benenden Blue, which he referred to as a lovely and very aromatic form, near Bonifacio in Corsica. The variety named for him he had collected in Majorca. It has stiffer leaves but equally beauti-

ful flowers. He added that both had been lost in his garden due
to freezing weather. A report in the California Horticultural Society Journal of 1963 describes the latter as two feet tall and six
feet across in California. Its flowers are a deep and striking true
blue color and its leaves a darker green. Last year my young plant
had only a few blossoms, but this year I hope to enjoy its lovely
flowers.

My eighth rosemary came to me at Santa Barbara, long ago,
and I heard it was discovered there. Its botanical name, I learned
recently, is *R. o. Lockwood de Forest*. I wrote to Mrs. de Forest
in Santa Barbara (from whom I had secured cuttings of *R. o.
Collingwood Ingram*, which she had introduced from England)
and she explained that years ago they had *R. officinalis* and *R. o.
prostratus* growing in their garden. Her husband, a noted landscape architect, discovered a seedling growing in their rock garden that was different from either. It grows about two feet tall,
has a branching and spreading habit with flowers the color of
prostratus, but with leaves larger and more sparsely arranged. It
now bears the name of its discoverer. My records show it has the
longest blooming period, only a few summer months without
flowers.

All of the other rosemaries have come originally from the
Mediterranean region, but this one is California's contribution
to the rosemary family, and we are very proud of it.

These eight rosemaries are growing in the Southern California
Unit's Herb Garden at the Arboretum in Arcadia. For years *R. o.
prostratus* has bordered the road past our garden, *R. o. Lockwood
de Forest* covers the slope and Tuscan Blue forms a border at the
top. A bed within the garden contains specimens of all eight varieties. And there are seedlings growing in many places where
they do not belong.

There are several varieties of which I have read but have
never found a source of plants: *R. o. pyramidalis*, gilded or
golden (unless our *roseus* is this), Silver-striped, Heavenly Blue,
Broad-leaved, Double-flowered, and Miss Jessup's Upright. Perhaps some day we will grow them all here and call them by the
proper botanical terms.

As the climate of Southern California is much like that of its natural habitat, the Mediterranean area, rosemary grows out of doors in the ground with no trouble. It prefers poor, well drained soil and requires little watering. All are easily propagated by seeds, though one can not be sure of the variety that will result, and by cuttings and layers. The latter method is the easiest and a drooping branch often layers itself so one can offer a plant to a herb friend with little effort.

Bloom is at its best with most varieties from November to April, the early months of the year, winter, a time when a garden wants color. And during these winter months the bees are always present, harvesting the makings of honey. How far the bees travel with their harvest no one knows.

Where its growth out of doors is possible the herb rosemary offers interesting green, fragrance, color, all with little effort. The larger growing varieties can be used as hedges or as accent plants in the garden, but they should not be pruned severely. The three lower growing varieties are most often suggested as ground covers, but not the kind one walks on, and are especially useful to cover gentle slopes for a permanent green cover.

In Praise of Sage

MARJORIE WARVELLE BEAR

In herbal literature the rose, lavender, thyme and artemisia families are extolled, not to mention the allium, viola and pelargonium tribes. But what of sage? It is deeply rooted in antiquity and a present day thriving genus of the mint family. In fact, probably no other botanical word has as many connotations or nuances of meaning as well as varieties of colors, odors and uses as Sage.

Sage derives its name from the Latin salveo, to heal. In the earliest nomenclature we notice a number of Latin roots which are associated with salveo, having become blended in legend and fact and still showing kinship with sage.

There is salve, to anoint with salve; likewise there is salve, to hail as in Salve Regina. Lastly there is sabio, to be wise, hence a sage. Even in this different meaning of sage, it has an herbal nuance with salve and salveo in that one could become a sage after being anointed with this herb of wisdom and healing or from having partaken of a sage tisane.

Gerard mentions sage ale — "no man need doubt of the wholesomeness of Sage ale, being brewed as it should be with Sage, Betony, Scabions, Spikenard, Squinnette and Fennel seed."

The double meaning of sage is mentioned in the "English Man's Doctor," 1607:

> "Sage strengthens the sinews, feavers heat doth swage
> The palsie helps and rids of mickle woe
> In Latin (Salvia) takes the name of safety
> In English (sage) is rather wise and crafty
> Sith then the name betokens wise and saving
> We count it nature's friend and worth the having."

Sage covers a broad field even beginning with these roots and stems. Today the salvia family numbers over 500 species and there is an extended listing of uses. Roughly it may be divided into culinary, chemical, medicinal, horticultural and decorative groups.

129

Going back to the source book of man's civilization, the Bible, we find a lowly sage, salvia judaica, grew in Palestine and was the inspiration for the Hebrew seven branched candlestick.[1] Exodus 37. 17-18. "And he made the candlestick of pure gold: of beaten work made he the candlestick: his shaft, and his branch, his bowls, his knops and his flowers were the same. And six branches going out of the sides thereof; three branches of the candlestick out of one side thereof, and three branches out of the other side thereof."

Thus sage takes its place along with the acanthus leaf, the lotus flower, the pomegranate and the papyrus as an enduring motif for decorative and symbolic art forms.

In the culinary and household adaptations sage can be traced from one particular genus, salvia officinalis. It thrived in its native habitat, the Mediterranean shores, and was one of those plants probably growing in Solomon's and Charlemagne's gardens. It was cloistered in the mediaeval monastery gardens. It thrived too, in China and was associated with Oolong and Pekoe teas. Sage as well as tea was introduced to Britain as a beverage in the sixteenth century.

John Evelyn wrote in "Acetaria": " 'Tis a plant indeed with so many and wonderful properties that the assiduous use of it is said to render men immortal." While John Hell wrote in his "Virtues of British Herbs": "Just when the flowers of sage begin to open there is in their cups a fragrant resin, highly flavoured, balmy, delicate and to the taste one of the most delicious cordials that can be thought, warm and aromatic . . . sage properly prepared will retard the rapid progress of decay that treads the heels so fast in the latter years of life, will relieve that faintness, strengthen that weakness and prevent that sad depression of spirits . . . will prevent the hands from trembling and the eyes from dimness and make the lamp of life, so long as nature lets it burn, burn brightly."

This lengthy discourse may have been influenced by the mediaeval saying: "Why should a man die whilst sage grows in his garden?" In Ram's "Little Dodeon" 1606, there is this advice: "To

[1]Harold and Alma Moldenke, *Plants of the Bible*, pp. 218.

comfort the brain, smell chamomile, eate sage, wash measureably, sleep reasonably."

Just as rue and rosemary were used as herbs of grace and remembrance in religious ceremonies, so was sage. Pepys in his "Diary" mentions that "sage mitigates grief" and for this was planted on graves.

While other sages were used in the household such as clary sage for bright eyes and wood sage for throat disorders, still salvia officinalis is to be credited whether to eat, drink, bathe or salve.

Today, gardenwise, this herb is known as Holt's Mammoth Sage and the newer varieties of Red Sage, S. officinalis purpurea. Commercially the best salvia officinalis comes from Dalmatia, where the distilled oil is a national industry. During World War II when the imports to United States were cut off, American farmers and herb growers attempted to relieve this shortage. However, the cost of production for distillation has been too great and the crops are sold as dried leaves for flavoring mainly to meat packing houses and spice companies. The virtues of that herb remain with us, truly a national ingredient in the Thanksgiving Day turkey.

The other great commercial sage used in the perfume industry is clary sage, salvia sclaria, grown and distilled in southern France and the Russian Crimea. In American gardens it is a majestic but difficult specimen to grow as it tends to be a biennial although it is a perennial in mild climates. The odor of the plant and its oil is reminiscent of ambergris and muscatel wine. The oil is used as a flavor, especially in wine bouquets and as a perfume fixative.

There are praises for many sages. Here are a few from the Golden West which might thrive in colder regions if given winter protection. Zane Grey's "Riders of the Purple Sage" is a composite name for many grey-green sages and their neighbors, the sage brushes, mostly artemisias. The local designations of black, blue, purple or white sage may represent a dozen different species, each of importance to insects, birds, beasts and men. All salvia of the West have an aromatic odor, usually pleasing; they furnish bee nectar to produce sage honey which is as choice as clover or orange blossom varieties. Black sage, S. mellifera, and white sage, S. apiano, are two used in commerical apiaries.

The pioneer Spanish padres led by Fra Junipero Serra, who established Missions along the El Camino Real in California, found the native sages most useful and beneficial. With the help of the native Indians whom the padres were Christianizing, many of these plants were grown in the compounds or cloister gardens. Today in the restored Missions the sages and other native herbs grow once more while in the State's botanical gardens they make spectacular specimen plants.

Among those in Southern California are purple sage, S. leucophylla, a dense four foot bush with whorled heads of light purple corolla and soft grey leaves. Another is humming bird sage or crimson sage, S. spathacea, a most robust plant with large bright green crinkled leaves and whorls of chocolate red flowers. The more delicate S. columbariae with prickly blue flowers was grown by the Mission fathers for its seed, used for a fever or poultice dressing.

Perhaps the most appealing of all the western sages is S. clevelandii, a rare plant indigenous only to the San Diego region. It is a modest, nondescript small-leaved plant which like mignonette perfumes the area around it with a most delicate and pleasing scent. Like the sweet grass of the east coast, and the vetiver root of Louisiana, this salvia is also gathered for sachet and closet bags of enduring fragrance.

The last category of sage to praise is the decorative or horticultural salvias. This group overlaps with some of the plants already described since many types of salvia are decorative to the garden-minded. The word salvia usually conjures up the old-fashioned scarlet sage, S. splendens, with its vivid red tassels which, like the Oriental red poppy, clashes with many flower tones. However, S. spendens has new muted tones of salmon now just as the poppy has. Two old standbys in the blue class are S. patens and S. farinacea, while S. pitcheri is a hardy perennial of cobalt blue and blends well with the crimson corolla of pineapple sage, S. rutulans, and the carmine flowers of S. grahami. These last two varieties add fragrance. S. argentia with its silver wooly leaves and pastel blooms adds a delightful color variation and S. haemotodes with its bushy dark green foliage and ultramarine flowers makes an ideal background.

Since the family of salvia is so far flung over the world and thrives under such wide ecological conditions it is understandable why sage as a word is both a noun and an adjective. It shares with the rose the honor of having more prefixes and appellations than any other two members of the plant kingdom.

While the rose delineations may be more colorful and romantic, the sage prefaces are more earthy and embracing. The two colors, rosy red and sage green represent the two forces of catabolism and anabolism, as one compensates the other.

Study your dictionary under rose and sage as well as looking out your window on a summer's day — a rosy sunrise or sunset — again, look and see the green blanket which covers the landscape or seascape. Depending on its mood the greens will vary, but always there is a blending of sage tones, basic and comforting. In that protective covering in the West, called sagebrush, one could find a hen or cock, grouse, hare or rabbit, sparrow or thrasher, all prefixed with Sage. Surely Sage deserves our praise anywhere in this wide world.

NOTES ON A FEW SAVORIES

By HELEN M. FOX

THE longer one grows herbs the more species one acquires, and soon seeds of plants related to herbs are ordered to see what they look like, and how they smell and taste. These relatives will not be as potent in flavor, fragrance or medicine as the true herbs. However, their similar shapes and habits of growth cause them to harmonize with the fluffy, fragrant plants with predominantly gray foliage and daintily colored flowers, that grace the herb garden.

As to the Savories, the best known is *Satureia hortensis,* an annual that has elements of spice and thyme in its taste of savory. It is easy to raise by sowing it right in the garden in early spring, and in a short time amber tinted stems brown at the base will come up, having narrow pointed leaves that can be stripped off to use in cooking. Cutting back will thicken it a little but the plant is not leafy and some of the plants do not stand too much cutting of stems. It is a good idea to have a second sowing to insure the continuance of a supply. By early summer the first batch will begin to flower and be ready to cut for drying.

A few sprigs of savory put into soups, stews, hamburgers, tomatoes or beans provide a delectable flavor. In salads, the chopped up herbs are mixed into the dressing but in hot dishes such as roast lamb, roast or broiled chicken, steaks or fish I put the herbs in a few minutes before the meat has finished cooking, for when they are put in too soon, the essential oil evaporates into the air instead of staying in the food. However, other cooks get equally good results from different methods. When using savory I like to add a bit of basil and thyme, and for fish, steak or chicken use tarragon instead of basil. Here I must repeat what I have written often, that a little onion should go into soup or meat where herbs are used, just enough to act as a warm undertone to their spiciness.

A second annual savory, very pretty for the herb border, is *Satureia acinos* which self-sows faithfully and can be depended on to return to the same spot year after year, and eventually to come up becomingly among other plantings. *Acinos* is a bushy little plant that grows to ten inches high and perhaps twelve across and is dotted with lavender florets in scattered whorls. The leaves are small, obtuse and slightly toothed.

Second in importance to *hortensis* as a flavoring is *S. montana,* a perennial, shrubby plant from one and a half to two feet high. It is spreading with leafy branches, woody at the base, which turn up at the tips and have pale green side shoots. The tiny white flowers marked with lavender are scattered over the plant. The leaves are slender, pointed, without stalks. and bend inward as if folded on either side of the central vein, while the upper surfaces glisten and are dotted with glands. The whole plant smells of resin and spice and has a sharper taste than *hortensis.* There are forms with pale lavender, pink lavender and almost purple flowers. They do particularly well and spread out gracefully when grown in the interstices of a rock wall or on banks, situations similar to the ones prevailing in their native Alps.

When I first grew herbs, twenty years ago, they could not be purchased in the United States and seeds had to be imported either from nurseries or botanical gardens in Europe and Africa. At the time, Henri Correvon was alive and had a wonderful collection of seeds and plants in his nursery in Switzerland, where so many of them grow wild. It is from there that savories and thymes are brought down in donkey carts to Grasse high above the Riviera to be distilled for their oil after first having been dried in sheds. The principal ingredient of oil procured from savory is cavacrol, and it is used in making dentifrices and soaps and has medicinal virtues such as being tonic. It is also reputed to be aphrodisiac.

From Monsieur Correvon I received seeds of forms of *Satureia* which came to me under the headings of species, among them *cuneifolia, pygmaea* and *repanda,* which are classified nowadays as varieties under *Satureia montana.*

Seed of the first *cuneifolia* I grew came from Bulgaria. The plant is lower than the type, much branched, and the thin leaves are covered with stiff hairs. A form labelled *cuneifolia var. canescens* came from Almeria in Spain and was a smaller plant in every way. *Pygmaea* has the leaves more crowded on the stem than the type and has large flowers that appear to be lavender to violet. They grow in free standing crowded spikes. The plant is about seven inches high and sixteen across, and looks as if it had been sat on for it is so compact. The leaves are dark and hairy, and form a tiny spoonlike hollow and are fragrant.

In *S. repanda* the leaves are set flatly on the stems and form a starlike pattern, and my plants smelled of citronella. The flowers have a white throat and the rest is pink lavender.

An exceedingly pretty plant is *S. alpina.* The stems are recumbent and form a mat. They start from a center and spread out flatly and grow to ten inches long. The leaves are small with short petioles, are oval elliptic and toothed along the upper part of the margins or all the way, while the flowers are purple and grow in axils without a common stalk and usually stand up above the leaves. The calyx is oddly shaped, being humped at the base and contracted in the center, and is inclined. Moreover it is bristly with pointed teeth and hairs standing out from the margins. It is found in high mountains in the Swiss Alps, Pyrenees and North Africa, as also in the Balkans and Asia Minor.

To leave the Alps of Europe and come to America we find a dainty plant, namely *Satureia glabella var. angustifolia,* that grows in rocky situations and in the South among the mountains, from New York to Minnesota and south to Missouri and Texas. When I first planted out this savory the stems were square and much branched, four to nine inches high bearing the characteristic labiate flowers, here colored blueish violet and half an inch long. Later, under the plant a mat of green leaves developed on purple maroon stolons that rooted as they advanced over the surface of the soil. The leaves on these stolons are differently shaped from those on the stems, being oval and rounded at the tip while the stem leaves are linear and wider above the center. The whole plant smells sweetly of pennyroyal. The type, *S. glabella,* has large flowers and is robust. It was first found by André Michaux in 1803 on the banks of the Cumberland River near Asheville. John Torrey found the variety *angustifolia* at Niagara Falls in 1818. I have grown only the variety, and found that it does not stay long in the garden.

These are only a few of many savories to be grown in a herb garden.

THE TARRAGONS, CULTIVATED AND WILD

EDGAR ANDERSON

TWO distinct tarragons are now on the market in this country. One is sterile and does not produce seed; it must be propagated vegetatively. The other can be grown from seed but it is vastly inferior as a culinary herb. In the garden these two tarragons look very much alike; even to the trained botanical eye there is little outward difference between them, but to a real herbarist they belong in quite separate categories, for the sterile one is among the best salad herbs; the fertile one has a rank, disagreeable taste. In horticultural and botanical treatises, as well as in catalogues and nurseries, the two have been much confused.

Nature herself has made the problem difficult. All tarragons belong to a species allied to the wormwoods, *Artemesia Dracunculus,* a notoriously variable species of a notoriously difficult genus of plants. By modern botanists *Artemesia Dracunculus* is understood to include a vast group of plants native all the way from our own great plains and Rocky Mountains across Siberia to the eastern edge of Europe. With such a distribution it is scarcely surprising to learn that the species is a variable one. Some varieties are hairy, others are smooth. Some have a rank odor, some have no odor at all. It is nearly as complex a species as mankind itself which includes Blondes and Brunettes, Negroes, Eskimos, Malays, and Mongols in a complex grouping of races, subraces and tribes that defies exact and orderly classification. Among all the varying forms, Asiatic and American, which belong to the species *Artemesia Dracunculus,* there is apparently but one which has superlative qualities as a domesticated herb. This is the tarragon which may occasionally flower but never sets seed, the tarragon which is often known as " French tarragon " or " German tarragon " but which really was anciently domesticated somewhere in central Asia and did not reach Europe until towards the end of the Middle Ages.

Of the wild tarragons several may well be in cultivation at one place or another, though only one strain has been seen by the writer. This is a rank-flowered variety sometimes known as Russian tarragon or Siberian tarragon. In addition to its flavor and its ability to set seeds it has a few trifling differences from the cultivated variety. It is first of all more variable from plant to plant. On the average, the margins of the leaves are a little heavier and a little wider and there are a few scattered hairs. These are so few that one can hardly speak of the leaves as hairy. Though the soft white-hairs are easily seen with a hand lens there are seldom more than one or two to a leaf. The flower heads are furthermore a little larger in these wild tarragons and the stalks below the heads tend to be somewhat longer.

When one searches for the precise and correct botanical names for these two varieties which are now in our gardens he finds man-made confusion added to the original difficulties presented by nature herself. So few horticulturists and botanists have been inclined to go to the root of the matter that the confusion in the books is worse than that in the gardens. As early as 1749 Gmelin, in quaint but descriptive Latin, had detailed his troubles in classifying the variable Siberian tarragons. The Russian botanist, Ledebour, put the Siberian tarragons in a separate species and called them *Artemesia Redowski.* Willdenow likewise thought them worthy of a separate specific name and named them *Artemesia inodora.*

Few botanists today would agree with Ledebour and Willdenow in classifying the wild and cultivated tarragons in separate species. The majority would follow Besser, the Russian botanist who a century ago published a series of papers of great technical brilliance dealing with this difficult genus. The cultivated tarragons he classified as *Artemesia Dracunculus* L. var. *sativa* Besser. The more variable wild sorts he considered to be another variety of the same species, *Artemesia Dracunculus* L. var. *inodora* (Willd.) Besser. Unfortunately at the time he did his work there were not, as there are today, sets of international rules by which botanists decide upon the exact name to be used in such cases. This means that when some modern student takes up the problem where Besser left off, and gives us a comprehensive treatment of the

Asiatic Artemesias, the latter of these names will probably have to be changed again for purely bibliographical reasons. Until that time we had best use Besser's names, *Artemesia Dracunculus* var. *sativa* and *Artemesia Dracunculus* var. *inodora,* adding to them the identifying abbreviations for the authors [as was done above] when we wish to achieve the greatest possible precision.

The cultivated tarragon is only one of several instances in which a sterile but horticulturally superior variety of a garden herb has been spread around the world by vegetative propagation. The horseradish of our gardens may flower, but it never sets seed; if one wishes to see a fertile plant he must journey to central Asia, the ancient home of that herb. More than one of the finest watercresses is quite sterile and cannot be grown from seeds. Which means, of course, that when we take a plant of the true tarragon into our gardens and grow it, and at length divide the root, we are the last link in a long chain of such people. Just so did the man from whom we had the herb, and the man from whom *he* had it, and the man from whom *he* had it, and the man . . . It was indeed by a series of just such steps that the cultivated tarragon spread out of its original Asiatic home and across central Europe and finally around the world.

THYMUS

By HELEN S. STEPHENS

THYMES are among the most interesting and versatile of all the herbs to grow. They are upright and prostrate — have pointed leaves and blunt — are shiny and woolly — green, gray and golden — you can sit on them or walk on them or eat them, but you can't help loving them. We find they have been loved for ages.

In the first century, A.D., Dioscorides said, " Being eaten with meat, it avails for the dull sighted. It is good instead of sauce for the use in health." He prescribes it mixed with honey for a remedy for throat diseases and asthma. Crescentius, in the 13th century, adds that " if you drink the wine in which the herb is cooked, it will warm the heart, the liver and the spleen." The Romans are said to have given thyme as a sovereign remedy for melancholy persons, to enliven the spirits.

In the days of chivalry thyme was considered an emblem of courage; ladies embroidered the device of a bee hovering over a sprig of thyme on the scarves they presented to their knights. The affection of bees for thyme is well known, and the fine flavor of the honey of Mt. Hymettus, near Athens, was said to be due to the wild thyme with which it was covered. According to an old English writer, " Thyme for the time it lasted, yielded most and best honey, and therefor in old time was accounted chief."

In Richard Surflete's translation in 1600 of the French " Maison Rustique " we find " Thyme craveth a place upon the Sunne neare unto the sea . . . and also that it may grow the fairer and fuller leafe, it will be good to water the ground oft with water wherein hath been steeped for the space of one whole day drie Thyme somewhat bruised." In Wales, thyme was one of the sweet-scented plants used for planting on graves. An old tradition says that Thyme made the fragrant bed of the Virgin Mary on the night that Christ was born.

Thyme, in its Greek form, is derived from a word meaning "to fumigate," and its antiseptic properties have been recognized since the earliest days. Thymes belong to the *Labiatae* family, and there are two types — *Thymus vulgaris,* or garden thyme, and *T. serpyllum,* or wild thyme. *T. vulgaris* a perennial with a woody, fibrous root and an agreeable, aromatic smell, whose seeds (round and very small) retain their germinating power for three years. Mrs. Grieve says that it likes light, dry, stony soil and is best propagated by cuttings or divisions. The perfume of Lemon thyme is said to be sweeter if raised from divisions rather than from seed.

T. serpyllum, or wild thyme, is more thick-set than *vulgaris,* in dense cushions, but occasionally running up a slender stalk a foot high, which gives it a different appearance. Its name is derived from the Greek word meaning "to creep."

Mrs. Grieve says, "Thymes are indigenous to the greater part of the dry land of Europe, are found up to a certain height in the Alps, the mountains of Crete, the highest crags of the Pyrenees and the sun-baked Smyrnan hillsides, but are also happy in our own country from New England to California. They will grow cheerfully over rocks and in barren and dry soils, where many other plants would disappoint us. In warm climates, one need have no worries about winter care, but in localities that freeze, they should be protected with salt hay or straw and watched carefully and pressed down into the earth if they begin to heave."

Thyme was grown in many mediaeval gardens as an herb "for potage" but it is probably more popular now as a flavoring than it was then. It has held, however, an important place in English kitchen gardens for many centuries, especially before the introduction of Oriental spices. It was commonly cultivated in England before the middle of the 16th century and was well figured and described by Gerard. Many people of our day prefer its delicate flavor to that of sage in poultry stuffing. It is delicious in stews, meat loaf, turtle soup and Burgundy sauce, is considered the proper seasoning for clam chowder and clam juice, and is a fine complement to egg and cheese dishes.

The active principle of its oil, known as Thymol, is recognized as an effective ingredient in cough drops. The essential oil is mostly distilled in the south of France.

In the garden, its uses are legion, because of the variety in its manner of growth and the colors of its leaves. The upright ones are lovely in rock gardens, as a ground cover for bulbs, and around sun dials. The creeping types can be used for those same purposes and also between flagstones, to carpet banks, and to grow over stones and walls. We read of a Seat of Thyme designed by Butler Sturtevant, San Francisco architect, and built in a California garden, which came from 14th and 15th century paintings. Here the low brick seat (about 17 inches) serves as a retaining wall besides providing additional interesting space for guests adjacent to a brick-paved patio. In many of its mediaeval prototypes, the "upholstery" was of turf, but the woolly thyme (*T. serpyllum lanuginosus*) used here is more satisfactory, needing less care and moisture. It makes a thick, spongy cushion which, grown in a sandy soil with little water, is dry and comfortable to sit on; and both its soft gray appearance and cool fragrance are most refreshing.

It is interesting to grow as many varieties as possible, and some not too difficult to obtain are: *

Thymus angustifolius — tiny, spreader, reddish stems
  Adamovici — slender leaves, loose-growing carpeter
  coccineus splendens — large, shiny light green leaves
  Azoricus — neat, tiny light green leaves, lilac flowers
  Janke — large, shiny rounded leaves
  Britannicus — neat, soft green, good-sized lavender flowers
  Balticum — loose-growing, light green leaves
  comptus — tiny creeper, fast grower
  Croaticus — long slender leaves, fresh bright green
  cimicinus — red-stemmed, good over rocks
  citriodorus — lemon-scented, small dark green, whitish flowers
  glaber (chamaedrys) — large leaves, fine long-napped carpeting
  glabrescens loveyanus — grayish hairy leaves, lovely

* Interest has been expressed by correspondents in the Field Note in *The Herbarist*, No. 21, 1955, on "Twenty-four Thymes a Day," and we are glad to give Mrs. Stephens's list toward that number. *Editor.*

lanicaulis — gray alyssum-like leaves, pale lavender flowers, rapid
    grower
Marschalli — sprawly, narrow pointed leaves
micans — thick mound, light green, narrow pointed leaves
nitidus — attractive, upright growing
nummuliris — large dark green shiny leaves, large-headed lavender
    flowers
serpyllum — albus: darling, neat round light green leaves
    Annie Hall: similar to albus, more sprawling, white flowers
    nutmeg: small shiny leaves, very fragrant
    lanuginosus: woolly thyme, gray velvet foliage, lavender flowers
    lanuginosus, Hall's variety: more profuse blooms, not as gray
    roseus: similar to albus, bright rosy-lavender flowers
vulgaris fragrantissimus — gray foliage, fragrant, strong grower
argentus — variegated, silver-leaved, lemon-scented
aureus — variegated, golden-leaved, lemon-scented

According to Gatefosse, thyme is "a faithful companion of lavender. It lives together with it in perfect sympathy and partakes
alike of its good and bad fortune." And I think that Alice Morse Earle
must have had thymes in mind when she wrote in "Old Time
Gardens," "It is impossible to describe to one who does not feel
by instinct ' the lure of green things growing,' the curious stimulation,
the sense of intoxication, of delight, brought by working among
such green-growing, sweet-scented things."

REFERENCE BOOKS

Herbs for the Mediaeval Household — Margaret B. Freeman
Culinary Herbs and Condiments — M. Grieve, F.R.H.S.
Green Enchantment — Rosetta Clarkson
Old Time Gardens — Alice Morse Earle
Herbs: How to grow them and how to use them — Helen Noyes
    Webster

A POCKETFUL OF THYME

A countryman cannot bring back from an afternoon walk a pocket
filled with "odours from the spicy shore of Araby." But he can
gather a handful of wild thyme and let it dry in the leeside of his

capacious khaki jacket. It is a scent he loves. It is a sun-stored sweetness of a fading summer. On an upstate hillside it is a reminder of Hymettus, and the plant has, literally, a honeyed breath. For as many weeks as it takes the fragile stems, the tiny leaves and the bee-loved blossoms to turn to powder in his ambulant pockets, he will carry with him the same fragrance that is crushed beneath a heifer's feet in a Delaware County field. A boy herding sheep in ancient Greece smelt the same perfume. A bee in ancient Greece sipped the same nectar. If a man wanted to allow himself the playful license of a punning columnist, he would say that here is the past flowering in the present time. More eternal than crumbled Grecian temples, the plant endures.

Of course, when it comes to August perfumes, to pocketing the herbal scents of summer, a man is not restricted to wild thyme. Pennyroyal can be gathered to dry zestfully in a khaki herbarium. So can spearmint, reminiscent of juleps and chewing gum. These more widely spread and better known plants can bring their own spicy scents to a man's hoarding pockets, but they can never supplant in his affections the Sabaean odor of wild thyme. Pennyroyal, he thinks, is a little too medicinal. He once tasted pennyroyal tea. It became a child's bitter remembrance to be placed against a kitchen slice of bread deliciously coated with honey that wild thyme might have furnished to the homing pockets of a bee. Spearmint, perhaps, can be considered as appearing attractively in either iced tea or iced bourbon. But wild thyme needs no such liquid connections and supports. It has a beauty of flower, beauty in its way of growth, beauty in a man's memory and in a poet's line. While there is a bank whereon the wild thyme grows, there a man will sit him down and be happy and honey-aired.

Let the Pharisees give tithes of mint and win Bible mention. A man will keep wild thyme in his pocket and gain a joy ten times as great. Beauty, perhaps, is too often a pagan thing. It loses nothing of truth by this. A countryman is ready to believe that if Pan had chewed gum he would have preferred it flavored with wild thyme. If the god had been conveniently equipped with pockets, he would have let wild thyme wither in them, keeping the fragrance which such pasture saunterers as a countryman or a Guernsey heifer can know today.

From the New York Herald Tribune, August 14, 1955
Reprinted by kind permission of the Editor

ONE MORE WORD

Two of our members picked up the foregoing editorial from the *Herald Tribune,* and the reference to the honey of Hymettus reminded them of a wonderful sight in the United States. In the foothills of the Catskills, in New York State, there is a tract of acres and acres of rolling country, tinged at its season with the rich purple of wild thyme. From it comes the true honey of Hymettus; for the story is that the seed was brought to this country years ago in the wool of imported sheep who had grazed on those Grecian hillsides. From this small beginning the plants with their natural adaptability grew and spread, and many visitors go yearly to see the purple acres and taste the honey. Our member states that the claims for this classic honey are not exaggerated, and " with hot biscuit it is actually food for the gods!"

The Thymes

Description and Classification

ELAINE SAMETH

General Features

The thymes are small, aromatic, bushy or prostrate sub-shrubs, mostly under 14 inches high. They are natives of the north temperate zone from Greenland to southern Russia, but are most abundant in the Mediterranean region, with greatest diversity in the Balkan and Iberian peninsulas. Thyme has been grown in this country (U. S.) since Colonial days.

The leaves are oblong, ovate, or lanceolate, and are very small. For instance, the leaves of *T. vulgaris* measure three-sixteenths of an inch long and one-sixteenth inch wide. The leaves are entire, that is, they have no indentations, and they are dotted with glands that carry the scents. The bracts are also small and in most species they are little different from the leaves. The flowers are small and grow in whorls placed in the leaf axils. The calyx is cylindrical and two-lipped, the upper lip broader and divided in three. The corolla tube is two-lipped, with the lower one divided in three and the upper one notched. There are four stamens, usually protruding. The seeds are very small.

Colors of leaves and flowers: The leaves of the different species of thymus vary from gray-green to deep glossy green and the mossy greens of some serypllums, and there are, of course, several varieties dappled with gold, or variegated or edged with silver or white, such as *T. vulgaris* Silver Posie and *T. citriodorus* Silver Queen. The colors of the corollas include white, pink, lavender, purple, the reddish-purple of *T. Serpyllum splendens* and the crimson magenta of *T. coccineus.*

Range of scents and flavors: The fragrances and flavors of thymus also have a wide range. Among the more pleasant are lemon, pepper, mint, pine, licorice, caraway, and nutmeg. Some other odors, perhaps less pleasant, ascribed to certain varieties are camphor, citronella, turpentine (*T. comosus*), and varnish (*T. jankae*).

Unusual or interesting species: One of the most interesting species, although I have not actually seen it, is the caraway-

147

scented thyme, *T. Herba-barona*. It is described as a dainty plant with narrow leaves, tiny lavender flowers and yellow-green stems which creep close to the ground. Because of its strong aroma of caraway it is sometimes called "Seedcake Thyme." Another interesting plant is *T. carnosus*, described as being like a miniature Irish Yew. The resemblance to a tiny Yew is also ascribed to *T. nitidus*. A magnificent species is *T. coccineus*, with dark green foliage and crimson flowers.

Classification of Thymus:

The genus Thymus belongs to the Labiatae or Mint family and includes possibly as many as 100 species.

Garden thymes fall roughly into three groups:

1) the common thyme (*T. vulgaris*) grown for culinary purposes.
2) the bushy species grown for their habit or their flowers (e.g., *T. carnosus*, the one resembling a miniature Yew),
3) the prostrate carpeting species (such as *T. Serpyllum*).

Wild thyme is described in detail in Euell Gibbons' *Stalking the Healthful Herbs* — in fact, the author has devoted one chapter to this herb, the chapter heading being "How to Have a Wild Thyme." Gibbons gives the classification "*T. Serpyllum*" to wild thyme, and states that it is closely related to *T. vulgaris*, the common garden thyme. It is exceedingly abundant in the northern Catskills, as well as other sections of the country. It is a native of Eurasia, growing wild from Spain to Siberia, and is especially abundant in the Alps.

Names of Species of Thymus:

The most comprehensive listing of thymes that I was able to find is that of the Royal Horticultural Society of England in its *Dictionary of Gardening*. The Society named and described over 60 species of thymes, indicating related species and synonyms. I have attached the listing, simply giving the name of the species and any synonym. About half of the approximately 60 species had synonyms, and there were many other indications in the descriptions that many species are closely related. The Society, as well as others, point out that thymes are notoriously difficult to classify and identify — botanists often disagree as to whether plants should be treated as species or varieties, and this uncertainty is reflected in their nomenclature, not only in botanical literature but also in catalogues and in gardens. Fairly comprehensive listings and descriptions of various species of thymes are given in several sources other than the Society, chiefly the books of Mrs. Helen M. Fox and Margaret Brownlow, each including some not in the Royal Society's listing, and differing in nomenclature to some extent.

Availability of Seeds and Plants:

While I did not make a current survey of nurseries as to where thyme seed and plants could be obtained, I did check through a number of catalogues from herb nurseries which I happened to have at hand, some of them, however, being rather old. In general, not too many species are listed in the catalogues but it may be that more plants are available if one visited the nurseries. The largest number listed was that of the Village Hill Nursery with 32 varieties, but the catalogue was an old one, as were two others with fairly long lists: Plantation Gardens, with 25 varieties, and the Tool Shed Herb Nursery with 18.

The Royal Horticultural Society states that *T. Serpyllum* is often used to cover a large number of plants, which some botanists distinguish as varieties of subspecies and others as species. Some of these have been derived from *T. Drucei* and allies, others from *T. pulegioides* and allies. Plants sometimes treated as varieties of *T. Serpyllum* also include *T. lanuginosus, T. Marschallianus, T. nummularius* and *T. pseudolanuginosus.*

Various Species of THYMUS

Listed by the Royal Horticultural Society of England in its *Dictionary of Gardening* (Synonyms indicated by the Society in its list are indented in italic type)

acicularis
  striatus acicularis
alpinus
  Calamintha alpina
angustifolius
  Serpyllum
arcticus
aveyronensis
azoricus
  caespititius

Billardieri
  integer
Boissieri
bracteosus
britannicus
Broussonetii
caespititius
  azoricus [micans]
  Serpyllum micans

capitatus
  Coridothymus capitatus
capitellatus
carnosus
Celakovskyanus
Cephalotus
Chamaedrys
Chamaedrys var.
  comosus

ciliatus
cilicicus
citriodorus
comosus
　transsilvanicus
　Chamaedrys
　comosus
comptus
Doerfleri
　hirsutus Doerfleri
Drucei
effusus
ericifolius
　Micromeria varia
Funkii
glaber
Herba-barona
hirsutus
hyemalis
　Reuteri var.
　ericoides
integer
　Billardieri
lanicaulis
　longidens
　lanicaulis

lanuginosus
longidens var.
　lanicaulis
longiflorus
　Moroderi
Marschallianus
　Serpyllum var.
　Marschallianus
Mastichina
Membranaceus
　murcicus
micans
　caespititius
montanus
Moroderi
　longiflorus ciliatus
murcicus
　membranaceus
　murcicus
neglectus
nitidus
nummularius
　Serpyllum var.
　nummularius
odoratissimus
ovatus

Pallasianus
　odoratissimus
　of Bieberstein
pseudolanuginosus
pulchellus
pulegioides
Reichardii
Reuteri var.
　ericoides
　hyemalis
Serpyllum
　angustifolius
striatus
　acicularis
tenuifolius
　Zygis
Trachelsianus
　Serpyllum var.
　Trachelsianus
transsilvanicus
　comosus
villosus
vulgaris
Zygis
　tenuifolius

Bibliography

Brownlow, Margaret — *Herbs and the Fragrant Garden*
Brooklyn Botanic Garden — *Handbook on Herbs*
Clarkson, Rosetta — *Herbs, Their Culture and Uses, Magic Gardens*
Doole, Louise Evans — *Herbs, How to Grow and Use Them*
Dutton, Joan Parry — *The Flower World of Williamsburg*
Everet, T. H. — *New Encyclopedia of Gardening*
Foster, Gertrude B. — *Herbs for Every Garden*
Fox, Helen Morgenthau — *The Years in My Herb Garden*
Gerard's *Herbal*
Gibbons, Euell — *Stalking the Healthful Herbs*
Grieve, M. — *Culinary Herbs and Condiments*
Herbarist (The) No. 1 — The Herb Society of America
Royal Horticultural Society of England — *Dictionary of Gardening*
Webster, Helen Noyes — *Herbs, How to Grow and How to Use Them*

HERB GARDENS
1960 NOTES ON DESIGN

FLETCHER STEELE

THOMAS HYLL directed us in 1584 to plant herbs in separate equal-sized plots. Each plot was to be enclosed with stone curbing or boarding, and no bold herb was to be permitted to stretch beyond this outline. To prevent this, the sides were to be sheared hedge-fashion. Thus, continual trimming would bring out fresh young leaves, and both the tidy gardener and the cook would be satisfied. Appearance would be stiffly neat, and the young leaves best for flavor.

Several of these equal plots were grouped together in patterns to make the garden, thus forestalling Le Corbusier in Modular Design. To judge by our standards, a mechanical monotony must have ruled throughout, though a variety of sorts was furnished by the divers habits of growth, texture and color, always fascinating in herbs.

It would be a mistake to suppose that design based on equal-sized units used as common denominator all over the garden was confined to Herb Gardens in that period. Botanical Gardens were done the same way. It was logical, of course, because, in theory, confinement of one genus to its own plot made for ease, both of maintenance and for study. As a matter of fact, it did not work out in practice. For all plants of one genus do not grow the same size, and different members of the same family often require dissimilar habitats.

Nevertheless, when the landscape architect found a long narrow strip of land on which to plant an Herb Garden, one of Hyll's schemes proved to be best. He made a series of interlocking "L"s. Each "L" was built up of four herbs, each in its tile-edged square. The gardener was given strict instructions to shear the sides of each square rigorously. This was never done, of course. Modern lack

Courtesy of Mr. Fletcher Steele

Herb Garden

of discipline permitted intermingling of branches. Yet the blocks of changing color and foliage texture of the plants have been satisfactory from the first. Perhaps the effect was helped by the enclosing fence, with its espaliered peaches and cordon pears, and bold splashes of pleached *Magnolia tripetala* for violent contrast.

A marked trait of designers of contemporary works of all the arts has been the study and use of primitive elements. Such precedents were soon merged with the sophistication inevitable in our day. But the average observer cannot distinguish between the two. When he sees something smacking of the primitive, he gets mixed, and calls it modernistic.

In another garden, the landscape architect found nothing for design motive more primitive than a common factory flue lining. It must be unfamiliarity that makes it appear neolithic. When passing yards where contractors' supplies are stored, he has often been attracted by the shapes and colors of flue linings. They are toughened to bad weather and hard treatment; built to withstand heat and cold. They are thin, and thus avoid the coarseness of concrete pipes. They can be chipped away as wanted, and fitted to an irregular surface. They have frequently served him in toolsheds as bins for storing fertilizer and lime. But not until he came to build an Herb Garden on a rock, had he used them otherwise. This time he was faced by a ledge sticking up out of a lawn, about three feet at its peak. It did look rather footless for a big rock. Distinctly, it was not where it was wanted, yet scarcely worth the cost of blowing up with dynamite. This might cause trouble to a nearby house. So there it stood, until the owner asked one day for kitchen herbs.

The landscape architect had read the opinions of herbalists who declared that poor, thin soil just suited them. Bad conditions seem to improve their character, both in color and flavor. If that is true, he thought, herbs would do best on a rock, with next to no soil at all. He decided to cover the ledge with herb beds. But how to keep even a skin of earth on a rain-washed rock was a problem. To make tiny terraces on its slope would require walls. The whole place was small, and walls of brick would be clumsy. Boards would be difficult

HERB GARDEN

to fit to the ledge where it rose and fell. The only practical solution that sprang to mind was the neat, thin emptiness of flue tiles. An architectural checkerboard climbing up the rock in alternating plots of herbs and graveled paths. What more convenient for edging the checkerboard than big chimney flue tiles? They come twenty-four inches on a side and somewhat longer. The latter would allow plenty to be chipped away and so fit the rock base.

Fortunately, along came Frank, the invaluable mason. Interminable lines were drawn up, down, and across the ledge in all directions. When the tile were chipped and set in place, all held at least six inches of soil, and some a foot and a half. Each tile was set eight inches higher than the one in front, forming a garden pyramid under which the old ledge was quite forgotten. Most of the herbs liked the place from the first, although there were disappointments. According to the general rule of gardening since the world began, "you can never tell with a plant whether it will or it won't." The greatest surprise was the sulkiness of the thymes, supposedly the last standby. They balked from the first. Some were persuaded to settle down later. Some never liked the place.

In these two gardens, the designer has been accused of being modern. Perhaps they are, but his interest lay in making them practical to build and to maintain; and to have the herbs like them. His other herb gardens were, by comparison, old-fashioned. Old-fashioned, because he can think of no other word to contrast with modern. And, indeed, the two words mean very little to him.

Other schemes, based on similar modulars, occur to mind. One that he hopes to carry out some day is a miniature Greek Theatre, where the herbs would sit in a hemicycle, stepped up in tiers, on which the varying shapes, colors and textures would look their best. Such a garden would be prettiest if small fruits in cordon form were used for balcony railings and espaliered round about for walls. If all were backed with the rich dark green of *Arborvitae (Thuja)*, variety *plicata atrovirens,* one would have an enchanting doll-house theatre. Borrowed from ancient Greece, perhaps people would call this idea modern.

A VIEW OF THE AUTHOR'S GARDEN

COLOR IN THE HERB GARDEN

Helen M. Fox

THE outstanding character of herbs is their fragrance. Their other charms are the filmy effect produced by their much-cut divided leaves, many of them grey, and the daintiness of the flowers. The herb garden is an intimate place where the gardener knows the history, origin, and the benign or nefarious qualities of each plant.

Though the foliage of many herbs is grey there are others with entirely green leaves such as agrimony, mallows, savories, hyssops, and most teucriums. With few exceptions the glossy green-leaved herbs such as *Myrtus communis, Laurus nobilis,* and box are absent. However, the all-green leaves when used as borders, hedges, or accents, enhance the greyness of artemisias, certain thymes, and the foliage of carnations. The greys are further emphasized by plantings of green ground covers such as strawberries, vincas, and sweet woodruff.

Although peonies, hollyhocks, foxgloves, and daturas rank as herbs their large colorful flowers and strong leafy growth overwhelm the herb garden beds planted with thymes, savories, sages, and alliums, with flowers in dainty pinks, blue, and yellow, many of them white often marked with rose or violet lines to show the insects the path to the pollen. Beebalms, to be sure, come in deep shades and have large flower heads, but the color is muted by the presence of rose-shaded green calyxes, as is the case with primulas, while the purple of violets is modest, true to their reputation. Perhaps because of their fragrant leaves and flowers, herbs do not require brilliantly colored conspicuous flowers to attract the insects for fertilization.

Sometimes herbs are grey on both sides and again only on the

157

under surface, as with rosemary, or at the top as with *Pycnanthemum muticum* which though grey all over is almost white at the uppermost portions. Greys stand out in the moonlight and in the daytime when the wind blows and causes the branches to sway, the greys look silvery in the sunlight.

The grey appearance is caused by hairiness which is a means developed to prevent too rapid evaporation of water under hot sunshine.

The tints of grey change according to the season. In general, the hairiness is strongest in spring. By mid-summer the hairs begin to die and the plants turn slightly yellow, and in autumn and through the winter they are sometimes quite blue, as with lavender where the foliage and stems are almost violet. Then, too, the tints of grey vary in different plants. Silver thyme is yellowish; *Santolina chamaecyparissus,* with leaves divided pinnately into rounded leaflets which look like coral turned grey, is bluish; while *Artemisia ludoviciana* has almost white leaves as are the leaves of *A. stelleriana* shaped something like those of oak. The leaves of *A. filifolia* called silvery wormwood are pale green, cylindrical, and closely disposed on the stems. The grey leaves of *A. pontica* are so thin and incised they look like frost patterns. These grey-leaved herbs are frequently evergreen, which makes them appropriate subjects to put in with evergreen green plants intended to stay attractive all winter. These plantings are particularly suitable to have in gardens alongside public buildings such as libraries, churches, and hospitals.

A certain number of plants with red or red-tinted foliage are charming with the greys. Outstanding is *Salvia officinalis* var. *purpurascens* where the leaves have a wine-red cast, and when their puckered leaves catch the light they look like velvet. Then there are red basils, a few being attractive with the grey herbs. *Perilla frutescens* var. *crispa* is red and self sows, sending up its crimson stems and leaves hither and yon in the beds; while *Rosa rubrifolia,* with its red leaves, is a handsome background plant. There are also herbs with yellow spots or markings such as spotted sage, golden thyme which unfortunately loses its yellow by midsummer, and yellow spotted rue, and recently I have been given strawberry plants having foliage marked with pale yellow. Perhaps the spotting on apple mint is more grey than cream.

There are plants with particularly unusual foliage such as the much-divided skeleton geraniums; also tansies and parsleys with their leaf division curled and twisted until they resemble moss.

The herb garden comes into maturity later than most other plantings and does not attain full growth to cover bare spots left by die-backs or winter casualties until mid-June when the lavender begins to bloom. Lavender is one of the handsomest and most satisfactory of all herbs because of its fragrance, its neat habit of growth, and its charming spires of bloom in pale to deep lavender, or, as in Munstead dwarf, having white or sometimes pink blossoms as also violet and purple. The flowering stems branch out like arching streams of a fountain and after they are harvested and cut back the shrubby portion of the plant looks sturdy and architectural. For warm climates there are lavenders with much-cut foliage, like *multifida* and *canariensis* and with toothed leaves as in *Stoechas*. Blooming along with the lavenders there will be tall hairy plants of white flowers with white-tinted pink or green calyxes and bracts of *Salvia Sclarea* and others with entirely white bracts of *Salvia sylvestris*.

One of the early bursts of color is provided by iris coming in early May. The roots of all iris have medicinal virtues though they do not furnish orris root as does *Florentina*. For their beauty there can be low-grown species, such as iris *verna, cristata,* and color forms of *pumila* in shades of violet, yellow, cream, or blue, also the grey-flowered *Florentina*. Along with them will come a few shrubs of brilliant yellow-flowered brooms. They all grow on a slope in my garden and later in summer their spearlike leaves will be hidden by self-sown bushy plants of *Campanula rotundifolia,* and alliums. *Campanula rapunculus* is biennial and always turns up in unexpected places. From mid-May into June the hedge composed of old-fashioned and species roses will be in bloom. The flowers are so thickly disposed they cause the branches to bend way over. Later, flowers on the species will be followed by oddly shaped, glossy orange or scarlet fruits. The ground under white and yellow rose bushes which grace four corners in my garden is thickly covered with *Primula vulgaris* and *P. polyanthus*.

The next color comes from *Dianthus plumarius, D. arenarius,* and *D. caesius.* Over the years cuttings have been made of the most pleasing forms. They now form thick mats of spearlike grey foliage. When the plants are in bloom, the foliage is hidden by pink, white, and scarlet flowers and sometimes flowers with much-laced petals. They, too, grow on the bank in my garden and the grey spears persist all winter. Later this bank will appear to be covered with alliums, *ramosum, senescens* with white umbels, *pulchellum* with rosy violet, *flavum* with yellow, and *cernuum* with pink flowers. Earlier there have been clumps of *Allium Moly* with flowers of butter yellow but the whole plant vanishes as the summer proceeds not to reappear until next spring. Chives will have come in the borders with blue-violet blossoms and close relatives of theirs with rose-colored and white blossoms. Also in the beds, away from yellow, there will have been pyrethrums in tints from pale pink to deep red. *Allium tuberosum* having white-marked green umbels continues into September. In August the garden becomes gay with bushy plants carrying sky-blue flowers of *Salvia azurea.* In warmer countries there will be *Salvia Clevelandii* and *S. mellifera, S. patens,* and many others.

Meanwhile thymes in the many forms of *Serpyllum* planted on walks and lawns where the ground is too stony for a good lawn as also *vulgaris* have shown lavender, rose, and purple blooms. Almost the last blooms of summer are colchicums. They send up clumps of cup-shaped flowers from pale lavender to deep purple, without any foliage, straight out of the earth. And finally here and there amid shrubbery will come the dainty violet blossom with pendulous pistils of the autumn *Crocus sativus.*

Annuals have not been mentioned for lack of space. However, I personally have found that once a herb garden is under way the plants will have grown so rankly there is little space for the annuals and they have to be planted among the vegetables or in the perennial borders.

HERBS IN THE ROCK GARDEN
Stephen F. Hamblin

When planning a rock garden of herb plants, we may think first of the Mint Family — not of the true mints, for they are far too tall and invasive, but of some of dwarf stature and neat habits.

Perhaps the star performer for this rôle is thyme, in its many forms, some 200 or more species. Of their 600 or more names, many are synonyms or duplications; the universal Mother-of-Thyme *(Thymus serpyllum)* alone has some 200 names. Named clones are now recognized and there are several hybrids.

But we can make two general groups for garden use: the shrubby ones and the creepers. The shrubby species are represented by common thyme *(T. vulgaris)*, a wiry bush up to a foot or more in height and with greater spread in age. There are cultivated forms, as Broadleaf English, Narrowleaf French, variegated and the Sicily form. These make rounded bushes as a background and as contrast to large boulders. They are easily increased by cuttings and usually layer themselves. The flowers are small, lilac, and not as showy as on some other species. Similar erect shrubs are Zygis thyme with tiny, narrow, deep green leaves and rose-purple flowers in heads, the bush attaining 6 inches, with strong thyme odor. Winter thyme *(T. hyemalis)* rises to a foot in height, the pale green leaves narrow and nearly odorless, with recurved margin, the flower pale pink in narrow spikes. These three little shrubs will withstand sub-zero temperatures, though native to southern Europe. Mastic thyme *(T. mastichina)* grows a foot or

161

more tall, the leaves very white and strongly aromatic of camphor, the flowers whitish with pale green bracts, the effect very like our little rabbit-foot clover. Unfortunately it is not hardy to below-zero winters.

The creeping sorts are legion, typified by Mother-of-Thyme, in endless garden forms and varieties, and variable leaf form and flower color. All creep madly, rooting at every joint. Some are entirely smooth of leaf, others moderately hairy, and some are exceedingly woolly, such as the woolly thyme (var. lanuginosus), gray and hairy all over, which rarely flowers. There are other forms from pure white to pink, rose and purple, and even nearly spectrum red, blooming in early June or into late August. There are named varieties such as Annie Hall, very green of foliage, with clear pink flowers. The variegated foliage forms may be edged white or silvery, but most popular is Golden thyme (var. aureus), the young twigs yellow and the foliage wholly yellow or with yellow edges. This was much planted around sundials in Colonial days, for "Time is golden." The one fault of this group is its habit of soon outgrowing its allotted space, or appearing elsewhere in the garden as variable seedlings.

Other creepers are Caraway thyme (T. herba-barona), with strong caraway fragrance; Scandinavian thyme (T. glaber), with round, smooth, shining leaves, the flowers light rose in large oblong heads; Woollystem (T. lanicaulis), in a tumbled heap of downy gray stems and foliage, up to eight inches, with pale pink oblong heads in June, the whole plant with a strong camphor odor; and Conehead (T. capitatus), with narrow stiff foliage and long heads of bright lilac flowers in August-September, like crimson clover in its manner of bloom, the last thyme to blossom. These and many others are hardy to below-zero frost conditions, but many other species from around the Mediterranean are safer in mild climates.

Next, we transfer our appreciation to Lavender. Twenty species or more, including Lavandula dentata, L. stoechas, L. lanata, L. latifolia, L. multifida, L. pedunculata, L. pinnata — all grown to some extent in this country — are hardy where there is little frost, but make fragrant small shrubs in warmer climates. Only certain forms of true lavender

(L. officinalis or *vera)* will survive zero winters, particularly Munsted Dwarf or other forms of compact growth. The forms flowering in white, rose, or deep purple color rarely survive severe frost.

Of course, rosemary is a big bush for a small rock garden, where little frost is known, but the creeping form *(Rosmarinus officinalis var. prostratus)* will give a thyme effect in warm regions.

Now comes savory for use in the rock garden. Botanical confusion extends into the garden, and I am never wholly sure whether to label as Calamintha, *satureja, clinopodium,* or *micromeria.* Summer savory is an annual, useful for its fragrance; but Winter savory is an erect small shrub up to one foot, the narrow, bright green leaves nearly ever-green; the flowers are purplish, in mintlike whorls, in July-August, very late to bloom in the rock garden, and withstanding zero winter cold and extreme summer heat. What is sold as *S. rupestris* is a similar plant with white flowers. The Calamints have ovate leaves with true petioles, but are not evergreen, though more showy of bloom. Yerba Buena *(Micromeria chamissonis),* from our Northwest coast, cannot survive hard frost.

Of the true Mints I cherish *Mentha requieni,* a tiny creeper only an inch high, the whole plant strongly peppermint scented. It resembles a microscopic thyme, but with the coming of frozen ground conditions it departs to its native Corsica. I must have common balm *(Melissa officinalis),* deciduous, but reaching to a foot in summer, the hairy yellow-green leaves strongly lemon scented. In regions of hard frost, give good drainage or a winter covering. Hoarhound in many species is permitted, the whitish silvery leaves — green in some species — are usually fragrant, though scarcely so in common hoarhound which is of great medicinal value. Common marjoram is a rather weedy thymelike plant, spreading rapidly by its horizontal roots, the stems up to a foot or more, topped with panicles of little purplish flowers with showy purple bracts in July-August. It is rather too robust a grower for a small rock garden. Other species, such as the famed Dittany of Crete (formerly *Origanum dictamus*) are for mild climates.

To conclude the Mint list we may add Hyssop, the flowers purple, white, or rose, erect little shrubs partly evergreen; and investigate the great genus Teucrium (Germander), with many woolly shrubs, often not too hardy. Germander *(T. chamaedrys)* is favored as a low evergreen shrub with thick shining leaves, the flowers rose in August, the foliage not fragrant.

Leaving the Mints, try some of the species of Artemisia, the small relatives of sagebrush and wormwood, daisy plants quite unlike most composites, as the flowers are not showy, the interest being in the fragrant foliage. Of the woody species I suggest Old Man wormwood *(A. abrotanum),* an erect shrub up to 3-5 feet, the foliage extremely aromatic. This European shrub came with the first settlers to America. A second choice would be Fringed sagebrush *(A. frigida)* from our plains. Partly woody is Roman wormwood *(A. pontica),* but its underground roots creep widely and it must be restrained or thrown out. The finely divided foliage is very aromatic. The present favorite in this genus is Silver Mound *(A. schmidtiana var. nana),* a woolly silvery rosette up to some six inches, with little bloom (yellowish) and no fragrance or medicinal value; it represents the very dwarf species, ornamental until it goes brown in the middle and must be divided. I would like to grow *A. genipii,* from the Alps, famed as a medicine and tonic.

Some of the ornamental species of Allium would be the chief bulbous plants in this special garden, such as lily leek *(A. moly)* with yellow flowers in June, long known to herbalists of Europe; Keeled onion *(A. carinatum* or *pulchellum)* with pink flowers in clusters, or some of our native species such as *A. cernuum,* soft pink, or *A. bolanderi,* the heads deep ruby red, and the many strange species from vast Asia. Or we could compromise on plain chives with its many purple heads.

The most famous bulb plant for us is Saffron crocus *(C. sativus),* its stamens for color and dye, the lilac flowers coming in September-October; but the bulb seems not to last long in the New World and must be frequently replaced. Far more permanent is the famed Colchicum, autumn crocus with big crocus flowers of rosy purple on long necks in September-October; but in the spring its great cabbagelike foliage upsets the scale of the rock garden. It is better to naturalize it in the woods.

So far we have supposed full sun on this special garden, but with some shade and the emphasis on medicinal value, we have a long range of candidates for rock planting.

Dainty sweet woodruff *(Asperula odorata)* gets first place, its little yellow roots creeping and the narrow leaves in whorls of six-eight topped by flat clusters of fragrant white flowers in May. Other species can be weedy, such as the related yellow bedstraw *(Galium verum)*, and many dwarf species of asperula that are rarely cultivated. The shady garden can have such foliage plants as wild ginger *(Asarum)*, the European species, and those of Virginia and Oregon, or our northern deciduous *A. canadense*. All had medicinal value once and their foliage is still of interest. Or we may plant alum-root *(Heuchera)*, particularly our *H. americana*, its foliage marked with white. And there is hepatica, round-lobed and sharp-lobed, harbinger of spring and once helpful internally; and bloodroot for its medicinal value, and twin-leaf *(Jeffersonia diphylla)* with an oversized blossom above twin leaves, or golden-seal *(Hydrastis canadensis)*, its little greenish flowers in spring not showy — but see the crimson berries in autumn! Or you can go the whole way on size of leaf, in May-apple *(Podophyllum peltatum)* with its nodding white flower and big edible medicinal berry. These and others bloom before the shade of trees becomes heavy, but they really belong in the woodland, or the north shade of the house, rather than in the true rock garden.

With the extremely long list of plants that are of interest to the herbalist, from apple and orange to vegetables and some annuals, it is surprising how brief is the list for the rock garden enthusiast who is also herb-minded. It is a subject on which more research is needed.

HERBS IN KNOTS AND LACES

By HELEN M. FOX

◇❯◇◇

IT seems odd, from our point of view today, that gardeners of the Renaissance in France and Italy should have gone to pattern books intended for embroiderers to get models for the designs of their flower beds. However, in those days it was not thought unsuitable for the same patterns to be used by weavers working with wool or silk, by lace makers with linen thread, carvers on wood or gardeners with plants. Much of the detail of these designs had originated in classical Rome and Greece. The patterns continued in use from the 16th century until a more realistic approach to art and crafts came about late in the 18th century. Even today many of the forms are still used, but there is a realization that the design should be appropriate to the material. At the time when patterns were taken from the pattern books there was a special vocabulary devised to indicate the different lines with words such as tendrils, knots, beads, trefoils, plumes, frets, interlacing, also wreaths, and shells. Besides these there were vases, flower and leaf forms, garlands and heraldic symbols.

The gardeners of the Renaissance regarded plants principally as colors to use in design. The beds with their elaborate patterns were on a level space and generally in front of the house. In France these gardens were called *"parterres de broderie,"* and in England the patterns were called "knots," because of their origin.

Each gardener tried to outdo his colleagues in the elaborateness of his designs and the most complicated of all were created by members of the Mollet family, a garden dynasty who worked for kings and nobles from the 16th on into the 18th century. At the height of elaborateness it required great skill to outline the patterns on the ground. This was done with sticks and strings. At that time only the outlines were carried out with plants. For these, dwarf forms of box and yew were recommended and also juniper trimmed to stay low. To fill in the spaces between the outlines, colored earths were used, also finely crumbled clay and brick dust, and for black, "smith's dust," presumably iron filings. Then, too, colored pebbles gave cream, white or rose colors.

In his book *Théâtre des Plans et Jardinages,* Paris 1652, Claude Mollet says the flowers for these parterres should be low and close to the ground, and he recommends wood sorrel with white flowers,

LACE PATTERNS
From an old pattern book showing similarity to garden design
Courtesy of the Metropolitan Museum of Art

thyme with dove-colored flowers, double chamomile, double blue and gray violets, also white and red ones, and all kinds of marguerites, such as double, red, white and speckled forms, and also strawberries and double yellow crowfoot.

John Parkinson in his *Paradisi in Sole,* which appeared in 1629 and is as valuable today as any garden book published since that time, speaks of germander and hyssop for knots but objects to them because they need constant thinning. Of marjoram, savory and thyme he says they rot too quickly, which was undoubtedly true in the damp climate of England. He has a good word for lavender cotton. To enclose the whole garden he recommends hedges of Italian privet, probably *Ligustrum vulgare,* sweetbriar and also white thorn intermingled with several kinds of roses, and for bordering the beds speaks of lavender, rosemary, sage, southernwood and cornel tree, probably *Cornus mas,* which must be kept low, and *pyracantha.* Batty Langley, who came soon after Parkinson, speaks of walks bordered with primroses and violets. Thus it was in the English as also the French tradition to use herbs in laying out knots.

To come to the present time and the designing of herb gardens today, Montague Free brought back the knot patterns in the garden he laid out at the World's Fair in Flushing Meadows in 1939 for the Brooklyn Botanic Garden. These greatly simplified knots were carried out entirely with herbs and were charming with their different shades of gray and green. Knots similar to these, laid out in one part of the herb garden such as the central bed or at either end, bring an old-time atmosphere, and their strict adherence to a pattern is a delightful contrast to the generally floppy carriage and suckering habit of growth of many herbs.

Herbs used to outline a pattern should be sheared at least twice during the growing season and sometimes oftener. The herbs that stand shearing well are gray and green santolinas, dwarf lavender bushes, rosemary, the tall *Teucrium lucidum, Thymus vulgaris,* hyssop and winter savory, but these last two are short lived. Others that can be shaped and sheared are *Artemisia abrotanum* and *A. pontica.*

Artemisia stellariana and violets along with thymes and strawberries make good "fills." The forms of *Thymus serpyllum* are best for filling, particularly *albus,* which is compact and flat and has tiny white flowers; also *argenteus,* with the stem about four inches high and the leaves margined with white; *aureus* has lavender flowers and the leaves strikingly marked with bright yellow; *coccineus* has brilliant magenta flowers, while *splendens* has reddish purple flowers and is very flat; and lemon thyme, now listed as *Thymus serpyllum var.*

vulgaris, is characterized by larger leaves than most of the others and has them tinted decidedly a yellow green. Other herbs for filling in outlines are *Teucrium chamaedrys,* the small-leaved forms of *Hedera helix,* sweet marjoram and *Mentha requieni;* this last is for a well drained place. *Ajuga repens* is perhaps too invasive but good for a dry sunny place. As to the strawberries, the bushy forms such as Baron Solemacher can be used for outlines, while the dwarf forms which sucker are good for fills. The filling plants have to be cut back every so often and an edging knife is a satisfactory tool for this.

From the beginning there seems to have been a greater freedom of treatment in representations of flowers in embroideries than in other arts, and here will be found naturalistic renderings of foxgloves, borage which was very popular, primroses and pomegranates and roses, as also of carnations and violets. While looking over pictures of laces, besides the flowers just mentioned, I have identified lily of the valley, daffodils and forget-me-nots and of course many different forms of leaves. Often the flowers are arranged in vases, garlands and wreaths, especially in the 17th and 18th centuries.

On the whole, in the machine-made laces of today the designs of earlier handmade laces are reproduced, sometimes as in the narrow edgings, very successfully.

For those of us who embroider, there is an opportunity to design and to stitch patterns with herbs. This idea was the inspiration of this article, for we were discussing the possibility of holding an exhibition at the Annual Meeting, of work which depicted herbs, done by our members in needlepoint and painting.

Herb Symbiosis – Companion Plants

HELEN PHILBRICK

All gardeners are familiar with various examples of plant symbiosis and we should not let the technical sounding word frighten us. Symbiosis simply means the functioning together of two or more plants in a living situation for better or for worse, depending on the plants and their mutual reactions. A good example of symbiosis familiar to most of us is the plant parasite Gold Thread (*coptis*), which is unable to manufacture chlorophyl for itself, and must wrap itself closely around a living plant such as clover to absorb the nourishment which the clover can give. This is an example of symbiosis where the host plant gives and the parasite receives but gives nothing in return. Another kind of symbiosis is the saprophyte. An example is the mushroom group. Mushrooms are live organisms which grow on dead material in the woods, mostly on dead trees or on decaying leaf mold on the forest floor. Another example of a saprophyte is the lichen which clings to old tree trunks or to stones. The lichen itself is an example of symbiosis because it is made up of two parts: one is a fungus, the other is an alga which supplies the chlorophyl for the fungus.

Another more intricate and fascinating example of symbiosis is the clover or any other legume with its root nodules, which are easy to locate on the roots of a pulled up plant. The root nodules are caused by soil bacteria which enter the plant through its hair roots. In this case symbiosis is of mutual benefit to both the legume and the soil bacteria (which are a type of plant too). The soil bacteria capture and fix the nitrogen from the air. They carry this nitrogen into the plant roots and the plant receives it. At the same time the legume plant is manufacturing carbohydrates, which in turn give energy to the soil bacteria to enable them to get the nitrogen to supply the host plant. This relationship is connected with the protein cycle, which explains why the

170

legumes (such as clover and alfalfa) are so important for feeding milk and meat animals for the use of human beings. This in turn, in a way, includes human beings in the symbiotic exchanges of nutrients from plants and animals.

Several different kinds of symbiosis are already known. Among the plants, symbiotic relationships usually depend upon immediate touch or some other close connection. They may be caused by root secretions between two species of plants. They may be caused by leaf secretions. Finally they may even be caused by scent between two plants — or, as the books elegantly term it, "exhaled aromatic substances."

The first serious attempt to assemble all known information about herbal symbioses was begun around 1943 when Richard B. Gregg scanned the literature of the Bio-Dynamic movement, both here and abroad, and wrote the pamphlet entitled Companion Plants. This little booklet included many indications given by Dr. Rudolf Steiner about herbs and plants which enjoyed, or did not enjoy, each other's companionship. Since the publication of that first pamphlet many people have undertaken several special projects, observing these plant companionships, testing them, and watching for other plant combinations. I quote the outline which Richard Gregg used when he compiled the pamphlet because it will not only give a sort of structure for this article, but also because it will provide other ideas of what to look for in plant symbiosis. Not all plants like each other, even among the herbs, and you should know what to look for among the symbiotic activities that are taking place in your own garden. The subject is so vast that it must be limited here to a few experiences of particular interest and concern to herb growers.

The following outline comprehends most of the ecological relationships which can be included under the subject of plant symbiosis: I. Plants which aid each other directly; II. Plants which aid each other indirectly by enriching the soil; III. Plants which oppose or harm each other; IV. A small ratio of a certain plant that aids growth of others, and a larger ratio that hinders or harms; V. Plants which repel harmful insects; VI. Plants which attract useful insects; VII. Plants which repel animal pests.

Most gardeners know of many favorite combinations that grow well together — not only flowers which complement each other by their beauty or their colors, but plants which have some definite symbiotic reaction upon each other. Observant gardeners may also suspect some bad combinations if certain plants do not thrive together although they may do well when separated. For instance, plants growing near wormwood or any of the Artemisias may be adversely affected to a serious degree by the bitter principle which washed into the soil from the leaves of the wormwood.

Before giving further examples let me explain the latest breakthrough in the science laboratories.[1] The process of chromatography is a relatively new technique by which a substance dissolved in water is allowed to spread through a disc of filter paper through a wick set in the center of the disc. As the liquid spreads by capillary action through the filter paper, the substance in solution creates a "picture" of the substance. Every substance makes its own picture. Its pattern is constant and every time the substance is tested the picture is relatively the same. Plant extracts make beautifully colored chromatograms with many colors and forms determined by the substance being tested. These colors and forms made by a specific plant extract create a graphic record which can then be compared with other chromatograms. Having once discovered that one plant extract always produces the same picture, laboratory technicians have now experimented with combinations of plant extracts. Plants known to be mutually helpful produced a harmonious picture when extracts were combined. Plants having a harmful effect on each other produced pictures showing confusion or disharmony, or a cancelling out of the finer forms of the individual pictures. It is expected that this testing method will become more and more useful in determining compatability or noncompatability of symbiotic combinations. I add this bit of current information, fresh, as it were, from the laboratory bench because this method produces an actual picture of these symbiotic effects that we gardeners in our enthusiasm might sometimes suspect we only imagine. What we see in the garden is real. It is not "tissue of fancy." It is now provable by scientific methods in a biochemical research laboratory where everyone can see and measure it.

Now to get onto the familiar ground of all herb gardeners. The so-called aromatic herbs and our common garden vegetables (which technically are also herbs) include many time-tested examples of plant symbiosis.

Following the classic outline above, I shall mention a few personal experiences we have had in growing some of these plant combinations together. Under Item I: for plants which aid each other directly in the garden, we think immediately of carrots and peas. These are not only good companions on the dinner table but they are also happy growing in each other's company. It should be noted here that most of the legumes (peas and beans and clover and all other plants which have blossoms like a sweet pea) are beneficial to their neighbors. The one exception is onions. We used to plant onion sets near our early peas and we wondered why each did so poorly. Now we keep them widely separated and both do better. Peas and carrots being cool weather plants can be sown early. Leaf lettuce too belongs with this combination and there you have an example of herbal symbiosis in the spring garden.

Other favorite symbiotic combinations which are always compatible in the vegetable garden are celery, celeriac and leeks, sown two rows of each alternating. Beets like to grow with kohlrabi or with onions. We plant them in alternate rows or with plants alternating. Beans and sweet corn are so compatible that our predecessors on this continent, the American Indians, had already noted their affinity and often planted them together.

Asparagus grows better if the asparagus bed is also used for tomato plants. In years to come scientists will research this combination to try to discover why these two plants complement each other. Scientists have already isolated a substance named asparagin which has a good influence on tomato plants, especially for controlling some of the soil pests which may afflict tomatoes. We know from satisfactory experience that if you cultivate the asparagus bed sufficiently to grow tomatoes there regularly, you can circumvent that late summer chore of weeding the asparagus bed. Parsley also belongs in this combination, adding color and savor and a wealth of good garnish.

After the spring peas are sown, sow potatoes nearby and each will be aided by the presence of the other. Furthermore if it is an early enough variety of potatoes, this gourmet combination may also grace the early summer luncheon table. Have you ever tasted green peas and tiny "grablin'" potatoes with a dash of mint?

Many aromatic herbs such as peppermint, rosemary, sage vermouth, dill or chamomile (both *Chamomilla officinalis* and *Matricaria chamomilla*) and onions will prove immeasurably helpful if you are trying to grow cabbages. This is a prime example of herbal symbiosis that works in several different ways. First, the aromatic scents of the herbs themselves repel several harmful insects, the worst of all being the cabbage butterfly. This symbiotic effect is understandable. The cabbage butterfly is repelled just as other moths are kept away from woolens by newsprint or camphor or wormwood or other aromatic scent. Secondly, the finely cut, spritely, aromatic type of the herb plants helps to balance the heavy, solid, ballhead type of the cabbage plant which is mostly leaves. The cabbage, being a stodgy, almost phlegmatic type of plant which has been bred until it is now only a great mass of heavy leaves is far from its original plant type. It welcomes the close proximity and the balancing influence of the lively aromatic herbs. The latter grow tall and thin and sparse with a strong fragrance and with myriads of tiny blooms. These help to stimulate and enliven the leafy cabbage. After years and years of experimentation with these plant combinations, and with cabbages grown without the help of the aromatic herbs, we feel safe in asserting that the herbs are a great help to the cabbages in the process of growth.

Another plant which particularly helps the cabbage — and all the cabbage family — is the onion. The cabbage butterfly especially dislikes the onion scent. Also, during the short season when the cabbage butterfly is flying, if you take the extra trouble to place a sprig of any herb across the top of each cabbage plant, you will be rewarded for your work because the cabbage butterflies will not stop to lay eggs on your cabbages.

The now famous combination of garlic and roses[2] follows somewhat the same reasoning as the cabbage-onion symbiosis. (In following these indications, you should not try to substitute plants for the plants listed because other plants will not work as well. These are *rules* and if they are not followed, the results will not follow. Do not try to substitute onion for garlic because it will not work!) The rose has been bred and hybridized through countless years and now it has become a tender, rather sophisticated plant, subject to many troubles and far removed from the original tough and wiry wild rose types. Garlic on the other hand is just as opposite as it can be. It belongs to the lily family, it is strongly aromatic, and it has changed very little since its origin before the time of written history. A few bulbs of garlic planted around the base of the rose bush will strengthen and stimulate the rose. Over many years we have observed and heard other gardeners testify that this really works to produce better, healthier roses. Some growers even state that the roses have no more aphis. There is much work to be done by biochemical scientists to to analyze the reasons for these symbiotic effects which we gardeners can observe but as yet can hardly explain.

Among the herbs which are not always helpful in the garden is fennel (*Nigella sativa*). This has a harmful effect on bush beans.[3] Chromatogram pictures of beans alone and fennel alone show their respective characteristic patterns. Combined plant extracts result in a pattern showing "a disturbing of the bean picture by the fennel pattern. The finer form characteristics of the bean picture are lost."[4] Here we have laboratory proof of the "dis-affinity" which many gardeners have observed through the years.

Not only in the garden, growing, but wherever living fruits and vegetables are stored there are symbiotic effects. Even in the storage cellar if potatoes and apples are stored close together the apples will taste flat and the potatoes will not keep well. Apples give off ethylene gas which hastens the growth process in the stored potatoes. When tests were made in the laboratory it was ascertained that the potato pattern flattened out the delicate pattern of the apple extract, thus further proving the unhealthy effect of each upon the other in storage.

For years gardeners have known about the good influence of stinging nettle (*Urtica dioica*) upon tomatoes and its practical value to all backyard gardeners. Those who have diligently tried to drive all trace of stinging nettle off their property have deprived themselves of a valuable ally. The nettle — despite its stinging your ankles, your wrists and your ear lobes when you stoop to pick tomatoes — makes the tomato plants resistant to disease, increases the flavor and stimulates humus formation in the soil around the tomatoes. It is also believed that the preservative effect of the formic acid in the nettle carries over — perhaps through root interaction — to make the tomatoes keep longer and to keep them free from mold. This is a good demonstration of a symbiotic effect in process of living growth. In the laboratory, in a test tube, formic acid is a different kind of substance. In life, in the biotic process, the formic acid is a living entity which creates living reactions to other living substances. Experiments with dried nettle plants made into hay have shown that the nettle also helps preserve the good quality of fruits far into the winter if the fruit is stored in the nettle hay. Other experiments have shown that even the soil from the vicinity of nettle roots has an enlivening effect upon any soil. It can be used as a substitute for compost in an emergency. Nettle is rich in iron also and perhaps that is why some "old wives" have found it helpful to add nettle leaves to their breakfast tea! It has been reported that stinging nettles grown as companion plants with herbs such as angelica, valerian, marjoram, sage, and spearmint notably increased their essential oil content.[6]

To one who asks how to keep the nettle patch from spreading all over the garden the answer is simple: *eat it!* In early spring when the nettle plants are two to three inches tall, don your garden gloves and snip off each plant close to the ground. Nettle is much easier to wash than spinach. Cook the same as spinach in a glass or enamelled pan. (Stainless steel will turn the nettle dark.) Drain, season with butter, salt and pepper and you have a delectable spring green with a fine flavor, as tender as spinach, not as bitter as dandelion, with none of the prickles left after brief cooking. Best of all, your nettle patch will be kept under control. If you like nettle greens as well as we do, you may even encourage the patch to spread a little! Actually it is not hard to control the spreading if you pull up a few of the mature roots in late summer and add them to your compost pile to limit the size of the patch. If you get stung by nettle, rub your skin with sour dock or rhubarb juice or jewel weed or garden balsam.

Another effect of nettles upon nearby plants can be observed in a symbiotic situation where nettles are well established. We had a spectacular example in the Garden for Meditation at Lasell House in Whitinsville, Massachusetts (a conference center where my husband and I care for the walled garden). In the Bible Garden we had nettle — a plant mentioned in the Bible — and of course it spread. There was also a large ring of hyssop plants. About the third year the nettle roots had invaded the hyssop on one side of the ring. It was plainly visible that the hyssop plants in close association with the nettle were half again as tall as the hyssop across the ring. They also looked healthier. There were also two rue plants, which I had snipped very close because someone needed the rue for a herbal mixture. The rue nearest the nettle survived the snipping and "came back" in late summer. The other plant, outside the nettle influence, died. At other times we have observed tall plants in a border growing even taller and a deeper shade of green when they were near nettles and the whole row decreasing in height as it departed from the nettles.

We now have the advantage of modern scientific laboratories where research may be done to find out why plants react to other plants. Keen-eyed gardeners have been observing these effects for centuries. Shakespeare wrote in Henry V: "The strawberry grows underneath the nettle, / And wholesome berries thrive and ripen best / Neighbored by plants of baser quality." Strawberries also like borage and green beans growing nearby. They like lettuce and spinach and a little thyme as a border plant. But strawberries dislike cabbage.

Some 200 plants are listed in the book Companion Plants and How To Use Them[5] with information about their likes and dislikes, culled from scientific literature from all over Europe and Russia. In 1966 the list was up to date as far as possible. Since then many other examples of herb symbiosis have been recorded. It is our hope and belief that eager and observant herb gardeners and horticulturists will continue to watch their plants with special attention to plants' reaction to one another. Consistent similar reactions, year after year, should lead one to certain conclusions which should be recorded and studied. Be sure to write down what you observe each year and keep good records and you may make important contributions to man's understanding of herbal symbiosis from your own herb garden.

References

1. *Bio-Dynamics*, Winter 1968, No. 85, Plant Relationships as Made Visible by Chromatography, by Mrs. Erica Sabarth.
2. *Companion Plants and Herbs*, Bio-Dynamic Farming and Gardening Association, Inc., 1943.
3. *Companion Plants*, op. cit., p. 2 and p. 5.
4. *Bio-Dynamics*, op. cit., p. 14
5. *Companion Plants and How to Use Them*, Philbrick and Gregg, Devin-Adair Co., New York, 1966.
6. Ibid.

The Significance of Botanical Pesticides

STEVE HART

Today, "pesticide" has become a household word which is respected by those "in the know" and feared by those who base their opinions on unfounded, dramatized publicity.

The use of pesticides has increased dramatically since the end of the second World War. This is largely because of the needs of our monoculture agriculture and our burgeoning population, to control disease and nuisance pests.

There are a number of different types of chemicals used as pesticides; however, the botanical (or plant-derived) pesticides were of considerable value long before the advent of "artificial" chemicals.

Botanical pesticides[1] are usually insecticides and they will be discussed as such in the rest of this paper.

"More than 2,000 species of plants are said to have some value as insect killers. They belong to 170-odd families. Commercial insecticides of plant origin are found in five families: Nicotine in the *Solanaceae* family; pyrethrum in *Compositae*; derris, cube, and timbo in *Leguminosae*; hellebore in *Liliaceae*; and anabasine in *Chenopodiaceae*. Anabasine is also found in *Solonaceae*."[2]

It is very difficult to know exactly when botanical pesticides were first used. "The Romans divided poisons into three groups: animal, plant and mineral. They used two species of false hellebore in medicine, and in rat and mouse powders and insecticides. The Chinese discovered the insecticidal value of derris."[2] As early as 1690, water infusions of tobacco (containing nicotine) were used to kill sucking insects.[3] Pyrethrum or "insect powder," as it was called, seems to have been derived in the Caucasus and Northern Iran from *Chrysanthemum coccineum*. It was reportedly first manufactured in 1828.[3]

The importance of botanical pesticides reached its peak between the beginning of the 20th century and the second World War. From the start of this period, until shortly after the first

World War, nicotine was the one most widely used. Between the two wars, the use of pyrethrum and rotenone came into prominence.[4]

Since the second World War, the relative importance of this group of insecticides has declined considerably in the face of competition from cheaper, more effective synthetic chemicals. This is largely due to the time factor involved in growing a crop of insecticidal plants (two to four years or longer for pyrethrum) and the vulnerability of manufacturers to the whims of growers. In addition, these products are renowned for their broad-spectrum insecticidal qualities, while the present-day tendency is towards "specific" insecticides.

Following is a description of the origins, history and uses of three of the most widely used botanical pesticides:

Nicotine — is derived from the *Solanaceae* family, genus *Nicotiana*, which contains 50 or more species. In North America, it is manufactured as a by-product of the commercial tobacco (*N. tobaccum*) industry. In its pure state, it is a colorless, almost odorless, liquid alkaloid, which is used the world over as an ingredient in many insecticides.[3]

The known history of nicotine as a pesticide dates back to 1690 when it was used to kill sucking insects. In 1746, Peter Collinson, a noted English botanist, wrote to his American fellow botanist, John Bertram, suggesting ways to protect nectarines from plum curculio. "After suggesting the smoking of infested trees with burning straw," he continues, "if the trees were to be squirted on with a hand engine with the water in which tobacco leaves were soaked, either of these two methods, I should think, if they did not totally prevent, yet at least would secure as much of these fine fruits as would be worth the labor of people of circumstance who are curious to taste these delicious fruits in perfection."[3]

Nicotine is usually classed as a contact insecticide, although it probably acts mainly as a fumigant, even when applied as a dust or spray. It is much more active in its pure state than as one of its salts, and it is highly effective on a wide range of insects.

Alkali has no effect on nicotine preparations, other than increasing their toxicity. For this reason, nicotine is compatible with all insecticides and fungicides, except definitely acidic material.

It is frequently formulated as dusts, with alkaline carriers such as hydrated lime and limestone, because of their ability to release the alkaloid. Some inert carriers, e.g., gypsum and elemental sulphur, are sometimes used. Certain acidic dust diluents, e.g., pyrophyllite and talc, are also used on occasion. It is sometimes formulated as a spray.

Nicotine is one of the most deadly poisons known for higher animals. It can be absorbed through the tongue, the eyes and even unbroken skin. It is a highly volatile compound and usually breaks down very rapidly.[3]

Pyrethrum — is derived from the *Compositae* family, genus *Chrysanthemum*. It is extracted commercially from the flower heads of *C. cinerariafolium* and consists of four esters (Pyrethrin I, Pyrethrin II, Cinerin I, Cinerin II), generally called pyrethrins. These esters are viscous liquids, insoluble in water, but soluble in organic solvents and oil.[4]

The use of pyrethrum as an insecticide originated in the Caucasus and Northern Iran, where it was called "Persian insect powder." The nature of this powder, which was originally made from *C. coccineum*, was kept a secret for many years. Early in the nineteenth century, it was discovered by an American merchant, and was first manufactured in 1828.

The value of *C. cinerariafolium* was discovered in Dalmatia (now part of Yugoslavia) in 1840 and first used as "Dalmatian insect powder" in 1854. It was introduced into France in 1850 and the United States in 1858. Shortly after, it was introduced into several other countries with the result that Japan, Brazil and several African countries became major producers.[3]

Ground pyrethrum flowers were previously used as "insect powder," but a great deal of waste occurred as the insecticide was locked in the plant cells. Today, the pyrethrins are usually extracted and made into dusts and sprays which are used in households, on domestic animals and for horticultural purposes.[3]

Pyrethrum is a safe effective pesticide which is non toxic to warm-blooded animals.[2] It tends to break down rather rapidly in the atmosphere.

Rotenone — is derived from the *Leguminosae* family, of the genera *Derris* and *Lonchocarpus*. It is extracted from the roots of

D. elliptica (far East) as derris powder and *L. utilus* and *L. urucu* as cube (Peru) and timbo (Brazil). It is a white, mostly crystalline solid, almost completely insoluble in water, with a melting point of 163°C.[4] As early as 1747, derris was used as a fish poison in Malaya. Its first recorded use as an insecticide was in 1848 in the same country. The first evidence of use in the Western World were some British patents covering derris extracts in 1911. The insecticidal qualities of cube root were reported in Peru in 1910, and those of timbo in 1924. However, it was not until the chemical nature of rotenone was discovered after 1930, that these insecticides were standardized.[3]

The use of the fresh root of *D. elliptica* as a fish poison in New Guinea, is described in the following fascinating quotation from Holland (1938) reported in Shepard's book, "The Chemistry and Action of Insecticides"[3]: "The native dives on a reef until he locates a large rock cod or groper in its hole. He goes ashore and procures the root which can be found growing almost anywhere. He chews the root, dives down, and ejects the contents of his mouth into the hole. He then comes to the surface, washing out his mouth with sea water, and waits a few minutes. He dives again and draws the stupefied fish from his hole."

Derris and cube are widely used as finely ground plant material, diluted with an appropriate non-alkaline product to provide a suitable strength of rotenone dust. The active constituents of rotenone-bearing roots are the extractives known as derris or cube resins. They usually contain 30-40 percent rotenone, as well as certain other, less active rotenoid compounds such as deguelin, elliptone, toxicaral and tephrosin. Due to the toxicity of these extractives, it is usual for both rotenone and total extractive content to be taken into account when evaluating the insecticidal property of roots.[3]

Rotenone, due to its complex structure, is much more unstable than nicotine or the pyrethrins. It is extremely potent against a number of insects and it acts both as a contact insecticide and a stomach poison. A considerable amount of the activity of derris and cube extractives is due to the non-rotenone portion.

Rotenone is extremely poisonous to fish and also to higher animals such as swine, especially when taken in drinking water.

However, when properly used on food crops, rotenone-containing insecticides possess little hazard to higher animals. Inhaling of rotenone dusts can cause vomiting, numbness of throat, lips and tongue.

Botanical pesticides have contributed greatly to our present overall knowledge in the pest control field. A lot of the synthetic chemicals used today are based on the structure of some of the naturally occurring pesticides. It was first necessary to determine the chemical structure of these materials and then apply this knowledge in the synthesis of similar chemicals. The relative value and quantity of botanical pesticides used today, in comparison with synthetic chemicals, continues to fall. However, we must always remember the enormous direct and indirect contribution they have made in our battle to control pests.

References

[1]Haller, H. L. — How Insecticides Are Mixed, pages 202-204 of "Insects." *The Yearbook of Agriculture*. 1952, United States Government Printing Office, Washington, D. C.

[2]Feinstein, Louis — Insecticides from Plants, pages 222-229 of "Insects." *The Yearbook of Agriculture*. 1952, United States Government Printing Office, Washington, D. C.

[3]Shepard, Harold H. — *The Chemistry and Action of Insecticides*. First Edition 1951, McGraw-Hill Book Company Inc., New York, Toronto, London.

[4]Brown, A. W. A. — *Insect Control by Chemicals*, 1951, John Wiley & Sons, Inc., New York, Chapman Hall, Limited, London.

Herbs of the Mediterranean

MARY WELLMAN

The shores of the Mediterranean are really the source of most of the herbs we commonly use. They have reached us in many different ways, usually wandering across France and England, though a few came because American seamen liked some of the foods of Southern France and Northern Africa, and probably asked their wives why they didn't produce them.

One especially, bouillabaisse, is possibly a remote ancestor of our fish and clam chowders, which is no doubt why New Yorkers insist on including tomatoes in the recipe. It came to us from Marseilles, where it was carried by the Phocaean colonists with the name of Kakavia. It originally contained saffron, which was greatly used by the ancient Greeks. One finds in the Museum at Heraklion a beautiful fresco of the saffron gatherer, and the flower blooms in many parts of Attica. At the present day Italy and Spain are the great users of this herb, though Turkey knows it under the name of "Safran."

Many dishes attributed to Italy originate in Lebanon and Syria, such as the pizza. Do you know that shallot owes its name to Ascalon? One can imagine a pilgrim or the follower of a Crusader bringing home the bulbs. In the Christian countries of the Near East basil has a religious significance. At the time of the feast of Saint Basil people put small jars of it on doorsteps or in windows and the taxi drivers in Beirut all carry sprigs in the vases in their cars. St. Basil has a particularly noisy festival there, with firecrackers exploding all over the city.

The Spice Market at Istanbul, lying next to the Great Bazaar is a lovely place in which to wander. It is a great arcade in which many shops are glass fronted and one may watch the distilling of attar of rose or the delicious lemon extract with which Turks wash their hands when no water is available. Other little booths are open, and full of huge baskets of "Kekik" (thyme) and the "Nane" (mint) used especially in yogurt soups.

There are also "Adagay", our old friend sage, "merzengu" (oregano), "maydanoz" used in all dishes, which we would recognize as parsley ... and countless others, familiar and unfamiliar to us.

Those who have been in any Middle Eastern or North African country are familiar with the sight of small boys dashing about the streets with lovely brass trays, which look like small cake stands, carrying tiny cups of Turkish coffee, from the nearest coffee house, to a shop where a customer is to be entertained. In some cases these cups may contain mint tea. This idea of mint tea has become a great habit in France also and if you go to the famous cheese place in Paris and consume as many as you can of the 120 varieties they carry, you can wash them down with mint tea.

As we walked toward the palace of Minos at Knossos, one hot August day, a most pungent heady odor surrounded us. One can readily understand how thyme came to be used as an incense, after that experience of treading the dried and powdering plants of dittany.

On a visit to the Island of Hydra while lunching with a Greek family, the man arose shouting "My rigani, where is my rigani?" Instead of being slightly mad, he was just indicating that he couldn't eat his tomatoes without a sprinkling of oregano.

Rosemary is such a precious plant that one likes to think of perfume made from it in France — however, it is awfully good to flavour almost everything including "Mediterranean soup."

I would like to see some of the famous Western Reserve cooks serve up a "Dolma" with parsley, dill and mint or a spinach pie with dill and tomato. What about a "soupe à l'oseille" to start with or an "omelette fines herbes" and top off with a few sesame seed cookies and perhaps a taste of "ouzo" or "raki" if you like the flavour of anise, or "cinzano" if you prefer wormwood.

Sage is of such vital importance in our country, to spicemakers and meat packers, that I would like to mention the project carried on during the Second World War by the Herb Society of America. We found that all sage used commercially here was imported from the Dalmatian coast and Greece; this was of course stopped during the war years. With her inimitable vision Mrs. Edward B. Cole decided that the H. S. A. had a marvellous opportunity to find an outlet for energy and an inlet for money, to many people who might be small "cottage" growers. In her careful and scientific approach to the subject we wrote to thousands of willing and eager growers. The spice manufacturers were most cooperative but the study ended with facts such as these: a) the only sage which could be grown here is the English-Broad leaved . . . which is not acceptable commercially. b) Each pound of sage we could grow cost forty-four cents, while the Mediterranean sage cost seven cents, duty paid, on the docks in New York! Meanwhile the war was at an end and commerce resumed. If anyone has seen sage gathered wild on the hillsides abroad, by the children, and tossed into white washed pits to dry in the hot sun, one can readily appreciate the reasons for the difference in price.

To go back to the mention of herbs in our apéritifs and liqueurs, one of the most exciting experiences is to visit the great factory of the Chartreux fathers at Voiron, France. It is a rather modest looking building fronting on a delightful courtyard. Inside are monster stills of copper, and in a cool vaulted cellar are the great vats where the liqueur "develops".

The Carthusian Monastery which was founded by Saint Bruno in 1684 lies nearby in a rather inaccessible part of the Savoy alps, on a mountain called the Grande Chartreuse. There the Fathers maintained a hospital for the surrounding countryside and in the "Pharmacie" was perfected in 1735 a recipe which had been in their archives since 1605. This medicine was used in yellow form as a stomachic remedy and in the green color as a nerve tonic.

One of the first steps in the production, is the steeping of 130 herbs, many of which are gathered in the mountain slopes. No visitors are allowed into the still room.

The care of the entire operation is given to three monks who are detailed for life to this service. From time to time they are allowed to return to the Monastery, which is a closed order, to resume their religious duties.

Since about 1848 "Chartreuse" has been widely known. Through a brief period in the early nineteen hundreds, at the time of the separation of Church and State in France, the Fathers carried on their work at Tarragona in Spain. Now, back again, in their old Monastery, the fame of their "Elixir" carries the fragrance and the flavour of herbs everywhere.

A LIST FOR AN OLD ENGLISH

WORT GARDEN

ELLEN GREENSLET

WORT is a word that has been in the English language since Anglo-Saxon times, meaning originally a root. Later it was transferred to any kind of plant, whether growing wild, or cultivated in a garden. Although a wort is not necessarily an herb, as we use the term today, yet long before Chaucer's time, in those early days when "herb" carried a less specialized significance than it does at present, the two words were practically synonymous, and so remained until the early 17th century. Indeed, throughout their entire history, most of the worts have come well within our modern usage and definition of "herb."

During the middle decades of the 17th century "plant," as a general term, took the place of the earlier "wort" and "herb," and "wort" gradually fell into disuse, except in the names of certain old plants, where it had been used as a suffix, or as a "second element," as some authorities prefer to speak of it. Many of these names are now used in everyday speech only in out-of-the-way corners of Great Britain, though a few have lingered on as the common names of certain genera and species. Except for this latter usage, many of these vernacular wort-names are found today only in old herbals and gardening books, in folk literature, and in scholarly treatises and lists, where their origins and evolution may be studied.

Hunting for these early worts is an interesting form of indoor botanizing; but it is a study which, to be entirely accurate in its results, would call for highly specialized and detailed research, which would necessarily develop into a lengthy article. The following list is the result of a weeding-out process, fifty or more worts having been discarded as ineligible either because of their modern "book

187

names," or because they were not known in Jacobean England. There is, however, sufficient material to serve as a nucleus for the study — either indoors or out — of these old plants of the country-side, all of them valued or loved because of their association in Chaucer's and Shakespeare's time.

"A GALLANT HERB"—Waywort or Pimpernel

(Anagallis Arvensis, Linn.)

" There are twoe kindes, differing in the flower, for that which hath an azure flower is called the femall, but that of a Phœnician colour is called the Male."
DIOSCORIDES, *Englished by John Goodyer,* A.D. 1655.
Edited and First Printed, A.D. 1933.
By Robert T. Gunther. Oxford, 1934.

This drawing of one of the oldest known worts, as reproduced in Mr. Gunther's edition, very much reduced in size from the original, is found in the Aniciæ Julianæ, a beautifully illustrated Byzantine manuscript of about 512 A.D., now preserved in the Vienna Library. This is one of several of its illustrations based upon originals by Crateuas, a celebrated Greek rhizotomist of the second century B.C., who described, and drew from nature, a number of medicinal plants. A few of those descriptions are known to us, having been quoted by Dioscorides in his Greek Herbal written in the first century A.D.

The bare bones of a list show so little result for all the pleasant and far-reaching ramifications of reading that have gone into its make-up. But it has been a peculiarly rewarding study in many ways, and it is hard to imagine a pleasanter bypath to follow when winter gardening has to take the place of one's outdoor summer activities.

Worts have a confusing habit of sharing their names with each other, one plant, such as the Greater Celandine, often having several wort synonyms. Any one of these, in its turn, may apply to two or three entirely distinct and quite unrelated plants. Bloodwort is an example of this, being a name used for White Clover, Centaury, Yarrow, Smartweed and Tormentil. There is also great divergence of opinion as to the Latin names of certain species. In the main, unless the balance of opinion seems to be against it, Mr. Britten's nomenclature has been followed.

Bibliography

Many interesting books, both old and new, have been consulted, but the list cannot be given for lack of space. The following six have been used constantly for reference:

EARLE, J.: *English Plant Names from the Tenth to the Fifteenth Century*. Oxford, 1880.

PRIOR, R. C. A.: *Popular Names of English Plants*. London, 1870.

BRITTEN, J., AND HOLLAND, R.: *A Dictionary of English Plant Names*. London, 1886.

BENTHAM AND HOOKER: *Handbook of the British Flora*, 1924 Edition.

MRS. LEYEL'S AND MRS. GRIEVE'S *Herbal:* A number of worts are considered. New York, 1931.

HORWOOD, A. R.: *British Wild Flowers*, 6 volumes, 1919. This work has been especially valuable. It treats of a number of plants from the standpoint of ecology and bionomics. Excellent "Life Histories" of a number of worts are found among the species described. London, 1919.

A LIST FOR AN OLD ENGLISH WORT GARDEN

Adderwort.....Snakeweed.....*Polygonum Bistorta, L.*
All Saints' Wort Tutsan.....*Hypericum Androsæmum, L.*
Axwort.....Axweed.....*Coronilla Varia, L.*

Bairnwort.....English daisy.....*Bellis perennis, L.*
Banewort.....Deadly nightshade. *Atropa belladonna, L.*
Banwort.....Sweet violet.....*Viola odorata, L.*
.....Wallflower.....*Cheiranthus cheiri, L.*
.....Centaury.....*Centaurium umbellatum, Gilib.*

Barrenwort...Heart'sease.....*Viola tricolor, L.*
Bearwort.....Bishop's hat.....*Epimedium alpinum, L.*
Beewort.....Meu or spignel.....*Meum athamanticum, L.*
Birthwort.....Sweet flag.....*Acorus calamus, L.*
.....Birthwort.....*Genus Aristolochia*
.....*Aristolochia clematitis*

Bishopswort...Herb Gerard.....*Ægopodium podagraria, L.*
Bitterwort.....Wood betony.....*Stachys Betonica, Benth.*
.....Water mint.....*Mentha aquatica, L.*
.....Gentian.....*Gentiana amarella, L.*
.....Dandelion.....*Taraxacum officinale, Weber*
Blackwort.....Boneset.....*Symphytum officinale, L.*
.....Comfrey
Bladderwort...Hooded water milfoil *Utricularia vulgaris, L.*
Blawort.....Harebell.....*Campanula rotundifolia, L.*
.....Cornflower or Blue-
.....bottle.....*Centaurea cyanus, L.*
Bledewort.....Red poppy.....*Papaver rhoeas, L.*
Blisterwort.....Celery-leaved Crow-
.....foot.....*Ranunculus sceleratus, L.*
Blodewort.....Waterpepper.....*Polygonum hydropipra, L.*
Bloodwort.....Whiteclover.....*Trifolium repens, L.*
.....Smartweed.....*Polygonum hydropiper, L.*
.....Yarrow or Common
.....Milfoil.....*Achillea Millefolium, L.*
.....Centaury.....*Erythraea Centauria, Pers.*
.....Tormentil.....*Potentilla erecta, Hampe*
Bogwort.....Cranberry.....*Vaccinium Oxycoccus, L.*
Bridewort.....Meadowsweet.....*Spiræa Ulmaria, L.*
Brimstonewort Milk parsley.....*Peucedanum palustre, L.*

Broadwort.....Water figwort.....*Scrophularia aquatica, L.*
Broomwort.....Water betony.....*Scrophularia aquatica, L.*
.....Pennycress.....*Various species of Thlaspi*
Brosewort.....Common henbane. *Hyoscyamus niger, L.*
Brotherwort.....Wild thyme.....*Thymus serpyllum, L.*
Brownwort.....Self-heal.....*Prunella vulgaris, L.*
.....Water figwort.....*Scrophularia aquatica, L.*
Bruisewort.....Yellow-horned
.....poppy.....*Glaucium flavum, Crantz.*
.....Comfrey.....*Symphytum officinale, L.*
.....Common daisy.....*Bellis perennis, L.*
Bullwort.....Water betony.....*Scrophularia aquatica, L.*
Burwort.....Lesser Celandine.. *Ranunculus ficaria, L.*
Butterwort.....Common Butterwort *Pinguicula vulgaris, L.*

Cankerwort.....Dandelion.....*Taraxacum officinale, Weber*
Chafewort.....Cudweed.....*Filago germanica, L.*
Chickenwort...Chickweed.....*Stellaria media, L.*
Christ's-wort...Christmas rose....*Helleborus niger, L.*
Churchwort.....Pennyroyal.....*Mentha pulegium, L.*
Clovewort.....Buttercup or crow-
.....foot.....*Ranunculus acris, L.*
Cnop-weed.....Knot-weed.....*Centaurea nigra, L.*
Cocowort.....Shepherd's purse.. *Capsella Bursa-pastoris, Medik.*

.....Avens or Herb
.....Bennett.....*Geum urbanum, L.*
Colewort.....Cabbage or Kale... *Brassica oleracea, L.*
Colickwort.....Parsley Piert.....*Alchemilla arvensis, L.*
Coughwort.....Coltsfoot.....*Tussilago Farfara, L.*
Cow's-wort.....Marsh red rattle.. *Pedicularis palustris, L.*
Cowthwort.....Motherwort.....*Leonurus cardiaca, L.*
Crosswort.....Crosswort.....*Galium cruciata, Scop.*
Cudwort.....Cudweed.....*Filago germanica, L.*
Culverwort.....Columbine.....*Aquilegia vulgaris, L.*
Curdwort.....Yellow bedstraw... *Galium vernum, L.*

Danewort.....Dwarf elder.....*Sambucus ebulus, L.*
Deadwort.....Dwarf elder.....*Sambucus ebulus, L.*
Dragon-wort...Snake-root.....*Polygonum Bistorta, L.*

Dropwort........Dropwort........*Spiræa filipendula, L.*

Edder-wort........Dragonwort........*Arum Dracunculus, L.*
Ellwort........Elecampane........*Inula Helenium, L.*
Ers-wort........Mouse-ear hawkweed........*Hieracium pilosella, L.*

Fellow-wort........Herb Robert........*Geranium robertianum, L.*
Felonwort........Greater Celandine........*Chelidonium majus, L.*
........Bittersweet........*Solanum dulcamara, L.*
Feltwort........Aaron's rod........*Verbascum thapsus, L.*
Felwort........Autumn gentian........*Gentiana amarella, L.*
Feverwort........Centaury........*Erythræa Centaurium, Pers.*
Field-wort........Autumn gentian........*Gentiana amarella, L.*
Figwort........Water figwort........*Scrophularia aquatica, L.*
....*Genus Scrophularia*

Filewort........Lesser Celandine........*Ranunculus ficaria, L.*
........Field cudweed........*Filago minima, Pers.*
Filwort........Centaury........*Erythræa Centaurium, Pers.*
Fingerwort........Foxglove........*Digitalis purpurea, L.*
Fleawort........Ploughman's spikenard........*Inula conyza, DC.*

Flewort........Ribwort........*Plantago lanceolata, L.*
Flirtwort........Feverfew........*Pyrethrum parthenium, L.*
Flixwort........Flixweed........*Sisymbrium sophia, L.*
Flowkwort........Marsh Pennywort........*Hydrocotyle vulgaris, L.*
Foalswort........Coltsfoot........*Tussilago Farfara, L.*
Frogwort........Purple orchis........*Orchis mascula, L.*

Gallwort........Common Toadflax........*Linaria vulgaris, L.*
Garlick-wort........Jack-by-the-hedge........*Alliaria officinalis, Andrz.*
Gipsy-wort........Water horehound........*Lycopus europæus, L.*
Glasswort........Saltwort........*Salicornia herbacea, L.*
Goosewort........Silverweed........*Potentilla anserina, L.*
Gout-wort........Herb Gerard........*Ægopodium podagraria, L.*
Grape-wort........Herb Christopher........*Actea spicata, L.*
........Common Bryony........*Bryonia dioica, Jacq.*

Hammer-wort........Pellitory-of-the-wall........*Parietaria officinalis, L.*
Hazelwort........Asarabacca........*Asarum Europæum, L.*
Heart-wort........Common melilot........*Melilotus officinalis, Wild*
Hartwort........Hartwort........*Tordylium maximum, L.*
Hertwort........Hertwort........*Various species of Aristolochia*
........Ash tree........*Fraxinus excelsior, L.*

Lungwort:
Bullock's........
Cow's........⎱Great Mullein........*Verbascum thapsus, L.*
Clown's........

Madderwort........Madwort........*Genus Alyssum*
Madderwort........Wormwood........*Artemisia absinthium, L.*
Madwort........Madwort........*Genus Alyssum*
....*Asperugo procumbens, L.*
Marshwort........Cranberry........*Oxycoccus palustris, Pers.,L.*
........Bogwort
Masterwort........Masterwort........*Peucedanum ostruthium, Koch.*
........Pellitory-of-Spain........*Imperatoria ostruthium, L.*
........Herb Gerard........*Ægopodium podagraria, L.*
Maudlin wort........Ox-eye daisy........*Chrysanthemum leucanthemum, L.*
May-wort........Golden Crosswort........*Galium cruciata, L.*
Meadwort........
Medewort........⎱Meadowsweet........*Spiræa Ulmaria, L.*
Meadow-wort........
Mekilwort........Deadly nightshade........*Atropa belladonna, L.*
Michelwort........White Hellebore........*Veratrum album, L.*
Milkwort........Common Milkwort........*Polygala vulgaris, L.*
Mingwort........Mugwort........*Artemisia vulgaris, L.*
Money-wort........Creeping Jenny........*Lysimachia nummularia, L.*
........Bog pimpernel........*Anagallis tenella, L.*
Moonwort........Moon fern........*Botrychium lunaria, L.*
........Greater Stitchwort........*Stellaria holostea, L.*
Moor-wort........Wild rosemary........*Drosera rotundifolia, L.*
Motherwort........Mugwort........*Artemisia vulgaris, L.*
........Motherwort........*Leonurus cardiaca, L.*
Mothwort........Immortelle........*Helichrysum stoechas, DC.*
Mudwort........Mudweed........*Limosella aquatica, L.*
Mugwort........Mugwort........*Artemisia vulgaris, L.*
Nailwort........Rue-leaved saxifrage........*Saxifraga tridactylides, L.*
........Whitlow Grass........*Draba Verna, L.*
Navel-wort........Wall pennywort........*Cotyledon umbilicus, L.*
Nettlewort........Nettlewort........*Whole order of Urticaceæ*
Nipplewort........Nipplewort........*Lapsana communis, L.*
Nipwort
Oderwort........"The Herb Dragance" Snakeweed........*Polygonum Bistorta, L.*
Opopanewort........Marsh Woundwort........*Stachys palustris, L.*

Helfringswort....Common Bugle....*Ajuga reptans, L.*
Hillwort....Wild thyme....*Thymus serpyllum, L.*
....Pennyroyal....*Mentha pulegium, L.*
Hip-wort....Common navelwort.*Cotyledon umbilicus, L.*
....Pennywort
Hoarwort....Cudweed....*Filago germanica, L.*
Horewort
Homewort....Common houseleek *Sempervivum tectorum, L.*
Honewort....*Trinia glauca, Dumort.*
....Corn parsley....*Petroselinum segetum, Koch.*
Honeywort....A hawkweed....*Hieracium cerinthoides, L.*
....Maywort....*Galium cruciata, Scop.*
Hoodwort....Skull-cap....*Scutellaria galericulata, L.*
Hornwort....*Ceratophyllum demersum, L.*

Iron-wort....Mayweed....*Anthemis cotula, L.*
Ivy-wort....Ivy-leaved toadflax *Linaria Cymbalaria, Mill*
*Juph-wort....not identified—used in Markham's "English Housewife." 1637.

Kelpwort....Prickly Saltwort..*Sakola kali, L.*
Kenningwort....Greater Celandine..*Chelidonium majus, L.*
Kernelwort....Figwort....*Scrophularia nodosa, L.*
Kidneywort....Navelwort....*Cotyledon umbilicus, L.*
Knight's-wort..Water-soldier....*Stratiotes aloides, L.*
....Woundwort
....Knight's Pondwort
Knot-wort....Knotgrass....*Polygonum aviculare, L.*

Lagwort....Butterbur....*Tussilago Petasites, L.*
Langwort....White or False
Lingwort....}Hellebore....*Veratrum album, L.*
Latherwort....Soapwort....*Saponaria officinalis, L.*
Leadwort....Common Leadwort..*Plumbago europaea, L.*
Leechwort....Ribwort Plantain..*Plantago lanceolata, L.*
Lichwort....Pellitory-of-the-wall *Parietaria officinalis, L.*
Limpwort....Viscid Campion...*Lychnis viscaria, L.*
Lithewort....Brooklime....*Veronica beccabunga, L.*
Liverwort....Wayfaring tree....*Viburnum lantana, L.*
....Common Agrimony *Agrimonia Eupatoria, L.*
....*Marchantia polymorpha, L.*
Longwort....Pellitory-of-Spain..*Anacyclus pyrethrum, L.*
Lousewort....Marsh red rattle...*Pedicularis palustris, L.*
Lungwort....Lungwort....*Pulmonaria officinalis, L.*
*This wort, taken from Mr. Britten's "Plant Names," is given in the hope that some one who may have run across it elsewhere can identify it for me.

Palsywort....Cowslip....*Primula veris, L.*
Peachwort....Persicaria....*Polygonum persicaria, L.*
Pearlwort....Pearlwort or Spurry *Genus Sagina*
Pennywort....Navelwort....*Cotyledon umbilicus, L.*
....Ivy-leaved toadflax *Linaria Cymbalaria, L.*
Pepperwort....Peppergrass....*Lepidium campestre, Br.*
Pestilence-wort..Butterbur....*Petasites officinalis, Moench.*
Peter's wort....Hard Hay....*Hypericum tetrapterum, L.*
Pewter wort....Rough horse-tail...*Equisetum hyemale, L.*
Pilewort....Lesser Celandine..*Ranunculus ficaria, L.*
Pipe-wort....Pipewort....*Family Eriocaulaceae*
Pond-wort....Water-soldier'....*Stratiotes aloides, L.*
Pricksong-wort..Honesty....*Linaria biennis, L.*
Purplewort....Marsh cinque-foil..*Comarum palustre, L.*

Quidwort....Cudweed....*Filago germanica, L.*
Quillwort....Quillwort....*Isoetes lacustris, L.*
Quincywort....Squinancy-wort...*Asperula cynanchica, L.*

Ragwort....Ragweed....*Senecio Jacobaea, L.*
Ribwort....Ribwort....*Plantago lanceolata, L.*
Rybwort
Rupture-wort...Rupture-wort....*Herniaria glabra, L.*

St. James' wort.Ragwort....*Senecio Jacobaea, L.*
St. John's Wort.St. John's Wort....*Hypericum perforatum, L.*
St. Peter's Wort.Cowslip....*Primula veris, L.*
....Square Stalked St.
....John's Wort....*Hypericum quadrangulum, L.*

Saltwort....Sea Thrift....*Salsola Kali, L.*
Sandwort....Sandwort....*Genus Arenaria, L.*
Sapwort....Dog's Mercury....*Mercurialis perennis, L.*
Saw-wort....Saw-wort....*Serratula tinctoria, L.*
Scabwort....Elecampane....*Inula helenium, L.*
Scallewort....Clary....*Salvia sclarea, L.*
Scourwort....Soapwort....*Saponaria officinalis, L.*
Sealwort....Common Solomon's
....Seal....*Polygonatum multiflorum, All.*
Setterwort....Bear's Foot....*Helleborus viridis, L.*
....Green Hellebore
Sharewort....Sea Aster....*Aster tripolium, L.*
Sicklewort....Self Heal....*Prunella vulgaris, L.*
....Bugle....*Ajuga reptans*
....Herb Carpenter

Sight-wort.... Greater Celandine.. Chelidonium majus, L.
Skir-wort..... Skirret or
    Water parsnip... Sium sisarum
Sleepwort..... Lettuce.......... Lactuca virosa, L.
Smallwort..... Lesser Celandine.. Ranunculus ficaria, L.
Smerewort..... Good King Henry.. Chenopodium Bonus Henricus, L.
Smearwort
Snapwort...... Greater stitchwort. Stellaria holostea, L.
Sneezewort.... Yarrow, Milfoil.. {Achillea millefolium, L.
Nesewort   Achillea Ptarmica, L.
Soapwort...... Scourwort........ Genus Saponaria
Somerwort..... Birthwort........ Genus Aristolochia
Sowdwort..... Columbine....... Aquilegia vulgaris, L.
Spearwort..... Spearwort........ Ranunculus flammula, L.
Sparewort..... Spearwort........ Ranunculus flammula, L.
Spiderwort.... Spiderwort....... Tradescantia virginica, L.
Spleenwort.... Maidenhair fern... Asplenium trichomanes, L.
Spoonwort.... Common scurvy
    grass........... Cochlearia officinalis, L.
Springwort.... Any so-called Keyflower
    Spring flowers
    Flax............. Linum perenne, L.
    Cowslip.......... Primula veris, L.
    Field Madder..... Sherardia arvensis, L.
Spurwort......
Squinancy-wort Quincy-wort...... Asperula cynanchica, L.
Stabwort...... Wood sorrel...... Oxalis acetosella, L.
Staggerwort... Ragwort.......... Senecio Jacobæa, L.
Stammerwort
Standelwort... Early PurpleOrchid Orchis mascula, L.
Starchwort.... Lords and Ladies.. Arum maculatum, L.
Starwort...... Starwort......... Genus Aster
           Genus Stellaria
Steepwort..... Common Butterwort Pinguicula vulgaris, L.
Sticklewort... Agrimony........ Agrimonia Eupatoria, L.
Stickwort..... Wood Sorrel...... Oxalis Acetosella, L.
Stitchwort.... Starwort......... Genus Stellaria
Strikewort...   Stellaria holostea, L.
Strapwort..... .... Corrigiola littoralis, L.
Stubwort...... Wood sorrel...... Oxalis acetosella, L.
Sulphurwort... Sulphur-weed..... Peucedanum officinale, L.
Swallow-wort.. Greater Celandine. Chelidonium majus, L.

Tent wort.... Wall rue........ Asplenium Ruta-muraria, L.
Tetter wort... Greater Celandine.. Chelidonium majus, L.
Thimble-wort.. Foxglove.......... Digitalis purpurea, L.
Throatwort.... Knotted Figwort... Scrophularia nodosa, L.
          Various campanulas
Thrumwort.... Thrumwort....... Amaranthus caudatus, L.
Toothwort..... Shepherd's purse.. Capsella Bursa-pastoris, Medik.
          Genus Dentaria
Toywort....... Shepherd's purse.. Capsella Bursa-pastoris, Medik.

Wallwort...... Dwarf elderberry.. Sambucus ebulus, L.
    Wall pepper....... Sedum, acre, L.
    Pellitory-of-the-wall Parietaria officinalis, L.
    Pennywort........ Cotyledon umbilicus, L.
    Navelwort........ Cotyledon umbilicus, L.
Walwort or.... Dwarf Elder...... Sambucus ebulus, L.
Walwort....... Dwarf Elder...... Sambucus ebulus, L.
Wartwort...... Sun Spurge....... Euphorbia helioscopia, L.
    Turnsole
    Greater Celandine.. Chelidonium majus L.
Waterwort..... Maidenhair....... Asplenium Trichomanes, L.
          Genus Elatine
Waywort....... Scarlet pimpernel.. Anagallis arvensis, L.
Whitewort..... Feverfew......... Pyrethrum parthenium, L.
    Whorled Solomon's
    Seal............. Polygonatum multiflorum, Moench.
Wildwort...... Lungwort—
    Our Lady'sMilkwort Pulmonaria officinalis, L.
Willow-wort... Great yellow
    loosestrife....... Lysimachia vulgaris, L.
Wolfs-wort.... Monkshood....... Aconitum Napellus, L.
Woundwort.... Kidney Vetch..... Anthyllis vulneraria, L.
    Golden Rod....... Solidago virgaurea, L.
          Species Stachys
Wreathe-wort.. Purple orchis..... Orchis mascula, L.
Yellow-wort... Yellow Centaury.. Chlora perfoliata, L.
Youth-wort.... Sundew.......... Drosera rotundifolia, L.

Now that the herb garden has again come into its own it may be interesting to consider some of the designs used in the early 18th century as a possible motif for our present-day gardens. "The Complete English Gardner," written in 1704 by Leonard Meager, presents "Divers forms or plots for gardens," a few of which are shown here.

SOME HERBS FROM THE OLD WORLD AND THE NEW
THAT WILL GROW IN NEW ENGLAND

ALICE T. WHITNEY

"From Greenland's icy mountains,
From India's coral strand."
and from elsewhere—far and near, North and South, East and West.

     *   *   *

". . . and such gardens are not made
By singing:—'Oh, how beautiful!' and sitting in the shade."
(From: *The Glory of the Garden*—KIPLING)

THE list of herbs following includes everything that grows at our Milton place, whether it had been there for a century or more, or for a week or less, when the ground froze up for the winter this past December. It includes things whether there for years; whether got for ornament only; whether got because they were native to this region—or whether got just because they *are* "herbs."

The authorities referred to as to "what *is* an herb" are:

A Modern Herbal by Mrs. M. Grieve and Mrs. C. F. Leyel, 1931.

A Synopsis of Medical Botany of the U. S. by J. M. G. Carter, M.A., M.D., Ph.D., Sc.D., 1888.

And a similar book by Charles A. Lee, M.D., *A Catalogue of the Medicinal Plants, Indigenous and Exotic, Growing in the State of New-York,* 1848.

A Manual of Botany by Laurence Johnson, A.M., M.D. (from a series, "Wood's Library of Medical Authors"), 1884.

195

Missouri Botanical Garden Bulletin, Vol. 10, No. 4, April, 1922.
Professors Carter and Miller are very spacious in their opinions as to what they call "Medicinal Plants," which generous latitude has caused this list to become so incredibly long, but they really did write as if nearly "*Anything* green that grew out of the mould (in these U. S.) was an excellent herb to our fathers of old."

Other books have been consulted, but any information as to what is what that others may give is included in those above.

For botanical information the following books have been continually referred to:

Bailey's *Encyclopædia of Horticulture,* 1922.
Bailey's *Hortus,* 1930.
Gray's *New Manual of Botany* (Seventh Edition), 1908.
A Manual of Weeds by Ada E. Georgia, 1931.
Standardized Plant Names, 1924.
The Flower Finder by George L. Walton, M.D., 1930.

Also many others in the past, but only those above just now while hastily compiling these lists.

Herbs, native to the U. S., at Winter Valley, Milton, Massachusetts. (As of December, 1934.)

Actæa alba	White Baneberry
Actæa rubra	Red Baneberry
Anemone virginiana (and other sp.)	Thimbleweed
Anemonella thalictroides	Rue Anemone
Aquilegia canadensis	American Columbine
Aralia hispida	Bristly Aralia
Aralia nudicaulis	Wild Sarsaparilla (Bamboo Brier)
Aralia racemosa	American Spikenard (Indian Spikenard)
Aristolochia Serpentaria	Virginia Snakeroot
Asarum canadense	Wild Ginger
Asclepias incarnata	Swamp Milkweed
Asclepias tuberosa	Butterfly Weed (Pleurisy Root)
Baptisia australis	Blue Wild Indigo (Blue False Indigo)
Baptisia leucantha	White Wild Indigo
Camassia esculenta	Quamash (Common Camas) (Eastern Camas)
Caulophyllum thalictroides	Blue Cohosh (Papoose Root)
Chelone glabra	Balmony (White Turtlehead)
Chelone Lyoni	Pink Turtlehead
Chenopodium blitum (Blitum capitatum)	Strawberry Blite
Chimaphila umbellata	Pipsissewa (Princess Pine)
Cimicifuga racemosa	Black Snakeroot (Black Cohosh) (Bugbane)
Coptis trifolia	Goldthread (Canker Root)
Corydalis glauca	Pale Corydalis (Pale Fumatory)
Corydalis aurea	Golden Corydalis (Golden Fumatory)
Cypripedium pubescens (and other sp.)	Yellow Ladyslipper (American Valerian)
Dentaria diphylla	Crinkleroot (Toothwort) (Pepperroot)
Dentaria laciniata	Cut Toothwort
Dicentra canadensis	Squirrelcorn (Turkey Corn)
Dicentra Cucullaria	Dutchman's Breeches
Dicentra eximea	Wild Bleeding Heart
Drosera rotundifolia	Roundleaf Sundew
Erythronium albidum	White Dogtooth Violet
Erythronium americanum	Dogtooth Violet (Adder's Tongue) (Troutlily)
Eupatorium aromaticum mellissoides	Melissa Thoroughwort
Eupatorium celestinium	Mistflower
Eupatorium urticæfolium (E. agratoides)	White Snakeroot (Snow Thoroughwort)
Euphorbia corollata	Flowering Spurge (White Purslane)
Ferns:	
Adiantum pedatum	Maidenhair Fern (American)
Athyrium Filix-femina	Lady Fern
Polypodium vulgare	Common Polypody
Phyllitis Scolopendrium (Scolopendrium vulgare)	Hartstongue
Gentiana Andrewsii	Closed Gentian (Bottle Gentian)
Gentiana Saponaria	Soapwort Gentian
Gentiana Porphyrio	Pine Barren Gentian
Geranium Robertianum	Herb Robert
Geum rivale	Purple Avens
Gillena trifoliata	Bowmanroot (Indian Physic)
Goodyera repens	Rattlesnake Plantain
Helenium autumnale	Sneezeweed
Helianthus annuus	Common Sunflower
Helianthus tuberosus	Jerusalem Artichoke
Hepatica acutiloba	Sharplobe Hepatica (American Liverwort)
Hepatica triloba (Anemone hepatica)	Roundlobe Hepatica (American Liverwort)
Heuchera americana	Alumroot
Hydrastis canadensis	Goldenseal
Hydrophyllum virginianum	Virginia Waterleaf (Boston Cabbage)
Jeffersonia diphylla	Twinleaf (Rheumatism Root)
Liatris scariosa	Button Snakeroot (Blazing Star)
Liatris scariosa alba	White Snakeroot (White Blazing Star) (Excellent ornamental plant for Sept. and Oct., until heavy frost)

Liatris spicata.........Spike Gayfeather (Button
  (and other sp.)   Snakeroot)
Lobelia cardinalis......Cardinal Flower
Lobelia siphilitica.....Great Lobelia (Great Blue
                   Lobelia)

Lycopodium clavatum.....Common Club Moss
  (and other sp.)

Medeola virginiana......Indian Cucumber Root
Mentha aquatica.........Wild Water Mint
Mentha arvensis var.
  canadensis (M. canadensis)...Canada Mint (American Wild
                   Mint)
Menyanthes trifoliata...Bogbean (Buck Bean, etc.)
Monarda fistulosa.......Wild Bergamot
Monarda punctata........Horsemint

Oxalis violacea.........Violet Woodsorrel
Osmorhiza longistylis...American Sweet Cicely

Panax quinquefolium.....Dwarf Gensing (Gound Nut)
Panax trifolium.........Gensing
Pedicularis canadensis..Early Wood Betony (Lousewort)
Physostegia virginiana..False Dragonhead
Phytolacca decandra.....Pokeweed
Podophyllum peltatum....Mayapple (American Mandrake)
Polemonium reptans......Greek Valerian (Abscess Root)
Polygonatum biflorum....Small Solomon's Seal
Polygonatum commutatum..Great Solomon's Seal
Potentilla Anserina.....Silverweed
Pyrola americana........Roundleaf Pyrola

Sagittaria latifolia....Arrowhead (Wampee) etc.
Sanguinaria canadensis..Bloodroot
Sanguisorba canadensis..American Burnet (Canadian
                   Burnet)

Satureia vulgaris
  (Clinopodium vulgaris)...Wild Basil (Hedge Basil) etc., etc.
Scutellaria galericulata...Common Skullcap
Silene virginica (and other sp.)...Fire Pink (Catch Fly)
Silphium laciniatum.....American Ipecac (Rosin Weed)
Silphium trifoliatum....Cup Plant (Rosin Weed)
Solidago odora..........Fragrant Goldenrod
Stylophorum diphyllum...Celandine Poppy

Thalictrum dioicum......Early Meadow-Rue
Tiarella cordifolia.....Foamflower (Coolwort) (False
                   Mitrewort)
Tradescantia bracteata..Spiderwort (Pink)
Tradescantia virginiana.Spiderwort (Common)
Trillium erectum........Purple Trillium (Beth Root)
Trillium nivale.........Dwarf Trillium
Trillium grandiflorum...Snow Trillium
Triosteum perfoliatum...Horse Gentian

Verbena hastata.........Blue Vervain
Vernonia noveboracensis.Tall Ironweed
Veronica Virginica
  (Leptandra Va.)...Culver's Root (Black Root) etc.
Viola palmata...........Wild Okra
Viola striata...........White Violet
  (and many other sp.)

Herbs not native to the U. S., at Winter Valley, Milton, Massachusetts. (As of December, 1934.)

Alchemilla vulgaris.....Ladies' Mantle
A. alpina...............Ladies' Mantle, Alpine
Allium Cepa.............Onion
Ajuga reptans...........Bugle
Anemone Pulsatilla
  (Pulsatilla)...European Pasqueflower
  (and other sp.)
Armeria maritima........Common Thrift
  (Statice Armeria)

Arnica montana..........Arnica
Artemisia mutellina.....
Asparagus officinalis...Asparagus
Asperula odorata........Sweet Woodruff

Linum alpinum ....Alpine Flax
L. austriacum...........Austrian Flax
Lupinus polyphyllus.....Lupine (Washington Lupine)
Lysimachia Nummularia...Moneywort
L. vulgaris.............Golden Loosestrife (Yellow
                   Loosestrife)
Lythrum salicaria.......Purple Loosestrife

Mentha requieni ....Corsican Mint (Requiem Mint)
  (Thymuscorsica)   (Grows like a weed here and
                 much of it survives worst
                 winters)

Bellis perennis............English Daisy

Chenopodium bonus henricus. Good King Henry ("Mercury") etc.
Cimicifuga fetida simplex... Kamchatka Bugbane
  (C. racemosa simplex)
Clematis recta.............Ground Clematis
Colchium autumnale.........Meadow Saffron
Convallaria majalis........Lily-of-the-Valley
  (and 2 vars.)
Convallaria majalis rosea... Pink Lily-of-the-Valley
Crocus sativus.............Saffron Crocus

Dictamnus Fraxinella.......Dittany
  (D. albus)

Ephedra sp.................Ephedra (Jointfir) (Mah Huang)

Fumaria officinalis........Common Fumatory

Galanthus nivalis..........Snowdrop
  (and other sp.)
Gossypium hirsutum.........Upland Cotton

Helianthemum mutabile......Sunrose
  (and other sp.)
Heliotropium peruvianum....Heliotrope
  (Hort. vars.)
Helleborus niger...........Black Hellebore (Christmas Rose)
Hemerocallis fulva.........Orange Day Lily
Herniaria glabra...........Burstwort
H. hirsuta.................Burstwort
Hesperis matronalis........Rocket (Sweet Rocket) (Dames' Rocket)
Hieracium auranticum.......Orange Hawkweed ("Grim the Collier," etc.)

Iris florentina............Orris
I. germanica...............Orris
I. pallida.................Orris
I. pseudoacorus............Yellowflag Iris

Lamium album...............White Dead Nettle
L. maculatum...............Dead Nettle
Linaria origanifolia.......(A delightful creeping plant in shade. Well worth while.)
Linum usitatissimum........Flax (The flax of commerce)

Myosotis scorpiodes........Forget-me-not (True)
  (M. palustris) (and other sp.)
Muscari botryoides.........Grape Hyacinth
  (and other sp.)

Narcissus Jonquilla........Jonquil
  (and hybrids)
N. poeticus...............Poets' Narcissus
N. Pseudo-narcissus.......Daffodil (Trumpet) (Common Daffodil)
  (Many vars.)

Paonia officinalis.........Peony
  (and Hort. vars.)
Polygonum bistorta.........Bistort
Primula elatior............Oxlip.
P. veris..................Cowslip
P. vulgaris...............Primrose, Common (English Yellow)

Pulmonaria angustifolia
cærulea (or: P. a. azurea).. Lungwort (Blue) (A most delightful, easy and indispensable spring plant—very hardy)
P. maculata...............Lungwort, Common

Radicula Armorica..........Horseradish
  (Cochlearia Armorica)
  (and now: Armorica rusticana)
Radicula Nasturtium-aquatica. Watercress

Sanguisorba officinalis....Burnet
Satureia croatica......... Can find no English name but it should be called "Croatian Savory." A delightful, creeping plant, very much like Linaria origanifolia
Scilla mutans (Scilla nonscripta)
  (Hyacinthus nonscriptus).. English Bluebell

Taraxacum officinale.......Dandelion (This is deliberately grown in a row in vegetable garden for spring salad and, mysteriously, seems not to add to the usual weed dandelions on the place!)
Thymus belgradensis
T. chamedrys
T. lanicaulis
  (also all the sp. we grow at Woods Hole)
Tusilago Farfara...........Coltsfoot

Valeriana officinalis.......Valerian
Vinca minor.......Periwinkle (Myrtle) (Joy of the
    (Blue, White and "Red")   Ground)
    (Also "Bowles Variety,"
    an extra good and robust
    blue.)

Viola odorata (Several vars.). Sweet Violet
V. tricolor.......Heartsease (Johnny-Jump-Ups)
    etc., etc.

Herb plants and shrubs found growing wild at Winter Valley, Milton, Massachusetts. Nearly all are the most arrant weeds, some are villainous and a few are attractive and desirable.

N = Native U. S.

N Achillea Millefolium.......Yarrow (Milfoil)
N Acorus Calamus.......Sweet Flag (Sweet Sedge)
N Agrimonia mollis.......Soft Agrimony
N Agropyron repens.......Quack-Grass (Couch-Grass) etc.
N Alisma Plantago-aquatica...Water Plantain
N Ambrosia artemisiifolia...Common Ragweed (sic) (That
    enemy of the human race!)
    (ALAS!)
N Ambrosia trifida.......Great Ragweed (Giant Ragweed)
N Anaphalis margaritacea....Pearl Everlasting, etc.
N Anemone quinquefolia......Wood Anemone
N Apocynum andros-
    æmijolium.......Spreading Dogbane
N Apios tuberosa.......Wild Bean (Ground Nut)
N Arisæma triphyllum.......Jack-in-the-Pulpit
N Asclepias syriaca.......Common Milkweed
N Aster cordifolius.......Blue Wood Aster
N Aster novæ-angliæ.......New England Aster
    (and other sp.)

Barbarea verna (B. præcox). Early Winter Cress (Scurvy Grass)
N Barbarea vulgaris.......Winter Cress (St. Barbara's Cress,
    etc., etc.)

Brassica nigra.......Black Mustard

N Caltha palustris.......Marsh Marigold
N Capsella Bursa-pastoris...Shepherds' Purse
N Cerastium vulgatum.......Mouse-Ear Chickweed
N Chelidonium majus.......Greater Celandine
N Chenopodium album.......Smooth Pigweed (Lambs'
    Quarters, etc.)

Chrysanthemum
    Leucanthemum.......Common Daisy (Ox-Eye Daisy,
    etc.)
Cichorium Intybus.......Chicory

Daucus Carota.......Wild Carrot (Queen Anne's Lace,
    etc.)

Nepeta Glechoma.......Ground Ivy, etc., etc.
    (N. hederacea)
N Oenothera biennis.......Evening Primrose
    (and other sp.)
N Oxalis stricta.......Wood Sorrel

Plantago lanceolata.......English Plantain (Ribwort) (a
    curse anywhere)
Plantago major.......Common Plantain
N Polygonum Hydropiper.....Smartweed
N Polygonum hydropiperoides. Mild Water Pepper
Polygonum Persicaria......Lady's Thumb, etc.
N Portulaca oleracea.......Purslane, etc., etc.
N Potentilla argentea.......Silvery Cinquefoil
N Potentilla canadensis.....Common Cinquefoil
N Potentilla monspeliensis...Rough Cinquefoil (Norway Cin-
    quefoil)

N Prenanthes alba.......White Lettuce (Rattlesnake
    (Nabalus alba)   Master, etc.)
Prunella vulgaris.......Selfheal (Prunella) (Carpenter's
    Herb)

Ranunculus acris.......Tall Buttercup
N Ranunculus repens.......Creeping Buttercup
N Rubus sp.......Wild Blackberry
Rumex Acetosella.......Field Sorrel (Sheep Sorrel)

N Senecio aureus.......Golden Groundsel (Life Root)
    (Squaw Root)
N Smilacina racemosa.......False Solomon's Seal
N Solidago sp.......Goldenrod (any and all are
    "Herbs," apparently)
N Spiræa latifolia.......Meadow-sweet
N Spiræa tomentosa.......Hardhack (Steeplebush)
N Stellaria media.......Common Chickweed
N Symplocarpus fœtidus.....Skunk Cabbage

N *Equisetum arvense*	Common Horsetail (Field Horsetail)
N *Erigeron annuus*	Daisy Fleabane
N *Erigeron pulchellus*	Robin's Plantain (Blue Spring Daisy, etc)
N *Eupatorium perfoliatum*	Boneset (American) (Thoroughwort, etc.)
N *Eupatorium purpureum*	Joe-Pye Weed (Gravelroot, etc.)
N *Fragaria* (Sp. unknown)	Wild Strawberry
N *Galium asprellum*	Rough Bedstraw
N *Geranium maculatum*	Wild Geranium (American Cranesbill Root)
N *Gnaphalium polycephalum* . .	Common Everlasting (Old Field Balsam), etc.
N *Gnaphalium uliginosum*	Low Cudweed
N *Hypericum mutilum*	Dwarf St. Johnswort
N *Hypericum perforatum*	Common St. Johnswort
N *Hypoxis hirsuta* (*H. erecta*) . .	Yellow Star-Grass(Goldeye-Grass)
N *Impatiens fulva* (*I. biflora*) . .	Spotted Jewelweed (Spotted Touch-Me-Not)
N *Iris versicolor*	Blue Flag Iris (Larger Blue Flag)
N *Lactuca canadensis*	Wild Lettuce
N *Leontodon autumnalis*	Fall Dandelion
N *Linaria vulgaris*	Common Toadflax (Butter and Eggs)
N *Lobelia inflata*	Indian Tobacco
N *Lycopus virginicus*	Bugleweed (Water-Horehound) etc.
N *Lysimachia quadrifolia*	Four-Leaved Loosestrife (and other sp.)
N *Malva rotundifolia*	Dwarf Mallow (Cheeses, etc.)
N *Mollugo verticillata*	Indian Chickweed (Carpetweed) (A dreadful pest)
N *Monotropa Hypopitys*	Pinesap (False Beechdrops)

Tanacetum vulgare	Tansy
Taraxacum officinale	Dandelion
Typha latifolia	Cat-tail (Common)
N *Urtica dioica*	Stinging Nettle (Great Nettle)
N *Uvularia sessilifolia*	Little Merribells (Bellwort) (*Oakesia sessilifolia*)
N *Verbascum Thapsus*	Common Mullein
N *Veronica officinalis*	Common Speedwell (The most charming and useful of weeds. Makes a fine, nearly-ever-green ground cover in shade where *nothing* else will grow.)
N *Veronica serpyllifolia*	Thyme-leaved Speedwell (Even this is useful, in shade-leaves so much like V. repens that have often to stop and look to make sure whether or not it is the latter—advise everyone not to scorn either of these two friendly and pleasant weeds.)
N *Viola blanda*	Sweet White Violet
N *Viola cucullata*	Blue Marsh Violet
N *Viola papilionacea*	Butterfly Violet
Vicia sativa	Common Vetch (Tare)

FERNS

N *Onoclea sensibilis*	Sensitive Fern
N *Osmunda cinnamomea*	Cinnamon Fern
N *Osmunda regalis*	Royal Fern
N *Parthenocissus quinquefolia* (*Psedera quinquefolia*) (*Ampelopsis quinquefolia*)	Virginia Creeper (Woodbine, etc.)

SHRUBS

Rosa sp.	Wild Rose?
N *Rhus glabra*	Smooth Sumach
N *Rhus Toxicodendron* (Alas) .	Poison Ivy
N *Rhus typhina*	Staghorn Sumach
N *Sambucus canadensis*	Elder (American)
N *Smilax rotundifolia*	Greenbrier (Horse Brier, etc.)
N *Viburnum dentatum*	Arrow-Wood
N *Vitis sp.*	Wild Grapes

Tree, shrub and vine "herbs" at Winter Valley, Milton, Massachusetts. (As of December, 1934.) All native to the U. S.

Abies balsamea	Balsam Fir	*Acer rubrum*	Red Maple
Abies Fraseri	Frazer Fir	*Acer saccharinum*	Silver Maple (White Maple)
(and other sp.)		*Acer saccharum*	Sugar Maple
Acer negundo	Box Elder	*Amelanchier canadensis* . . .	Shadbush (Downy Shadblow) etc.

Amelanchier laevis................ Allegheny Shadblow
Amelanchier stolonifera....... Running Shadblow
Aralia spinosa.................... Hercules Club (Angelica Tree)
Arctostaphyllos uva-ursi...... Bearberry

Benzoin aestivale................ Spicebush (Benjamin Bush) etc.
(Lindera Benzoin)
Betula lenta....................... Sweet Birch
Betula lutea....................... Yellow Birch (Gray Birch)
Betula papyrifera............... Paper Birch (Canoe Birch)
Betula populifolia.............. Gray Birch

Calycanthus floridus.......... Sweetshrub (Strawberry Shrub)
(Carolina Allspice)

Carpinus caroliniana.......... American Hornbeam
(C. americana)
Cassia marilandica............. American Senna
Ceanothus americanus........ New Jersey Tea (Red Root)
Celastrus scandens............. American Bittersweet (Wax-work)
Celtis occidentalis.............. Hackberry (Sugarberry)
Cephalanthus occidentalis.... Buttonbush
Cercis canadensis............... American Judas Tree
(American Redbud)
Chiogenes hispidula........... Creeping Snowberry
Chionanthus virginiana....... Fringe Tree
Cladrastis lutea................. Yellow-wood
(Virgilia tinctoria)
Clematis virginiana............ Virgin's Bower
Clethra alnifolia................ Summersweet (Sweet Pepperbush)
Comptonia asplenifolia........ Sweet Fern
(Myrica asplenifolia)
Cornus Amomum................ Silky Dogwood (Kinnikinnik)
(C. seriaca)
Cornus circinata (C. rugosa).. Roundleaf Dogwood
Cornus florida................... Flowering Dogwood
Corema Conradi................. Broom-Crowberry
Corylus americana.............. Hazelnut (American)
Crataegus coccinea............. Thicket Hawthorn
Crataegus phenopyrum........ Washington Thorn
(C. cordata)

Diervilla rivularis.............. Georgia Bush-honeysuckle
Diervilla trifida................. Dwarf Bush-honeysuckle
Diospyros virginiana........... Persimmon (Common)
Dirca palustris.................. Leatherwood

Empetrum nigrum............... Crowberry

Larix laricina.................... American Larch (Tamarack)
(Hackmatack)
Ledum grenlandicum.......... Labrador Tea
(L. latifolium)
Linnaea borealis americana... Twinflower
Liquidamber Styraciflua....... Sweet Gum (Bilsted)
Liriodendron tulipifera........ Tulip Tree
Loiseleuria procumbens........ Mountain Azalea

Magnolia acuminata............ Cucumber Magnolia
Magnolia glauca................. Swamp Magnolia (Sweet Bay)
Mahonia Aquifolium............ Oregon Hollygrape
(Berberis Aquifolium)
Malus coronaria................. Wild Sweet Crab
(and other sp.)
Mitchella repens................. Partridgeberry (Squaw Vine)
Myrica carolinensis............. Bayberry
Myrica Gale...................... Sweet Gale

Nemopanthus mucronulatus... Mountain Holly
Nyssa sylvatica.................. Tupelo (Sour Gum) (Pepperridge)

Oxydendrum arboreum......... Sorrel Tree (Sour Wood)

Physocarpus opulifolius........ Ninebark
Pieris mariana................... Staggerbush
(Lyonia mariana)
(Andromeda mariana)
Pinus Banksiana................ Jack Pine
Pinus resinosa................... Red Pine
Pinus rigida...................... Pitch Pine
Pinus Strobus.................... White Pine
Populus balsamifera............ Balsam Poplar (Old Field Balsam)
(Tacmahac)
Populus deltoides................ Cottonwood (Necklace Poplar)
(P. canadensis)
Populus tremuloides............ Quaking Aspen
Prunus serotina................. Wild Black Cherry
Prunus virginiana.............. Chokecherry
Ptelea trifoliata................. Hop Tree (Wafer Ash)

Quercus alba..................... White Oak
Quercus bicolor.................. Swamp White Oak
Quercus coccinea................ Scarlet Oak
Quercus palustris............... Pin Oak
Quercus rubra.................... Red Oak

Epigœa repens...........Trailing Arbutus (Mayflower)
Euonymus americanus......Strawberry Bush
Euonymus atropurpureus...Burning Bush (Wahoo)
Euonymus obovatus........Running Euonymus (Trailing Wahoo)

Fagus americanus.........American Beech
Fraxinus americana.......American Ash (White Ash)

Gaultheria procumbens....Wintergreen (Checkerberry) (Teaberry)
Gaylussacia baccata......Huckleberry
(and other sp.)
Gleditsia triacanthos....Honey Locust (Black Locust)
Gymnocladus dioica.......Kentucky Coffee Tree

Hamamelis ternalis.......Vernal Witch-hazel
Hamamelis virginiana.....Witch-hazel
Hichoria ovata (Carya ovata). Shell-bark Hickory
Hydrangia arborescens....Smooth Hydrangea (Seven Barks) (Hills of Snow)
Hypericum prolificum.....Shrubby St. Johnswort

Ilex glabra..............Inkberry
Ilex lœvigata............Smooth Winterberry
Ilex monticola...........Mountain Winterberry
Ilex opaca...............American Holly
Ilex serrata.............Finetooth Holly
Ilex verticillata........Common Winterberry (Black Alder)

Itea virginica...........Sweetspire

Juglans cinera...........Butternut
Juglans nigra............Black Walnut
Juniperus communis depressa. Prostrate Juniper

Kalmia angustifolia......Sheep Laurel (Lambkill)
Kalmia latifolia.........Mountain Laurel
Kalmia polifolia.........Swamp Laurel (Bog Kalmia) (K. glauca)

Rhododendron maximum......Rosebay Rhododendron
Rhus canadensis..........Fragrant Sumach
(R. aromatica)
Rhus Cotinus.............Smoke Bush
Ribes aurea..............Flowering Currant
Rubus deliciosus.........Boulder Raspberry
Rubus odoratus...........Flowering Raspberry

Sadix discolor...........Pussy Willow
(and other sp. unknown)
Sassafras sariifolium....Sassafras
(S. officinalis)
Symphoricarpus racemosus...Snowberry
Symphoricarpus vulgaris...Coralberry (Indian Currant)
var. Chenaulti

Taxus canadensis.........American Yew
Thuya occidentalis.......American Arbor Vitae (Yellow Cedar)
Tsuga canadensis.........Hemlock
Tsuga caroliniana........Carolina Hemlock

Ulmus americana..........American Elm
Ulmus fulva..............Slippery Elm

Vaccinium corymbosum.....Highbush Blueberry
Vaccinium pallidum.......Dryland Blueberry
Vaccinium pennsylvanicum.Lowbush Blueberry
Vaccinium macrocarpum....Cranberry (American)
Vaccinium Vitis-idea.....Cowberry
Vaccinium Vitis-idea minor. Mountain Cranberry
Viburnum alnifolium......Hobblebush
Viburnum americanum......American Cranberry Bush
Viburnum cassinoides.....Withe-Rod
Viburnum Lentago.........Nannyberry (Sheepberry)
Viburnum prunifolium.....Black Haw

Zanthorrhiza apiifolia...Shrub Yellowroot
Zanthoxylum americanum...Prickly Ash

Trees, shrubs and vines which may be classed as "Herbs" but are not native to the U. S., at Winter Valley, Milton, Massachusetts.

Acer platanoides.........Norway Maple
Acer pseudo-platanus.....Sycamore Maple
Æsculus Hippocastanum....Common Horsechestnut
Aristolochia sipho.......Dutchman's Pipe

Berberis vulgaris........Common Barberry
(and other sp.)
Calluna vulgaris.........Heather
(and vars.)

Castanea vesca	Chestnut (A Chinese sp. said to be blight-proof)
Corylus Avellana	Filbert
(and hort. vars.)	
Crataegus Oxyacantha	English Hawthorn
(and other sp.)	
Daphne Mezereum	Mezereon (February Daphne)
Erica carnea (and vars.)	Heath
(and other sp.)	
Euonymus europaea	Spindle Tree (European Burning Bush)
Fagus sylvatica	European Beech
Fraxinus Ornus	Manna Ash
Hamamelis mollis	Chinese Witch-hazel
Hedera helix	English Ivy
Hedera helix baltica	Baltic Ivy
Hedera helix conglomerata	Bunchleaf English Ivy
Hedera helix gracilis	Baby English Ivy
Laburnum alpinum	Scotch Laburnum
Laburnum vulgare	Common Laburnum (Golden Chain)
Larix europaea	European Larch
Larix leptolepis	Japanese Larch
Lonicera fragrantissima	Fragrant Honeysuckle
(and other sp.)	
Malus sylcestris (Hort. vars.)	Apple
Morus tatarica alba	Russian Mulberry
Philadelphus coronarius	Mock Orange
(and other sp.)	
Picea excelsa	Norway Spruce
Pinus Cembra	Swiss Stone Pine
Pinus densiflora	Japanese Red Pine
Pinus montana	Swiss Mountain Pine
Pinus montana mughus	Mugho Pine
Pinus nigra	Austrian Pine (Indispensable, a joy always)
Pinus nigra var. calabrica (in "Hortus") (Poiretiana —in "Stand. Plt. Nms.")	Corsican Pine (A poor, unhappy thing here)
Pinus sylvestris	Scotch Pine
Prunus glandulosa (Hort. vars.)	Flowering Almond
Prunus tomentosa	Nanking Cherry
(and other sp.)	
Pyracantha coccinea (and var.)	Firethorn
Quercus robur	English Oak
Rhamnus Frangula	Glossy Buckthorn (Elder Buck-thorn)
Rosa rubiginosa	Sweet Brier (Eglantine)
Salix alba	White Willow
Salix caprea	Goat Willow (European Pussy Willow)
Salix pentandra	Laurel Willow
Sorbus Aucuparia	European Mountain Ash (Rowan Tree)
Styrax japonica	Japanese Styrax
Syringa vulgaris	Common Lilac
(and Hort. vars.)	
Taxus baccata repandens	Spreading English Yew
Ulmus campestris	English Elm
Viburnum Carlesii	Fragrant Viburnum
Viburnum fragrans	Fragrant Viburnum
Viburnum Opulus	European Cranberry Bush
Viburnum Opulus sterile	Common Snowball
Vitex macrophylla	Chaste Tree
Vitex negundo	Negundo Chaste Tree
Vitex negundo incisa	Cutleaf Chaste Tree

GREENHOUSE HERBS

Osmanthus fragrans (Olea fragrans)	Fragrant Olive
Osmanthus Aquifolium	Holly Osmanthus
Thea sinensis (Camellia thea)	Tea
Viburnum tinus	Laurustinus

Herbs at Little Harbor Farm, Woods Hole, Massachusetts. (As of September, 1934.)

Agrimony	Agrimonia Eupatoria	Catsfoot (Pussytoes)	Antennaria dioica
Angelica	Angelica archangelica	Cedar, Red	Juniperus virginiana

Anise...........Pimpinella anisum
Avens...........Geum urbanum
Balm...........Melissa officinalis
Balm of Gilead
  (Mosquito Plant)....Cedronella cana (or C. triphylla)
Basil, Bush.......Ocimum minimum
Basil, Purple Bush...O. comosum
Basil, Sweet........O. Basilicum
Bedstraw, Hedge....Galium Mollugo
Bedstraw, Ladies'...G. verum
Bergamot
  (Bee Balm) (Oswego Tea)..Monarda didyma
  (Salmon Pink)......M. didyma var. salmonea
  (Pink)............M. kalmiana
  (White, Tall)......M. superba
  (Virulent magenta)..M. media
Betony, Wood (Woundwort)..Stachys betonica (Betonica officinalis)
Betony, Big.......Betonica grandiflora
Betony, Woolly....Stachys lanata
Bittersweet......Solanum Dulcamara
Blessed Thistle...Cnicus benedictus
Borage...........Borago officinalis
Box (Truedwarf)...Buxus sempervirens var. suffruticosa
Broom...........Cytisus scoparius (Genista scoparia)
Bryony..........Bryonia dioica
Burnet (Lesser or Salad).....Sanguisorba minor (Poterium sanguisorba)
Calamint, Alpine....Satureia alpina (Calamintha alpina)
Calamint, Lesser....S. Nepeta (C. Nepeta)
Camomile, English...Anthemis nobilis
Camomile, German...Matricaria chamomilla
Camphor Plant....Chrysanthemum balsamita (Balsamita vulgaris)
Catnip (Cat Mint)...Nepeta cataria
  N. lanceolata* (White flowers)
  N. nepetella* (Mauve fls.—tall, interesting plant resembling a refined and slender Clary)
  N. mussinii
  N. nervosa
  N. "Souvenir d'Andre Chaudron"

Centaury...........Erythraea Centaurium
Chaste Tree.......Vitex Agnus-castus
Chervil...........Anthriscus cerefolium
Chives...........Allium schaenoprasum
Cinquefoil.......Potentilla reptans
Clary...........Salvia sclarea
Clove Pink.......Dianthus caryophyllus ("Grenadine Red")
Clover, Yellow Sweet......Melilotus officinalis
  (Melilot)
Cornflower.......Centaurea cyanus
Corn Salad.......Valerianella olitoria
Costmary (Alecost)...Chrysanthemum balsamita tanacetoides
  (Bible Leaf)
Cupidone (Cupid's Dart)...Catananche caerulea
Currant, Black....Ribes nigrum
Currant, Red......R. rubrum
Currant, White....R. rubrum var. album
Dalmatian Powder Plant....Chrysanthemum cinerariifolium (Pyrethrum cinerariifolium)
Dill..............Anethum graveolens
Dyers' Greenwood.........Genista tinctoria
  (Woadwaxen)
Echinacea (Cone Flower)...Echinacea angustifolia
Echinacea (Purple Cone Flower)...E. purpurea
Edelweiss........Leontopodium alpinum
Elder, Dwarf......Sambucus Ebulus
Elecampane......Inula Helenium
Eryngo (Sea Holly)...Eryngium amethystinum
Flax, Perennial....Linum perenne
Foxglove.........Digitalis purpurea
Garlic...........Allium sativum
Geranium, Lemon...Pelargonium crispum
Geranium, Lemon...P. capitatum
Geranium, Nutmeg...P. odoratissimum
  (Apple Geranium)
Geranium, Oak-leaved...P. quercifolium
Geranium, Peppermint...P. tomentosum
Geranium, Rose (and 2 vars.)...P. graveolens
Germander.......Teucrium Chamaedrys
Goats' Rue.......Galega officinalis
Gooseberry, Red...Ribes grossularia

Gooseberry, White......... R. grossularia
Holly, English........... Ilex aquefolium
Hops.................... Humulus lupulus
Horehound (or Hoarhound). Marrubium vulgare
Hyssop................. Hyssopus officinalis
Indigo................. Indigofera tinctoria (Tropical plant—treat as an annual)

Juniper, Savin......... Juniperus sabina

Lavender, Spike........ Lavandula spica
Lavender, Sweet........ L. vera
Lavender, ——.......... L. pinnata (Tender, not hardy through winter)

Lavender Cotton........ Santolina Chamæcyparissus incana
Lemon Verbena......... Lippia citriodora
Lily, Madonna......... Lilium candidum
Lime Tree (Linden).... Tilia vulgaris (Tilia europæa)
Locust, Common....... Robinia pseudoacacia
Lovage............... Levisticum officinale

Mallow, Common or Blue.. Malva officinalis (M. sylvestris)
Marigold, Pot......... Calendula officinalis
Marjoram, Pot........ Origanum onites
Marjoram, Sweet...... O. Majorana
Marjoram, Wild....... O. vulgaris
Marshmallow......... Althaea officinalis
Meadowsweet........ Spirea Ulmaria (Filipendula Ulmaria)
Melilot, Blue........ Melilotus caerulea (Trigonella caerulea)

Mints
Curly Mint......... Mentha crispa
——?............ M. perfoliata saxonis
Peppermint......... M. piperita
Pennyroyal......... M. Pulegium
Applemint......... M. rotundifolia (Leaves dark green and very much rounder than those of any of the other mints)
Applemint (Variegated).. M. rotundifolia, var. variegata (Leaves variegated grayish-green and white, much crinkled and rather woolly.) Both of these smell very decidedly of apples and it is only when they are crushed that the mint fragrance becomes uppermost. These tally with the descriptions of each, and their names, both botanical and English, as given in "Hortus."
Spearmint (Lamb's Mint). M. spicata (M. viridis)
——?............ M. tomentosa

Thymes.................. Thymus azoricus*
T. cimicinus
T. erectus
Caraway-scented Thyme... T. herba-barona (Charming, delicious)
T. hyemalis
T. marshalliensis
T. micans*
T. nitidus (Charming, very useful in sunny wild garden)
T. nummularius (Fine, robust, spreading plant)
T. Serpyllum*
Thyme, Wild.......... T. Serpyllum albus
(Mother of Thyme)
Thyme, White......... T. Serpyllum carnosus
T. Serpyllum citriodorus
Thyme, Lemon-scented.. T. Serpyllum coccineus
T. Serpyllum languinosis
Thyme, Woolly........ T. Serpyllum minus (A treasure—tiny, flat, very dark green)
T. Serpyllum odoratissimus
T. Serpyllum pulchellus
T. Serpyllum roseus
T. Serpyllum villosus
T. Serpyllum zygis
T. vulgaris
T. vulgaris (No special botanical name given for this—a delightful heatherlike plant)
Thyme, Broad-leafed Eng.. T. vulgaris argenteus
Thyme, French........ T. vulgaris fragrantissimus
Thyme, Silver........

There is so much confusion about Thymes and so few definite descriptions given to distinguish one from another that these last four seem to require some notes. With us they are as follows:

T. vulgaris "Broad-Leafed English" Common Thyme: Leaves rather dark green. Fls. inconspicuous white. Ht. 6". Dies out in patches after flowering and must be severely pruned.

T. vulgaris "French variety." Leaves dark gray-green. Fls. same as above. Ht. 8-10". Robust, bushy plant almost exactly like our T. fragrantissimus and in the distance much resembling heather.

T. vulgaris argenteus. Again a lusty shrublet like the above in height. Variegated light gray-green and white. Not in the least of the T. serpyllum type although "Silver

Lemon Mint.............. *M. sp.*
(This English name is according to Mrs. Bardswell who gives no botanical name)
(Leaves variegated green and yellow and more smooth and shining than those of any of our other mints)

Mugwort................ *Artemisia vulgaris*

Nasturtium.............. *Tropaeolum majus*

Parsley................ *Petroselinum hortense*
Passion Flower.......... *Passiflora edulis*
(Purple granadilla)
Pellitory-of-the-Wall.... *Parietaria officinalis*
Plum, Beach............ *Prunus maritima*
Plume Poppy........... *Bocconia cordata*
Poppy, Opium.......... *Papaver somniferum*
Psylla................ *Plantago Psyllium*

Rampion............ *Campanula Rapunculus* (or *C. rapunculoides*) (have got seeds of both twice over and the plants from each seem to be both exactly alike)
Rosemary........... *Rosmarinus officinalis* "Heavenly Blue"
R. officinalis
Rue................ *Ruta graveolens*

Safflower... *Carthamus tinctorius*
(False, or Bastard, Saffron)

Sage.............. *Salvia officinalis*
Savory, Summer....... *Satureia hortensis*
Savory, Winter........ *S. montana*
Scurvy Grass....... *Cochlearia officinalis*
Soapwort(Bouncing Bet, etc.) *Saponaria officinalis*
Sorrel............. *Rumex acetosa* (or *R. patientia*— have both sp.)

Southernwood (Old Man).. *Artemisia Abrotanum*
(Lads' Love)
Stonecrop............ *Sedum acre* (and other sp.)
Sweet Cicely......... *Myrrhis odorata*

Tansy, Huron......... *Tanecetum huronensis*
Tarragon............ *Artemisia dracunculus*
Toadflax...........? *Linaria ericoides Hendersoni*
?....... *Linaria ericoides* "Canon J. Want"
(A delightful plant for border, rock garden or anywhere. Foliage grayish and heathlike, Fls. salmon pink)
?............. *L. pallida*
L. pallida alba
Ivyleaved Toadflax (Wall Pennywort, Kenilworth Ivy)............. *L. Cymbalaria*
Tobacco, Aztec........ *Nicotiana rustica*

Thyme" is almost always listed as *T. serpyllum argenteus.* Have seen one English catalogue which lists both kinds of "Silver Thyme," but otherwise our kind seems never to be mentioned.
T. vulgaris fragrantissimus: Almost exactly like our French Thyme. A little grayer and a little more fragrant.

Veravin.............. *Verbena officinalis*

Willow Herb........... *Epilobium angustifolium*
Woad............... *Isatis tinctoria*
Wormwood, Common.... *Artemisia absinthinum*
Wormwood, Beach..... *A. stelleriana*
Wormwood, Roman.... *A. pontica*
Wormwood, Saw-toothed.. *A. serrata*
Wormwood, "Silver King".. *A. albula*

WEEDS: (Dug up on the place and transplanted to top of wall above herb garden.)

Clover, Alsike......... *Trifolium hybridum*
Clover, Low Hop....... *T. procumbens*
Clover, Rabbit's Foot... *T. arvense*
Clover, Red.......... *T. pratense*
Clover, White........ *T. repens*
Cranesbill (Small-flowered) - *Geranium pusilium*

Feverfew............ *Chrysanthemum Parthenium*

Milkwort, Racemed..... *Polygala polygama*
(Bitter Polygala)

Pimpernel, Scarlet..... *Anagallis arvensis*
(Poor Man's Weather Glass)

Cedar, White........ *Chamaecyparis thyoides* (Little seedlings growing wild in moss in wall chinks, *not planted* there)
Liverwort (True)...... *Marchantia polymorpha* (*Not* put there on purpose—it just appeared)

* Asterisks after certain Nepetas and Thymes are to explain that the plants we have under these names actually do differ one from the other although, according to "Hortus," these different names apply to one and the same sp. Perhaps we were sent wrongly marked seeds or perhaps our labels got mixed.
This herb garden contains also 55 genera and 10 sp. of plants and 15 sp. of trees or shrubs which are not listed here because they are both happier at and more appropriate to our Milton place and so they are on the latter's list instead.

THE TUSSIE MUSSIE, AN HERBAL BOUQUET

Edna K. Neugebauer

What is a Tussie Mussie? This question is often asked. John Parkinson, in his *Paradisus Terrestris* of 1629, wrote of using flowers "to make a delicate Tussimussie, as they call it, or nosegay, both for sight and scent." It seems to have been a tight little bouquet of fragrant flowers and leaves placed in a filigree holder and was intended to be held in the hand so its warmth would release the aroma. In the old days it was thought that it warded off disease as well as counteracting the odors of a closed room. Another use was to carry a message from a young man to a maiden, perhaps a proposal of marriage, to which she could reply in like manner, signifying her interest or lack thereof. In Colonial days a Tussie Mussie was tucked in the Sunday bodice to wear to church.

In our day, the Tussie Mussie is usually made of herbs, both leaf and blossom, arranged artistically for color and form and placed in a small paper doily with a gay ribbon bow. Often it bears a message from the Language of Herbs. One can send sympathy and cheer to an ill friend or to strangers in a hospital, congratulate another on an accomplishment, or thank a hostess, as on the next page. These tiny bouquets can serve as luncheon favors, very appropriately for a gathering of herbalists. On her coronation, Queen Elizabeth II, following an old custom, was presented with a Tussie Mussie. And smaller arrangements can even be tucked into an envelope and sent across the country to convey one's feelings to a friend.

A MESSAGE TO OUR HOSTESS FROM OUR HERBS

We thank you for your

	Generosity — Honeysuckle
and	Courtesy — Marjoram
and your	Patience — Chamomile
also your	Activity — Thyme
and	Cheerfulness — Mint.
It was our	Luck — Lavender

which we shall always remember — Rosemary.

POT-POURRI ALBUM

By MARY E. BAER

◇◆◇

AS ELEANOUR SINCLAIR ROHDE has so aptly put it, "The summer flowers laugh and sing and the earth is filled with its gladness. No scents are alike, and yet how perfectly they blend in the garden. There is neither speech nor language but their voices are heard amongst them."

There is a medley of sweet fragrance also in the dried petals of roses, scented leaves, herbs and spices, a conglomerating of odors, most delightfully designated — Pot-Pourri.

The rose has been a favorite in many lands from time immemorial. Its portrait and praises appear in the very earliest literature and art, nowhere more so than in England, where it is the friendliest flower of the English countryside and the most famous flower of English tradition. When perfumes became the fashion during Elizabeth's reign it was to their gardens that the womenfolk turned and from out of their still-rooms and country houses many a family recipe for making pot-pourri comes down the ages. They form a fragrant link between the past generation and the present, when roses were valued more for their fragrance, sweet flavor and medicinal virtues than for the beauty of their petals alone.

There are two ways of preserving the flowers. In the "dry" method the petals are dried thoroughly and then the fixative, spice and perfume oils are added. The result will be as colorful and fragrant as a bouquet of living flowers. The other method is called the "moist" method and is the old-time one of pickling or preserving the partially dried petals by the addition of salt, thereby making what is called the stock, before the addition of the other ingredients. In this method the color is lost, due to the bleaching action of the salt or preservatives.

THE DRY METHOD

Gather the choicest blossoms from the garden, preferably in the morning just after the last trace of dew has disappeared from the petals. Carefully pull the petals apart from the flowers and spread them loosely upon a wire frame or window screen. If the screen is elevated the air currents can penetrate from the bottom as well as the top and this will help to hasten the drying process. During warm summer months this should not take longer than several days; providing of course that the drying takes place in a warm room, such as an attic or garage, but away from the direct rays of the sun. Be sure to turn the petals each day until they are chip dry, a state closely resembling corn flakes. Store the dried stock in covered containers.

The first step in making pot-pourri from stock is to add a " fixative," which is a material to absorb and help retain evaporation of the fragrant oils which are so volatile. There are two types of fixatives, those of animal origin and those of vegetable origin, of which the latter is more preferred for our purpose. Crushed orris root, calamus root or benzoin-Siam are fixatives which may be used singly or in a combination of all three. Several heaping tablespoons will be the right amount for several quarts of dried petals.

Crush the fixative in a mortar and add the spices. It is customary to use a mixture of crushed spice, generally the same proportion as the fixative. Those generally used are nutmeg, cinnamon, allspice and clove.

To the fixative and spices add the perfume oils, using just enough to create a fine, lumpy mass. It should be neither too moist to allow the oil to seep over the petals, nor too dry to have the powdered fixative and spices dust the leaves. If properly mixed, it will have the appearance of dampened ground corn meal, and when sprinkled over and through the jar will, in about one month's time, season each petal with a lasting bouquet and fragrance.

Oils for delicate scent of flower fragrance are synthetic rose, jasmin, sweet clover, orange flower, neroli, patchouli, mimosa, cassia and tube rose. Oils of greater strength which can be overpowering unless used

THE HERB GARDEN AT BREEZEWOOD, BRYN MAWR, PA.

Courtesy of Mrs. Walter Rebmann

for accent only are geraniol or rhodinol (both from the geranium), rosemary and sandalwood.

The spice oils of cinnamon and cloves and that of camphor, almond and eucalyptus are very overpowering and are quite apt to strangle those oils of sweet scent.

Other fragrant additions to both pot-pourris are: the ground seeds (with mortar and pestle) of coriander, cardamon and anise; also bits of vanilla beans and tonka beans, spicy slivers of orange and lemon rind about one-half inch wide and two inches long (using skin only) clove-studded with the large-headed Madagascar or Zanzibar cloves, sandalwood shavings, vetiver root, patchouli leaves, dried orange flowers, mullein flowers, along with pale and dark rosebuds and English lavender. All can be procured by the ounce or by the pound from the importer and are a fine addition to the scent jar.

On Other Methods of Drying

Flowers and petals can also be dried in borax or fine white sand, or in a slightly warm oven. They may also be pressed between the pages of a book. Flowers so dried are very beautiful accents for the pot-pourri jar because of their high coloring and natural appearance. However, they require very expert handling to insure good results.

Rose petals must always predominate in any pot-pourri in which they are an ingredient, for their very presence calls up the memory of their living scent. However, only the old-fashioned roses and lavender have any fragrance when dried. But you may desire to gather together the colors of your garden and make a spectrum arrangement. The following suggestions may be helpful.

Red: Roses, hollyhocks, geranium blooms, bee balm, peonies, berga-mot, carnation pinks.

Pink: Hollyhock, dittany of Crete, hyssop, roses.

Orange: Calendula, marigold, nasturtium, tansy, coreopsis, elecampane.

Yellow: Daisy, primrose, flag, camomile, mullein, cowslip, butter-cup, yarrow, pansies.

Blue: Cornflower, borage flower, larkspur, flag, anchusa, pansy, forget-me-not, delphinium.

White: Feverfew, hollyhock, yarrow, phlox, pansy.

Violet: Heliotrope, foxglove, lavender, pansy, flower heads of mint, rosemary.

Gray: Santolina, artemisia, peppermint geranium.

Green: Leaves of sweet-scented geraniums, sweet basil, sweet marjoram, bergamot mint, apple mint, orange mint, lemon thyme, rosemary, sweet woodruff, patchouli.

THE MOIST METHOD

For making this method, leave the rose petals on the drying frame just long enough to wilt them so that they will have lost about one-half their bulk. They will have a leathery appearance. Take a large wide-mouth crock and place one-half inch of the petals on the bottom, and add a like amount of table salt to cover them. Continue the process until the crock is almost full, stirring with a wooden spoon after each addition of petals. When filled, put a weight on top and allow it to remain for ten days. By then a solid cake mass will have formed. This may be taken out and broken into small pieces and mixed with the same type of fixative, spice and perfume oils as used in the dry method.

There are so many diversified recipes for making this type of scent jar that I am enclosing several for your trial and preference.

Recipe for Pot-Pourri from a letter in *English Country Life,* July 9, 1953.

". . . The recipe which is used here is the most lasting of any that I know, and some of the jars filled ten years ago are as fresh as those made today. Take a quantity of freshly opened fragrant rose petals, together with the yellow stamens, and an equal quantity of lavender blossoms (which can be bought). Place them in an earthenware bowl and cover them with ½ lb. orris root. To this mixture add 2 oz. bruised cloves (to every 2 lbs.), 2 oz. cinnamon, 2 oz. allspice and 2 oz. table salt. Allow it to stand for two weeks. It should be thoroughly turned over and mixed with the hands. Finally, it should be placed in bowls with covers, to ripen."

Recipe from
Sweet Scented Flowers and Fragrant Leaves,
Donald McDonald, 1895

" The following mixture is said to retain its fragrance for fifty years. Gather early in the day when perfectly dry a peck of roses, pick off petals and strew over them three-fourths of a pound of common salt. Let remain three days and if fresh flowers are added add more salt. Mix with the roses one-half pound of Bay salt, the same of allspice, cloves and brown sugar, also one-fourth pound gum benzoin, and two ounces orris root powdered. Add one gill of brandy and any sort of fragrant flowers such as oranges, lemon flowers, lavender, and lemon verbena. They should be perfectly dry when added. The mixture must be stirred occasionally and kept in close covered jars. The covers to be released only when perfume is desired in the room. If after a time the mixture seems to be getting dry, moisten only with brandy, as essences too soon lose their quality and injure the perfume."

The following two recipes are for the Dry Method.

Pot-Pourri — A Formula

Perfumes, Cosmetics and Soaps, W. A. Poucher, Vol. II, 1932

Flowers: Rose petals, lavender flowers, patchouli leaves.
Spices, etc.: Broken cinnamon bark, allspice, cloves, mace, coriander seeds, coarse sandalwood, vetiver roots, tonka beans.
Fixatives: Calamus roots, benzoin-Siam and orris rhisome.
Oils: Rose artificial, neroli, jasmine, ambrone and heloptropin (last two are powders).

Pot-Pourri — from Lady Blessington 1790-1845

From *A Book of Scents and Dishes,* Dorothy Allhusen, 1926

" Dried pale and red rose petals, one tumbler full of lavender flowers, acacia flowers, clove gilli flowers (pinks), orange flower petals, one wine glass of mignonette flowers and one teaspoon heliotrope flowers. Take one grain musk, thirty drops oil vetiver, five drops oil sandalwood, ten drops oil myrtle, twenty drops oil jonquille. Dry petals and flowers in the sun, then add the other ingredients and put in hermetically sealed jars for some time."

BIBLIOGRAPHY

Allhusen, Dorothy: *A Book of Scents and Dishes,* 1926
The American Rose Magazine: May-June, 1944
Clarkson, Rosetta: *Herbs, Their Culture and Uses,* 1942
Clarkson, Rosetta: *Magic Gardens,* 1939
Jekyll, Gertrude: *Home and Garden,* 1900
Jessee, Jill: *Perfume Album,* 1951
Leyel, Mrs. C. F.: *Herbal Delights*
McDonald, Donald: *Sweet Scented Flowers and Fragrant Leaves,* 1895
Poucher, W. A.: *Perfumes, Cosmetics and Soaps,* Vol. II, 1932
Rohde, Eleanour Sinclair: *Rose Recipes,* 1939
Rohde, Eleanour Sinclair: *The Scented Garden,* 1936
Toilet of Flora: Reprint, 1939

TASTES IN TEA

By Edna Cashmore

◇≻◇

TEA . . . a magic word that conjures up fantastic tales of romance and poetry; of clipper ships and trade routes; of intrigue and revolution. It is "the Plant of Heaven," the "froth of liquid jade"; it is the "pernicious weed," the "base exotick." It will keep you awake, it will put you to sleep. It will cure whatever ails you, it will cause your early demise. Some like it hot, some like it cold. It has been beset by shortages, high prices and taxation. Withal, it has survived and flourished through perhaps 4,000 years or so as the world's most popular (and, next to water, its cheapest) drink. It has helped to build an empire; it played an important role in the birth of a new nation.

Tea, in the classic sense of the word, refers to a single species of plant, *Thea sinensis,* a venerable shrub probably indigenous to China, where it was first cultivated. In its wider application, however, it might be said to be a drink made from brewing or steeping fragrant leaves, flowers, seeds, roots or barks in hot water. The development of a gigantic trade has carried China and India teas to the four corners of the world; but other teas are still popular in many countries. The French have always enjoyed their delicious herbal *tisanes,* with chamomile, *tilleul* (linden blossoms), and mint rating high. Many South American countries, including Brazil, which yields three-fifths of the world's coffee, are heavy drinkers of *yerba maté,* a member of the holly family. Then there are also the Australian Tea Tree (*Leptospermum laevigatum*), Philippine Tea (*Ehretia mycrophylla*) and others, not forgetting the early American Indians' and Colonists' herbal teas.

As with the discovery of many national foods and drinks, dates become somewhat obscure and confused, and legend and fact mingle carelessly. China, Japan and India long competed in claiming the origin of tea, as well as in the development of tea-drinking ceremonials and rituals. But China perhaps has the oldest tradition of all; there is a legend, slightly reminiscent of Charles Lamb's "A Dissertation upon Roast Pig," dating back to 2737 B.C. It tells of Shen Nung, the philosopher-emperor, known also as the first teacher of medicine and agriculture, who knelt before a fire, boiling water, when a few leaves from the branches above were blown into the water. Smelling the delightful aroma, he could not resist the temptation to taste it. "Ah, what flavor!" he cried. How could he have sensed the importance of that discovery! How could he have foreseen how that ancient wild tea plant would affect the customs and economics of the entire world! India, too, has its legend of the Buddhist priest Darma, and the Japanese version is similar.

The tea that has been considered a favorite drink by millions of South Americans for some four hundred years is *Yerba maté, Ilex paraguariensis**, which grows in the region of the Paraguay and Parana Rivers. The Guarani Indians, who taught the virtues of this tree to the white settlers who came later, drank it from gourds which they called *matti,* hence its name. Strangely, the word was shortened to *ti,* and is pronounced exactly like "tea" in English. Today it is not only a favorite beverage in South America, where it is a custom to drink it through a *bombilla* or tube, frequently made of or beautifully ornamented with silver, it is a growing economic factor, being exported to many other countries, including the United States.

There are three types of Asiatic teas: black, or fermented; Oolong, or semi-fermented, and green, or unfermented. India produces most of the black teas and China and Japan most of the green teas. At one time about 50% of the world's tea came from the Chinese mainland. Practically none comes into this country today, but Formosa, which formerly supplied only Oolong, is now trying to fill that gap. India

---

* Since the spelling most commonly found is *paraguayensis,* we wrote to Dr. George Lawrence, Director of the Bailey Hortorium, to see if the spelling in Hortus Second was intentional and correct. His reply was: "The name was originally spelled this way by St. Hilaire when the species was published by him in 1882, and it was correctly used by the monographer of the groups (Theodore Loesener) in 1901. The spelling *Ilex paraguayensis* is an unfortunate corruption of the original spelling that has been used by several uncritical authors. The Code of Nomenclature requires us to use the original spelling of a name unless it be shown to have been corrected by the original author as an orthographic error."

is the big tea producer today, with Ceylon, Formosa and Japan running close. Tea imports into this country jumped 11% in 1953, more
than 100 million pounds being used by Americans. The favorite is
black tea, an important matter to India, which produces nearly two-
thirds of the billion pounds of tea grown in the free world each year.
Among the many varieties, Darjeeling and Assam seem to be favored
most by tea connoisseurs.

It is paradoxical that while the tea plant grows most luxuriantly in
tropical heat, the finest quality is produced from leaves grown in
cooler altitudes of from 3,000 to 7,000 feet. Some of the world's
finest tea comes from India and Ceylon gardens over 6,000 feet high,
facing the snow-capped Himalayas. It is mostly the two leaves and
bud of the new shoots, or "flushes," that are picked by hand and put
through many complicated processes before they come to our tables.

The misconception of the meaning of "Orange Pekoe" is as universal as its mispronunciation. Orange Pekoe (pronounced peck-o,
not peek-o) is merely a designation to indicate size and has nothing
to do with the flavor or quality of the tea. Pekoe is the Chinese word
for "white hair" and was once applied to the earliest pickings in
China because of the white down on them. The Chinese sometimes
scented these with orange blossoms, which gave rise to our term,
Orange Pekoe.

The Pilgrim Fathers listed no tea on the menu of that first Thanksgiving dinner . . . only the wine made from wild grapes. (The
Colonists had learned, however, to brew a delicious tea from native
shrubs and plants, a knowledge that came in very handy a century and
a half later.) We are apt to forget that China and India tea was not
commonly known even in England at that time. While generally used
as a beverage in China from the 6th century on, it was not until the
middle of the 16th century that the dried herb was being imported
to Europe, after a scholar of Venice, then one of the chief commercial
ports of the world, published a story in 1559 that a Persian merchant
had told him of drinking tea in China. Fifty years later, in 1610,
Dutch merchants were bringing sizable shipments to Holland. Still
fifty years later the English began to show real interest. The history of

the British and Dutch East India Companies is another fabulous story in itself.

In the middle 1600's tea was too expensive an item for the common man to buy by the pound, though he could familiarize himself with the drink by buying a cupful at the public coffee house. It was England's Queen Catherine of Braganza who made tea a social event in the Western world, by introducing it to society in 1662 as a temperance drink.

It was about this time too that tea was first brought to this country. Ships plying between the Dutch colony of New Amsterdam and its mother country, Holland, it is believed, carried the first tea here about 1650. Despite the fact that it cost from $30 to $50 a pound, it quickly became fashionable. Hostesses of social standing brewed several different kinds of tea and sometimes offered saffron and peach leaves for flavoring. Tea took on English customs and manners from 1674 on, when New Amsterdam passed into the hands of the English. Tea gardens and tea parties became popular, though the custom of afternoon tea was not yet known; ladies went to parties each carrying her own teacup, saucer and spoon, the cups of the most delicate china and very small, holding about as much as a common wineglass. The first record of a tea table made in America was in 1705, and it was about that time that Madam Winthrop served tea in her house after a lecture. What could be more modern!

Tea was fast growing in popularity in other parts of the country too. The Swedish naturalist Kalm reported that when he visited Albany in 1749 everybody there drank tea for breakfast. The English Colonists had begun to use tea, to a limited extent, probably as early as 1670, but considering their early attempts at its preparation it is surprising that it survived and grew to such popularity. In Salem, Massachusetts, the tea leaves were boiled or simmered for a long time, as they still are by some Australians today, and the bitter concoction was drunk without cream or sugar. Then the leaves were salted and eaten with butter. This recalls the custom in certain parts of China and Thibet where the leaves, having been drained, are mixed with butter or other fat, molded into cakes and fried or baked.

The famous brew of 1773 when 342 chests of tea were dumped into the salty waters of Boston Harbor, while one of far-reaching significance, was but one incident in the history of taxation and smuggling so closely interwoven with the history of tea. It was one more proof of the old adage, "It's an ill wind that blows no good." It was not only one of the sparks that ignited the fires of the Revolution . . . the Colonists went happily back to brewing their herbal teas.

Duties on tea in England, which at one time reached 100%, were responsible for two centuries of smuggling. When in 1929 the moderate duty on tea was abolished by Winston Churchill, the exchequer lost six million pounds annually — an indication of the amount consumed there. By 1932 a people strained almost to the breaking point felt a sense of profound injustice when Mr. Chamberlain argued in favor of restoring the duty. "Punch's" charlady was their mouthpiece: "Well, mum, what I sez is, why need they put tea up? Why couldn't they tax whitewash, or something else that folks could do without?"

When taxes are high, when supplies are short and prices soar, then people look for substitutes or alternatives. The current coffee situation illustrates the point nicely. No one believes of course that the inveterate coffee drinker will give up his coffee indefinitely, regardless of price. But for the present his outraged feelings impel him to seek other products; so, while the consumption of coffee is currently declining, the consumption of tea is rapidly gaining. This coincides with a reviving interest in herbs, so that both India teas and herbal teas are riding on the crest, mixtures of both being used. One such favored commercial mixture of choice Ceylon teas, blended with orange rind and sweet spice, is based on a recipe from an old Southern plantation, dating back to the early Jamestown settlers. Other popular blends on the market consist of fine India teas and herbal ingredients such as marigold blossoms, strawberry and peach leaves, mint and spice. A well-known English blend dates back more than a century, to the time when an English Prime Minister on a diplomatic mission saved the life of a Mandarin who, in gratitude, gave him the secret of his specially blended tea that was so greatly admired.

It is still a secret, but experts say that the wonderful aromatic scent is imparted by a herb none other than the wild bergamot, *Monarda fistulosa,* that grows so profusely in our gardens and roadsides.

In "Herbal Remedies" (London, 1945) Mary Thorne Quelch says, "When tea cost eight or ten shillings a pound, as it did in the days of our great-grandmothers, numerous substitutes were found, many giving most excellent results. Lime flowers . . . provide a wholesome and palatable beverage either alone or mixed with an equal quantity of tea." Speaking again of lime-flower tea — and who does not know the relaxing properties of the fragrant scent who has sat under a lime tree in bloom? — Mrs. Quelch praised it as a very pleasant drink, soothing to the nerves, and said, "Recently the newspapers stated that lime-flower tea was becoming a universal drink in Eire as real tea was in short supply. *The general health should benefit by the change."* (The italics are the author's.) "Probably the best of all tea substitutes," believed Mrs. Quelch, "are the young leaves from the blackthorn bushes in the hedges. In the days when tea was at a prohibitive price these ' sloe leaves ' were commonly added."

That all sounds very familiar again today. Whether straight from our own gardens or from a commercially prepared mixture, more and more herbal teas, both blends and straight, are being used for the fragrant golden liquid that relaxes and refreshes. Hostesses who cherish their social reputation are serving after-dinner mint tea and other spicy teas as well as coffee. We are looking up again those teas which our great-grandmothers liked, and the "liberty teas" that served the patriotic American Revolutionists so well.

People realize today that herb teas need not be associated with lavender and old lace — or even lavender and arsenic! Herb teas, while all healthful, are not necessarily medicinal or bitter-tasting. (These have value, but require a chapter to themselves.) Many are drunk purely for their pleasant taste and their stimulating or relaxing effects. The various mints: peppermint, spearmint, lemon mint, apple mint, pennyroyal (*M. pulegium*) and many other varieties are good either hot or cold, or as fresh sprigs dropped into iced tea. Chamomile, lemon balm (*Melissa officinalis*), bee balm or Oswego tea (*Monarda didyma*), lemon verbena, lemon basil, lemon thyme, New Jersey tea (*Ceanothus americanus*), wintergreen, known also as teaberry or checkerberry, golden rod or Blue Mountain tea (*Solidago odora*), pineapple sage (*Salvia elegans*), anise seed — these are but a few of the long list that found favor in earlier days and are there awaiting our further pleasure.

The Chinese cannot understand why we import tea from them when we have sage. They use it with full appreciation of its wonderful value and have been willing to swap with us at a ratio of four to one. In this country sage tea sweetened with maple sugar is a Vermont tradition. In the South, sassafras has been particularly favored, not only as an ingredient (*Filé*) for creole gumbo. The ground root makes an especially pleasant tea with an aroma described by Henry David Thoreau as "that fragrance of lemons and a thousand spices." There is a legend that it was the odor of sassafras blowing off-shore that first indicated to Columbus that he was nearing land — the America that he was to discover. And it may have been sassafras mingled with other sweet herbs to which John Winthrop referred in his journal as he neared the unknown land in 1620: "And there came a smell off-shore like the smell of a garden."

The custom of dropping a few petals of jasmine or orange blossoms into the tea leaves, as practiced by the Chinese, was a pleasant one. Other pleasing accessories of the tea table if one is in an experimental mood are rose or violet petals, clove, pieces of vanilla bean (our grandmothers kept those in their tea caddies), cinnamon and many more. A good tea, however, can stand on its own, whether served in glasses from a samovar as in Russia and middle Europe, or over a Laplander's camp fire or from an Australian "billy can."

As all tea connoisseurs will tell you, the preparation of tea is extremely important. This applies as well to herb teas, which some people make carelessly. In general, the method is the same: boiling fresh water, a non-metal tea pot, and steeping for about six minutes. Since herb blends have not been the big business that China and India teas have, there is still room for a great deal of experimentation in their preparation and use. Another point to be remembered is that in all teas the color is no indication of strength. Teas are perhaps best served clear to reveal their own unique flavor. Sugar or honey improve their taste for some, and occasionally a slice of lemon—these are matters of individual preference; but most tea connoisseurs agree that milk or cream are taboo. J. B. Priestley once explained in a radio talk why his fellow countrymen "slop" milk into their tea. America, he said, gets all the good tea, and the English are obliged to corrupt theirs to make it palatable!

Though we suspect Mr. Priestley may have been speaking with his tongue in his cheek, there is nevertheless probably no country in the world today that enjoys a higher quality of tea than the United States, now that the lavish days of the extremely wealthy families in Russia are over. This is largely due to the high standards set by the U. S. Board of Tea Experts. When the tea, in aluminum foil lined chests, arrives in the principal U. S. ports of entry for tea, it is placed in bonded warehouses and cannot be moved until the Board of Tea Experts, composed of seven members, six from the trade and one from the Government, approve or disapprove. They meet in New York once a year, in February.

Then, for those admitted, comes the expert grading and blending, a fine art in itself. There are over 3,000 varieties of tea and an expert tea taster can identify between 1,500 and 1,600 different teas, often telling where they are grown, in what season they were picked and sometimes even from what tea gardens they come. An amusing story is told of a top-ranking tea taster in New York who dropped into the executive offices of the Tea Bureau. An enthusiastic junior executive rushed to him with a cup of tea, explaining that it was a new and highly recommended blend and they would be interested in knowing what he tasted in it. A judicial sip and the tea taster said, "I taste a rather good Assam, a trace of fine Darjeeling, one of the better Dooars, several nice South Indias, and, of course, the tea bag."

China and India may have their legends of tea, but America has its own interesting contributions to talk about. A young Englishman by the name of Richard Blechynden came from Calcutta to represent India and Ceylon teas at the St. Louis World's Fair in 1904. The weather turned very hot and the stifling crowds hurried past the steaming tea booths in search of iced drinks. In desperation Blechynden tried an experiment. He filled tall glasses with ice and poured the hot tea over it. Something new, and the crowds responded. The idea caught on and grew in popularity, until today it is estimated that of the 20 billion cups of tea drunk each year by Americans, at least six billion are iced tea.

Another American contribution, more questionable to some in the matter of taste, but a decided convenience in these busy days, is the tea bag, which has become big business. Only four months after the iced tea experiment a small wholesale tea and coffee merchant in New York, one Thomas Sullivan, decided it would be cheaper and simpler to send tea samples to his customers in little silk bags instead of tins. The response was wholly unexpected. The orders poured in— for tea in bags! He obliged, and today half the tea drunk is brewed in bags, but they are no longer of cloth. They are made of a special filter paper. One can even find herb teas in bags today. The golden anniversary of the tea bag was celebrated at a party in New York this winter. There was a hot tea punch, laced with rum and brandy. (What! No herbs?)

Lichilai, a poet of the Sung dynasty, where tea is a truly great tradition, once deplored the three great evils that had beset his country: the spoiling of gallant youths through bad education; the degradation of good art through incompetent criticism; and the waste of fine tea through careless making. Unfortunately, much of his complaint still holds today. But at least, with more concern for our selection and in all the phases of its preparation, we may be able to enjoy tea as did the Chinese poet, Lotung, who said, "When I drink tea I am conscious of peace. The cool breath of Heaven rises in my sleeves, and blows my care away."

SOME NOTES UPON THE USE OF HERBS IN NORWEGIAN HOUSEHOLDS

SIGRID UNDSET

THE minimum of herbs in a Norwegian kitchen garden is a bed of parsley and some tufts of chives. A box of parsley and chives is usually prepared to serve as a window garden in the kitchen during winter.

Norwegian housewives would rarely serve scrambled eggs without a sprinkling of chopped chives. A favorite dish, especially of boys, is called "Fleskepannekake." Fry slices of fat pork a crisp brown, distribute neatly in the skillet, pour over a batter of eggs and milk (no flour), and sprinkle liberally with chives. The pancakes should be thick, cut in triangles and served with boiled potatoes. "Sildepannekake" is made with baby herrings, packed closely in the skillet, so that less batter is needed. I have made these pancakes with small smelts—delicious!

Stuffing for poultry as used in America and England, we don't use. Roast goose we stuff with prunes and apples, unpeeled but cut in boats and cored. With roast chicken or hen we put some handfuls of fresh parsley, stalks removed, inside the fowl. Leg of mutton I used to lard with tufts of parsley, the way venison is larded with strips of pork, before putting into the oven. Pan-fried mackerel is very nice if it is filled with parsley and tied up loosely.

With us the test of the skill of a cook is—can she boil potatoes? As long as the potatoes are firm and good we boil them in their skin, peel tenderly and return to the hot and perfectly dry saucepan. Shake with a light hand over the fire for a minute or two. They must be served piping hot, absolutely dry, slightly cracked so that the mealy meat peeps through, and sprinkled with plenty of chopped parsley. (Fried or French fried, mashed or creamed potatoes are all right towards spring, when the potatoes are not very good. But potatoes boiled the right way are a treat, and we eat it every day).

Dill is common in our kitchen gardens. The umbels of flowers are a "must" with our homemade mixed pickles, which we prefer to make in good sized jars of stoneware. A layer of cherry- and black currant-leaves on the bottom gives a nice flavor to the pickles.

Mutton with dill is a favorite summer dish of mine. An earthenware pot is best. Cover the bottom with fresh green of dill, cut mutton in chop-sized pieces and dredge in flour. Layers of meat alternate with a thin spread of dill. Cover with water, salt to taste, and let simmer until the meat is tender. If the mutton is very lean lumps of butter should be put in. Serve in the pot. (If we have to use anything but an earthenware container we drape it chastely in a napkin). This dish may be made with veal, but the taste of dill is not nearly so "becoming" with veal as with mutton.

With cold cuts, steaks and chops we serve a heap of horseradish shavings. With boiled meat, horesradish sauce. Thicken one pint of the broth with a little butter and flour, season with one tablespoonful of vinegar and one teaspoonful of sugar, and grated horseradish to taste—plenty according to my taste. As the culture of horseradish is quite difficult, we usually buy this herb from the greengrocer's.

Marjoram and thyme are used in homemade sausages and with meat to be cured and smoked. Thyme is also used on yellow pea soup and thick soups made with salt broth and barley and vegetables. Also in a number of Spanish and Italian dishes of fish, rice or spaghetti, which have become popular in Norway— a by-product of our export trade in dried fish to the Mediterranean countries.

Thyme, marjoram and sage we pull up with the roots before they bloom, tie them in little bunches and let them dry in the sun. Hanged from hooks in the larder they are at hand when you need some sprigs, and they make the air in the larder fresh and sweet.

Sage is not much used for flavoring food, but we have a great belief in tea made from sage. According to the country people sage tea is good for almost all the evils our flesh is heir to, and they are probably right. A cup or two of sage tea taken in bed at night will calm upset nerves or stomachs, induce sleep, and sweetened with rock candy it is good for sore throats and colds on your chest. It is supposed to be good for children to have sage tea with milk with their supper. For tired or reddened eyes wads of absorbent cotton soaked in hot sage tea are very soothing (but if the redness lasts for more than a day, call the doctor).

Camomile tea and tea of the dried blossoms of the black elderberry tree serve the same ends, but they taste less pleasant. A shampoo of camomile tea keeps fair hair light and glossy. As a mild sedative however, nothing compares with tea made from the flowers of the common milfoil or yarrow (Achillea millefolium), which I have seen grow profusely in New England. Gather the flowers on a sunny day, rip from stems and dry on a tray in the sun. Store in paper bags in an airy place and use for tea whenever you suffer from sleeplessness. Unless the case is a very bad one, yarrow tea will make you sleep like a baby.

And thus we arrive at the several wild herbs we use during springtime.

The queen of pot herbs to all Norwegians is "Karvekal,"—caraway, the common Carum Carvi, in this country an immigrant from Europe. In Norway it is the commonest weed in pastures and meadows. And the first green things to sprout from the withered grasses of last year are the delicately cut young leaves of the caraway. Then we go out to dig "Karvekal," using a knife to get some two inches of the fleshy taproot with the rosette of leaves. Digging caraway is a lovely way to spend some hours of a sunny May morning, and as any number of children will call at your kitchen door offering "Karvekal" for sale, and women from the country take quantities of it to market in the cities, we may have "Karvekal" soup every day as long as this herb is in season,—that is, until the beginning of June, when the leaves become coarse and no good. Some years ago the truck gardeners did take up the cultivation of "Karvekal" under glass, so we might get it as early as February, but it was not nearly so good as the wild herb.

The brown skin is scraped from the roots, the plants carefully rinsed and passed through a vegetable chopper, put into the soup which should be kept at the boiling point for some five minutes before serving, but not permitted to boil. For Sunday or party dinner we use a strong, clear broth of veal. Place one poached egg in each plate, and pour. Crisp buttered toast is handed around with the soup. For everyday use inferior stock or even beef extract or cubes will do. Thicken somewhat and put into the soup whatever you have at hand—leftover meats diced, sliced hardboiled eggs, tiny dumplings or cubes of fried bread.

There will still be an abundance of caraway growing up and seeding. From the swathes made by the mowing machine the country people will gather armfuls of caraway with seeds not quite ripe, tie them in bunches and leave to dry on the fences. Some pounds of seed taken to the storekeeper's will bring the children pocket money, and the housewife will have caraway seed to put in homemade bread, in cheese, on boiled cabbage and a number of other dishes.

Almost, but not quite as good as caraway are the young shoots of the common stinging nettle. I never tried "to grasp the nettle firmly,"—gloves and scissors will do. We take only the topmost four or six leaves, and in June the nettles become too coarse to eat, though the farmers harvest them all summer to chop and boil with oatmeal for their cattle and pigs,—an auxiliary fodder which according to Norwegian veterinarians is

superior to most others.   Besides for soup, the young nettle tops
are good used as spinach.   They must be scalded well before
passing through the chopper.

"Spring soup" is made with four pints of thin stock, one cupful of chopped "Karvekal," one cupful of chopped nettle, one
cupful of chopped wild sorrel and the young leaves of bladder
campion (Silene latifolia), a few chopped leaves of strawberry,
black current and cherry, sprigs of tarragon and parsley. Serve
with poached eggs and buttered toast.   From June on we have
to make our "green soups" with chervil from the garden,—
which is good too.

My attempts to use stewed young leaves of dandelion did not
meet with the approval of my family.   I can still see the pitiful
face of my seven year old son and hear his plaintive voice: "Oh
Mother, this tastes as if it was awfully good for little boys!"
A green salad however of dandelion, bladder campion, tarragon,
parsley and chervil on lettuce is delicious.   Ready made salad
dressings seem to me one of the least attractive features of
American life.   We never use metal on lettuce, but break up the
heads, rinse and shake dry in a cloth.   Arrange in a bowl which
may or may not be rubbed with garlic, seasoning herbs on top.
According to the French prescription use olive oil like a wastrel,
vinegar like a miser, salt and pepper like a sage.   Stir and tear
a little with fork and spoon.   Made of horn, or shell mounted
in silver, or best of all handsomely carved in wood, salad forks
and spoons are prominent in all Norwegian gift shops.

If lettuce is to be served with fish we sometimes dress it with
sour whipped cream seasoned with horseradish.   We never mix
cucumber or tomatoes with lettuce.   Sliced tomatoes with a little
freshly made oil-and-vinegar dressing we use with "red" meat.
Cucumber salad goes with salmon, trout and fried chicken.   A
couple of hours before it is to be served the cucumbers are peeled
and shredded paper-thin, put in a deep plate and a second deep
plate with a weight placed on top, to squeeze out the moisture.

The usual dressing is poured on sparingly, and chopped parsley sprinkled on top.

Tarragon is quite popular, as a seasoning herb during summer and for making tarragon vinegar.

Finally, I should like to give the recipe for a herb tonic, which is not so much used in Norway as in Denmark, where the rural population believes in it as a cure-all: "Perkom-brandy." Gather the flowers and fullblown buds of St. John'swort (Hypericum perforatum) and dry on a tray in the sun. As it shrinks in drying you will need a lot, so pick a basketful every day on your morning walk. Fill dried flowers into bottles but do not press, and pour over Aquavit (or gin or vodka, I believe would do it). It is quite exciting to see how the fluid immediately turns a delicate pink. Cork and store for three months, and strain off the brandy which has now taken on a deep garnet color. Brandy may be filled on to the flowers a second time, but this brew will not turn out quite as strong as the first. As the liquor is very bitter it may be diluted like one does with Angostura. My maternal grandfather in Denmark, who otherwise never touched wine or hard liquor save twice a year, on his birthday and New Year's day, started every day of his adult life with a dram of Perkom bitter before breakfast. As he lived to be 93 years old and enjoyed splendid health at least till he was 87, it probably did him good. I wonder if Perkom bitter might not be introduced with advantage in some kinds of cocktail?

DYEING WITH HERBS

FRANCES T. NORTON

GIVING color to fabrics through the dyer's art is not so well known a use for herbs as the blending of sweet scents and healing lotions, or seasonings and flavors for the housewife's table. It will be found, however, that it is fully as interesting to study.

Practically all the herb plants when boiled in water will give infusions which impart color to textile fibres such as cotton, linen, silk, or wool. The infusions vary greatly in strength and color with the kind of herb, the part of the plant used and the time of gathering. They also vary in the readiness with which they are absorbed into the textile fibres and in the degree of permanence or fastness of the resultant colors.

It has been a common practice from earliest times to soak into the fibre, before treating it with a dye, some solution, usually of a mineral salt which will combine with the dye in the body of the fibre to give a strong and permanent color. These substances are called mordants and in many cases, if they were not used, the dye which soaked in with water would soak out again with more water. In other words, the mordant sets the dye in the fibre.

Some of the mordants not only fix the dyes but give to them characteristic colors. Most common of these are the salts of tin and iron. Alum, the most widely used of all mordants, has, in most cases, little effect on the colors of the dye. The natural chemical compounds contained in the vegetable dyes may be profoundly changed in color by the addition of small amounts of the common and better known acids and alkalies. The well-known change of blue litmus to red when it comes in contact with acid and its turning back to blue on the addition of ammonia is typical of the behavior of many of the herb dyes.

It is an interesting experiment to fill several test tubes with the dye liquor, adding a drop of acid to one, ammonia to another, and such salts as copperas and tin chloride to others and note the change of color in the solution. This will suggest what a wide variety of colors, unfortunately not all useful or permanent, might be hoped for from the considerable number of herbs growing in our gardens and fields.

The several kinds of fibres behave very differently in the dye solutions; for instance, cotton, silk, and wool boiled in the same dye liquor will usually differ appreciably in the readiness with which they take up the dye, and will not be of the same shade of color or brilliancy.

Wool yarn seems to be the most satisfactory medium for experimental dyeing. For convenience, the yarn may be wound into uniform skeins of a practical size for small pots of dye.

Since the wool must, in most cases, be mordanted before dyeing, a brief description of the process follows.

Alum, the commonest mordant, is dissolved in water to which cream of tartar is usually added in the proportion of four ounces of alum to one ounce of cream of tartar to one pound of wool. Enough solution should be used to completely immerse the amount of wool being mordanted, and this should carry enough alum and cream of tartar to bear the proper ratio to the weight of wool used. The wool, thoroughly washed, is entered in the mordant solution at about 100° F., heated to boiling point and simmered for an hour, then drained, squeezed gently, and rolled in a linen cloth to stay for several days when, after rinsing in water, it is ready for the dye pot.

The tin (stannous chloride) and iron (ferrous sulphate) or copperas mordants are usually added to the dye in addition to the alum mordant toward the end of the dyeing process. The yarn should be lifted from the dye pot and the tin or copperas thoroughly dissolved and stirred in the dye and the yarn returned to finish the dyeing. The tin mordant tends to brighten, and the iron to darken and strengthen colors. They should be used in the proportion of

½ oz. tin crystals to 2 oz. of cream of tartar ⎫
½ oz. copperas to 1 oz. of cream of tartar ⎬ to 1 lb. wool
⎭

The dye liquor is made from different parts of the several plants, blossoms, leaves, stems, berries, fruit, bark or roots boiled for a sufficient time in water to extract their color. In most cases the blossoms yield their color most readily but do not as a rule give as permanent a dye.

The plant material should be first finely chopped, added to a pot of cold water and brought slowly to a boil and simmered for one to three hours, according to the part of the plant used. When the color is strong enough the bath should be cooled to about 100° F. and the dampened wool entered and boiled slowly until the desired shade is reached. This usually takes from a half to two hours. It is left in the dye liquor until cold. Next it is drained and washed in cold running water until no color comes from the wool. A thorough washing in hot soap suds follows, after which the wool is hung up and when dry twisted into skeins. In this manner it has been found possible, this summer, to prepare from the common herbs, nearly a hundred skeins of attractive shades and tints, most of which appear to have at least a reasonable degree of permanency.

The equipment needed for home dyeing is plenty of young fresh plant material, a few agateware pots, one to be used solely for the alum mordant, some china spoons, a pair of scales, a stove, and plenty of running water. The list of supplies should include the following:

alum	ferrous sulphide
ammonia	stannous chloride
acetic acid	cream of tartar
citric acid	soap

To this must be added a generous supply of patience. A few colors which may be made with some of the common herbs:

BEDSTRAW (*Gallium boreale*) young roots with alum, red; deeper red with the addition of tin; long boiling, terra cotta

BARBERRY (*Berberis vulgaris*) stem and roots, yellow

GOLDENROD (*Solidago*) blossoms with alum, lemon yellow; chrome yellow with tin; brown with copperas

ST. JOHN'S WORT (*Hypericum perforatum*) flowers, yellow with alum; pinkish purple with acid; brown with copperas

BLACK ALDER (*Ilex verticillatus*) bark, dark green with copperas

HYSSOP (*Hyssopus officinalis*) leaves, grey green with copperas

TANSY (*Tanacetum vulgare*) young shoots, greenish grey, alum

SWEET CICELY (*Myrrhis odorata*) stems and leaves, green, alum; olive green with ammonia added

YARROW (*Achillea millefolium*) blossoms, yellow, alum

POKEBERRY (*Phytolacca*) blossoms, crimson with alum

LICHENS (*Ramalina scapulorum*) red brown with no mordant; grey brown with copperas

One of the most attractive things about herb dyeing is that there is small chance of its becoming commercially important. It is quite possible to go no further than your garden to find material for an infinite variety of shades suitable for dyeing enough woolen yarn for your own use, for such work as needlepoint or knitting.

Its charm lies in the simplicity of the work and in the pleasure which comes from the development of color from common and unpretentious things.

Bibliography

VIOLETTA THURSTON: *The Use of Vegetable Dyes for Beginners.* The Dryad Press, Leicester, 1930.

ETHEL M. MAIRET: *Vegetable Dyes.* St. Dominic's Press, Ditching, Hassocks, Sussex, 1916.

JAMES HAIGH: *The Dyer's Assistant in the Art of Dyeing Wool and Woolen Goods.* Poughkeepsie, P. and J. Potter, Printers, 1813.

CHARLES F. MILLSPAUGH, M.D.: *American Medicinal Plants,* 1887.

DYEING SKEINS OF WOOL
woodcut from:
PLICTHO DE L'ARTE TENTORI by Gianventura Rosetti, Venice, 1548
In which Indigo, then a rare dye imported from America, is discussed

INDIGO, THE TRUE BLUE

MARTHA GENUNG STEARNS

PERHAPS you will remember the little villages in Italy perched up on impossible rocks or clinging to a mountain-side, which have been sun-baked for so many centuries that they have mellowed to terra-cotta and merged with the sun-scorched rock. If you have climbed up to one of these primitive little places, you have come through a crumbling arched gateway into the village square, and there, up in the campanile of the church, you see a bit of intense blue, repeating the higher blue of the sky. It is the face of the clock, an ancient timekeeper, sometimes with but eight numerals, so that in the twenty-four hours its one hand must make the circuit three times. It marks only the hours, perhaps because minutes don't matter very much when you live above the world. The face is painted blue, the color of eternity, of infinity, to remind one who looks at it that time will one day cease to be.

It seems as if the most loved and familiar things in nature are one sort of blue or another; the distant blue of mountains and cloud shadows and the sea, and the same hue comes into our immediate foreground in many a bird and tiny flower, even to the little blue eggs of robin and hedge-sparrow. In all the handicrafts, the work of a man's hands is intimately bound up with nature, as he takes ma-terials which have grown out of the earth and brings them by simple processes to a useful and beautiful end. All through the history of the arts and crafts, we find indigo as a staple pigment and dye from the earliest days down to the present time; there is no other natural blue so reliable or running so true.

In Christian symbolism, which is really a picture language of astonishing range and richness, every color and almost every natural object has its meaning. Blue is not only the color of Our Lady's gar-ment in the works of the old painters: it is the soul's color, the color of faith. The flower of nigella, or love-in-a-mist, was a symbol of the soul, a blue blossom enclosed in a feathery green sheath, the veil of the mortal body. In the world's universal language green is the earth color and blue the symbol of heaven.

Blue, as we think of it in the arts, is almost synonymous with indigo. In the Middle Ages, there were three great natural sources of blue. One was mineral, a copper ore called Azurite, or lapis lazuli, which had to be reduced to powder and mixed with some vehicle which would carry the particles; and there were two plant sources, Woad, always considered as secondary, and true Indigo, which stood severe tests and was the colorist's standby. There was not much difference, chemically, between woad blue and indigo blue, and the woad which grew readily in northern countries was substituted for the Oriental indigo for domestic purposes. This was partly due to the fact that the ashes of woad, when the stems and waste were burned, were the best source of potash and lye; and as such, woad has been used down to the present day as an adjunct to dyeing with indigo in potash solution, so that the terms are sometimes interchanged and consequently puzzling. But woad was a disagreeable plant, exhausting the soil so that new tracts must constantly be given up to it, and also fermenting in the dyeing process and becoming extremely odorous. Daniel Thompson says, in "Materials of Medieval Painting,"

> " The other great blue that the Middle Ages inherited from antiquity was indigo, a colouring-matter known to the ancient Egyptians and imported by them, and later by the Greeks and Romans, from India (whence its name). It was extracted from certain plants native to India known to modern botany as *Indigoferae,* the bearers of indigo. It was used primarily as a dye, but as a by-product of dyeing with it a blue pigment was formed, the colour *indicus* or *indicum,* which became in Italian *endeco* or *endego,* and in English 'Indigo.' The importation of indigo from the Orient continued through the Middle Ages, and the best qualities in the European market were known as Bagdad indigo or Gulf indigo."

Indigo by itself is a dark purplish color and must be thinned and lightened to get a true, clear blue. Most of the indigo in the market still comes from its ancient home, India. The plant *indigofera sumatrana* is grown from seed sown about the end of April; by the

DESIGN BY ELIZABETH HARTWELL OF EDGARTOWN, MASS. 1786
IN THREE SHADES OF BLUE

middle of June it is from 3 to 5 feet high, and the first crop is cut then, another being ready by August in that climate. It is cut early in the morning, taken to the factory and steeped in water from 9 to 14 hours, when the liquid is run off into another vat, where it is violently beaten; the object of this is to bring as much air into it as possible, and in the hand-process this whipping was done with bamboo sticks. The precipitated indigo is allowed to settle like a sediment or mud to the bottom, and the water run off. After being strained and sterilized by boiling, it is dried and cut into blocks. The color comes from the leaves alone, the stems yielding practically none. In its dried cake form it is easily handled and exported, and thus it travelled over the world, coming to America in the days of the earliest settlements.

India brought dyeing to a fine art, and was the first Eastern country to export dyes into Europe. Italy was soon learning her secrets and was noted during the Ages of the Faith, when the Church was the great patron of the arts, for her magnificent fabrics, especially Florence, which was the city of master-dyers. By the slow progress of time and commerce, the art of textile weaving and dyeing moved northward by way of Lyons and Arras, Bruges and Spitalfields, and what would these fabrics have been without their glorious blues? Indigo was preëminently the dyer's color; in illuminated books and on canvas and especially for enamels, ultramarine was more desirable, a powder of ground lapis lazuli from Persia which went through long processes to reach the painter's brush in workable form. An Italian book on dyeing, printed in Venice in 1548, spoke of "endego" as a rare dye from the Americas, and the renowned traveller Marco Polo speaks of it.

When America entered the company of nations, indigo was well known, and the simple but laborious hand-processes went on for more than two centuries. What we call by the covering term of "Puritan gray" is said to have been a wool fabric woven by the formula of one part good white sheep's wool, one part black sheep's wool, and one part of "taglocks" and other discolored bits spun and dyed blue in the indigo pot, all three woven into a dull mixture of practical worth but little beauty. A blue dye-pot was said to see as much service as a teapot; and these old earthenware dye-pots with a blue sediment in the bottom only needed more water to be boiled up and used for many household needs, sometimes sweetened by flag-root to counteract the strong odor. In an austere society which frowned upon bright colors and display, the humble blue was allowed, and this accounts for the prevalence of the honest, hold-fast color in early needlework, woven bed-covers and garments. The indigo peddler appeared once or twice a year, bringing the dye in lumps, and the best quality cracked apart and showed a glint of gold. It was tied up in a cloth and pulverized by pounding, and a little went a long way. The depth of color depended on how long the fabric remained in the pot, or the number of dippings.

Eliza Pinckney, the energetic mistress of Belmont, near Charleston, South Carolina, demonstrated in 1744 that she could grow indigo successfully, and a minute description of her method is given in her life by Harriott Horry Ravenal. She obtained seed from the East Indies and devoted a whole crop to raising her own seed, much of which she gave away; she writes: "Out of a small patch of indigo . . . besides saving a quantity of seed, made us 17 pounds of very good indigo," and in 1753 the neighboring planters formed themselves into the "Winyah Indigo Society," which flourished for years and exported enormous quantities to England, receiving a bounty from the Crown.

A less successful experiment was conducted at the Pine Mountain settlement school in Kentucky in 1925, with seed from France. The old hand-process was carefully adhered to, a pound of leaves to a gallon of water; but the yield in dry weight of cake indigo from 12 pounds of leaves was just short of one ounce. Considering that Madras indigo can be bought for $2 per pound, it would not seem practical to spend the time, labor and expense necessary to extract indigo; but the fact has been established that it is entirely possible to get excellent indigo from American-grown plants and American seed.

Dyeing methods were revolutionized by the discovery in 1834 of the aniline process by a German chemist who noticed that a bright blue color resulted from the action of a bleaching powder on a distillation of coal-tar. Artificial indigo was worked out in 1878; and now the aniline process has displaced the old vegetable dyes, giving a vast range of shades; but with the passing of the old-time method, we have lost another contact with nature and her own soft and subtle shades which had so much charm.

EARLY AMERICAN DYEING

By E. McD. Schetky

EARLY dyeing in America was practised by the New England colonists, the German pioneers in Pennsylvania, the early settlers in New York and in the Southern Highlands. In the Southwest, the Spaniards introduced sheep to the Navajos in the late 16th century and wool fibre became available and was dyed with native plants and minerals and woven into Navajo rugs. The Indians had long been using colors for skins, baskets, quills used in decoration, and tattooing. Much of it we would call staining, but some produced permanent colors, and undoubtedly these experiences were of value to the white settlers. Comparatively little is known of the indigenous art of the New England Indians, especially of such perishable articles as garments.

In my search for the ways and means of early Colonial dyeing I approached many sources of information. The writers on New England home life, Earle, Rawson, Kamm and Crawford, writing in the 1900's, often had contact with elderly people who gave answers with many amusing references, beginning " I remember when . . ." " Why, we never talked about dyeing in the old days, we just colored our yarns. . . . If the indigo peddler didn't come, we used butternut. Butternut gave a different color each month of the year. Onion skins for yellowing, with indigo added gave a green. . . . For black, the ooze of walnut with copperas added and a handful of sumac berries to make it glisten. The roots and sprouts of walnut in the new moon in June . . . boil for ooze, copperas darkens it. Saffron, that aromatic and pungent favorite of old gardens, did its yellowing." In measuring, when asked " How much? " the answer was "All you can hold with two hands."

Colonial women came to these shores with knowledge of home crafts: spinning, weaving and dyeing. They found many plants, roots

243

and berries which they had known in their home land, and they experimented with new ones found in the new world.

Dyeing called for careful work and old diaries tell of long hours of preparation. First the washing, carding and spinning of the wool and gathering materials for the coloring. Then the long hours of preparing the yarn for the dye pot. Favorite colors were blue from indigo and red from madder. The plain colors for everyday use came from native plants or trees such as walnuts and butternuts. The nuts might have been gathered and dried on a loft floor, or covered with water in a large crock or wooden tub until ready for use. The swamp maple, oak, alder, sumac were available, goldenrod flowers, St. John's-wort, elderberries and pokeberries. Seeds of broom (*Genista tinctoria*) were brought over prior to 1628 for Governor Endicott and this plant is now an escape from Salem gardens. Broom did its yellowing.

Practically all the dyeing in the homes was done after the wool was spun into yarn. Every family had one large kettle, the so-called 5-pail size, of brass, copper or iron, which was used for dyeing. The one exception was the indigo pot of earthenware glazed inside and kept on the hearth by the fire.

Indigo dyeing was a long process. The first step was mordanting, a term applied to the special process of preparing the wool to receive the dye. They used wood ashes, soda, salt, vinegar, sumac, hemlock, iron and tin filings to "set the color." Animal fibres, feathers, bone, horn and ivory have properties resembling those of wool and behave in a similar way in dyeing. These too came within the range of the housewife. She knew that certain plants, barks or roots gave more lasting colors, without any knowledge of the chemical properties as we know them today — the tannin astringent principles contained in sumac, oxalic acid in sorrel, salicylic acid in the lichens. Some colors do not exhaust in the dye bath, and she learned from experience when the yarn was the desired color.

The domestic load was gradually lifted with the setting up of carding mills and with itinerant weavers arriving at the homesteads when the family had accumulated sufficient wool, spun and dyed.

Massachusetts had a fulling mill in 1654; the workers had been clothiers in England.

Turning the pages of old books reveals a wealth of information. During the 16th and 17th centuries there are recorded 23 books on dyeing; the first half of the 18th century produced 27, while the second half produced 75, due in great measure to the beginning of the industrial age. Progress from the family dye pot to the mills was inevitable for those families in the towns; country people were not so fortunate and depended on their old methods. One book of the 18th century, "The Country Dyer" by Asa Ellis, printed in Brookfield, Massachusetts, in 1798, gives much information of the period, the names of colors, the use of imported dye materials, and includes instructions for the home dyer. I quote to retain his flavor and understanding:

"With regard to our manufacture of cloth women and children commonly dictate the colors to be impressed on them. But they frequently make injudicious choice, the color which they dictate fades, the coat is spoiled and thrown aside. True colors retain the complection that is impressed on goods. False ones on wearing and exposed to the sun and air lose all their original tints."

Imported dyestuffs in his recipes include logwood, fustics, cochineal, camwood and green wood. Logwood from Mexico was introduced into Europe by the Spaniards early in the 16th century. It was used in dyeing purple, blue and black. Young fustic, often called Venetian sumac, is the smoke tree, *Rhus cotinus;* it imparted colors varying from bright yellow and orange to brown and dark olive. (There is no botanical connection between young and old fustic.) Old fustic, *chlorophora tinctoria* of the mulberry family, grew wild in the West Indies and Central America and was introduced into Europe by the Spaniards in the early 1500's. The color imparted to wool varied from gold to lemon color. Cochineal, an insect, *coccus cacti,* considered to be a natural dye, came from Mexico; the Spaniards found it being used there about 1518. The Spanish Ministry ordered Cortez to take measures for this valuable commodity to be sent home, and by 1587 it is computed that 400,000 pounds were shipped annually.

Mr. Ellis regrets that our own Government doesn't consider it worthy of their attention to encourage able chemists to explore the qualities of our fossils, woods, barks, shrubs, plants, roots, weeds and minerals. He feels that the advantages derived would indemnify the Government for the extra expense. His regrets are echoed 15 years later by Partridge in Philadelphia, who says "Of late the shrub sumac employed to lay the ground in paper staining has been ground in Mills, constructed for that purpose, put in casks and sent to Europe. This affords a handsome profit. The Indigo has been the only article for dyes that has been exported toward balancing the imports of other dyestuffs."

Samuel Wilson wrote in 1682 in Charles Town, "Indigo thrives well here and very good hath been made." We know of indigo culture in South Carolina through the letters of Eliza Lucas Pinckney. Lt. Colonel George Lucas sent indigo seed from Antigua, West Indies, to his daughter Eliza in Charleston; later he sent an overseer from the Island of Montserrat to superintend the harvesting and the difficult preparation of indigo. In 1744 Eliza had her first indigo and in 1747 the first was exported to England. In 1748 the British Parliament passed an act allowing a bounty on indigo from the British Colony, to exclude French indigo from her markets. Before the Revolution, over a million pounds of the dye were annually shipped from Charleston.

Mr. Ellis describes various native plants which produce yellow. "Among them the root of the upland dock, the herb Peterswort, but in a particular manner the arsmart (*polygonum*) gives a beautiful yellow. If fermented before it is employed in dyeing it will impress a permanent color.... Not only those who profess the art but private families may embrace the advantages of the following directions and color their own yarn, woolen, worsted, thread and small pieces of silk as beautifully as the dyer. The principal dyes which people in common will at present wish to reduce to a small quantity which may be required for one pound are: Navy blue, cinnamon and London brown, Black, Saxon green, scarlet and crimson." He gives directions for each one.

Indigo supplanted the woad plant for blue. I found very few references to the woad plant being used in America. It had been grown in the area of Hartford, Connecticut; but one dyer writes of the error committed in packing woad too moist after couching. Its main asset was in combination with indigo in setting the indigo vats.

"Saxon Blue," much used in England, was first discovered in Saxony about 1740. Among the workmen in American dye houses it was called Chymic. This was made from the compound of indigo and oil of vitriol (sulphuric acid), bottled and kept for months. Asa Ellis refers to Saxon green obtained from the chymic with fustic for the yellowing necessary to obtain green.

The American oak had taken its place in the dye world. Edward Bancroft, one of the founders of the Medical Society of London, was a scientist and chemist. In 1794 he published "The Philosophy of Permanent Colors." He had visited both North and South America, and introduced the American oak into England in 1775 as a substitute for weld (*Reseda luteola,* wild mignonette): he advised then that oak contained 8 to 10 times more coloring matter than weld. Many men of trained experience were coming to America in the 19th century; some had published books in England and we find them reprinted in America. "The Family Dyer and Scourer" by William Tucker was printed in Philadelphia in 1817 from the 4th London edition.

"Partridge on Dyeing" by William Partridge was entered in the Clerk's Office in New York in 1834, a second edition was printed in 1847. He names seven native "drugs," as he calls goldenrod, sumac, bark of swamp maple, black oak, alder, chestnut and butternut. He recommends the growing of *Monarda dydima* for coloring pink as nearly equal to the safflower.

Among most dyers swamp maple was used for hats and leather dyeing; barberry roots and bark were used almost entirely for coloring leather. "The Dyers Companion" by Elija Bemiss, printed in New London, Connecticut, in 1815, is written in old-time English, and his introduction is quaint. "I am well perſuaded the greater part of my fellow functioners have labored under the ſame embaraſſments as there has not to my knowledge, any book of this nature ever before been publiſhed in the U. S." His book names the colors being used:

claret, portable red, maroon red; the browns are legion: London brown, reddish brown, Spanish brown, London smoke, cinnamon brown, liver brown, snuff brown, bat wing brown and drabs.

Typical of all these old dye books is the wealth of information they also contain for the household in general: how to clean copper, to make ink, paint for their houses, furniture polish, wine, etc. To keep weevil from wheat, use Elder flowers. To remove corns, two ivy leaves soaked in vinegar 24 hours, apply one at a time.

The old foundation of the first fulling mill in Rhode Island is on my own homestead in East Greenwich. A neighbor's library contains an original copy of "The Domestic Manufacturer's Assistant and Family Directory of weaving and dyeing," by J. and R. Bronson, printed in Utica, N. Y., in 1817, used when weaving was carried on here. Of barks and plants useful in dyeing he lists a durable yellow from arsmart, alder and peach leaves for the domestic dyer, black birch bark for Nankeen, maple bark a durable cinnamon, walnut or hickory a more durable bright yellow than fustic, yellow oak, a better yellow on cotton, linen or wool than any other native plant, yielding more coloring matter than either fustic or weld. Oak bark was being exported at that time from New York for $45 to $60 a ton. Sumac was used in dyeing black. Lombardy poplar gave a tolerable yellow. His directions contain these dyestuffs: Annatto, Brazilwood, cam wood, cochineal, fustic, logwood, madder, Nicaragua, nut galls, woad (employed for the fermenting of the indigo), weld, turmeric used to give an orange tint to scarlet.

He also thinks of the needs of the household with recipes for inks, isinglass glue, staining woods, staining horn to imitate tortoise shell, how to prepare oil for gilding, and gilding the edges of books, how to soften horn, how to remove carriage-wheel grease from woolen cloth and so on.

After the middle of the 19th century aniline dyes from coal tar products were casting shadows of the future, and now in the 20th century dyeing from natural plants, roots and barks is left for those interested in the handicrafts.

INSTRUCTIONS FOR DYEING

The instructions of 150 years ago are the same for today's dyeing. Soft water is preferred, and scales that are true in order that dyestuffs will never be used without strict attention to their weights. The U. S. Department of Agriculture's Booklet, "Home Dyeing with Natural Dyes," Miscellaneous Publications No. 230, will give the beginner excellent instructions. Needless to say there is much more to dyeing than meets the eye; it is not a craft to be done hurriedly.

Some plants have the properties to dye wool, cotton and linen, such as walnut, broomsedge, indigo and sumac berries. Some will only dye wool. Cotton, linen and other vegetable fibres do not absorb metallic mordants as readily as silk and wool, and require different preparations. For today's dyer, the mordants used are: alum, tin, chrome and iron. In some cases different mordants produce different colors from the same plant. Cream of tartar is used to brighten colors. The standard mordant recipe for one pound of wool is 4 ounces of alum, one ounce of cream of tartar; there are exceptions for very fine wool; less alum is used.

Weigh all wool when dry. To prepare for the dye, thoroughly wet the wool, squeeze out excess water and immerse in a large kettle holding 3 to 4 gallons of cold soft water in which the alum and cream of tartar have been thoroughly dissolved. Bring gradually to a boil, then let it simmer for an hour. Leave in the mordant water over night. Remove, squeeze gently (do not wring), put in a bag and and hang in a cool, dark place for four or five days. Rinse well before it enters into the dye.

Preparing Plant Material. — In the light of the experience of early dyers, barks and roots offer the most permanent colors. Berries and fruits are not satisfactory. But for today's dyer, there are many more plants tested and found to give beautiful permanent colors. Plants in different sections, and gathered in different seasons, will vary in shades.

Generally 1 pound of roots, 1 to 2 pounds of fresh plant material, 2 pounds of nut hulls are needed for 1 pound of wool. A large kettle is essential. Enamel is a substitute for the copper and brass kettles of the past; iron is not used, as it tends to darken the colors. It is often recommended to soak barks and roots over night, then boil one to two hours, strain, and the liquid is ready for the next step. Add enough water to the dye liquid to have 3 to 4 gallons in the dye pot. When it is lukewarm, enter and spread the wet, mordanted wool quickly, so that it absorbs the color evenly. Simmer or boil ½ to 1 hour depending on the directions for different plants. Stir gently but constantly with a long-handled wooden spoon, or sticks, or glass rods. Sometimes wool is left in the dye bath to cool, more often it is removed at once. The first rinse water is the same temperature as the dye bath, and each succeeding rinse is cooler. Rinse until no color remains in the water. Squeeze, roll in a towel to absorb excess moisture. Hang in the shade to dry.

Once in the dye pot, the mysteries of color become more fascinating. The old saying " dyed in the wool " was never truer than for the dyer herself. " The proof of the pudding is in the eating," and I go forth in a dress dyed with cochineal. Mr. Ellis would describe it as " full of lustre, and glares full of blazon."

Happy dyeing to all amateurs!

A NOTE ON THE ILLUSTRATION. — This reproduction of an early American " Keeping Room " was part of an exhibit by four New England Garden Clubs on the theme, " Our Garden Heritage," at the International Flower Show in New York, 1954. Several members of the H. S. A. were concerned in the project, which was hailed with enthusiasm by judges and public alike, and Mrs. Schetky's Keeping Room with its display of dye-plants, methods and samples of dyed materials won two medals as being outstanding for its educational value and historical accuracy. She was assisted by Mrs. Jastram and Mrs. Campbell of the New England Unit.

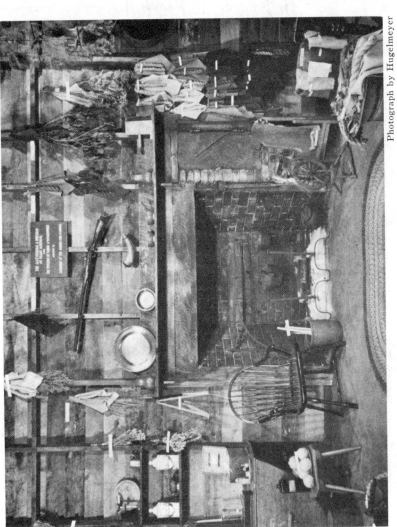

The Exhibit of the Process of Vegetable-Dyeing
which won The Garden Club of America's Medal of Merit

In Praise of Herbals

ELIZABETH REMSEN VAN BRUNT

Reading a recipe, perhaps for a Quiche Lorraine, may whet one's appetite, but hardly satisfy one's hunger. It might inspire a trial run at the creation of that culinary masterpiece, the ingredients of which are, traditionally, pastry, fresh eggs and cream, cheese, shallots, and bacon, with, of necessity, a dusting of sweet basil from one's own garden. Mouth-watering to read, spurring to action in the kitchen. But the taste and savour is only second-hand. The Missourian quips, "Show me---!" and to a child, a picture is worth a thousand words, just as is the actual tart to the reading of the recipe. Rudyard Kipling wrote, "Scents are surer than sights or sounds to make the heart strings crack," and the scents, the savours of actual food are important to our appetite and our health. So to the herb enthusiast — or to one unfamiliar with the growing and using of herbs — books which compile, quote and transcribe second-hand descriptions lifted bodily from the writings of those who have painstakingly experienced and studied the plants, should be spurs to one's interest. They may create not only an appetite for actual work with those plants, but contact with those who wrote of them. Those who wrote of herbs in meticulously descriptive words, recorded their life and death, their color, shape and growth, their roots, their flower and fruit, so that after many years identification is possible and that basic knowledge is before us. For plants were found valuable to mankind for healing, for flavor or for fragrances — they could alleviate the pain of a blow, the bleeding of a wound, dispel the humours of winter or make fragrant the homes of man, as well as assuage the hunger of a child.

We read, slothfully seated in a comfortable armchair, of the findings of those explorers of the plant world, often briefly collected in digests, very pleasant, inexpensive and easy reading because briefly transcribed and (comparatively) cheaply printed. But the herbals of the past, assembled by trial and error, minute

descriptions, reports of plantings, of virtues and of faults sometimes, it is true, lifted bodily from a previous author, have the
spark of authenticity, of personal experience and sincerity, the
ring of truth. Each, in its time, was very important; there was a
need, and filling that timely need, each stood alone. Today we
have an oversupply — a multiplicity of 'digests,' too easily acquired.

Probably the earliest herbal known to man is comprised of
stone tablets; examples are in the Metropolitan Museum in New
York City, dating from 3000 B.C. These ancient Sumerian
archives delineate, cut in the stone, crudely, but recognizable,
chamomile, thyme, roses and violets and elder. The Chinese and
the Egyptians of that same period recorded medicinal uses of
plants — *ephedra*, for one — did we fatuously believe our present-day scientists had discovered the value of ephedrine? I am
no student of mankind's history, but the fact that these earliest
existing records are all of the period 3000 B.C., seems to place
the date of the Great Flood just before that approximate date.
The Greek philosophers wrote of herbs in the third century
before Christ, and Dioscorides, the personal physician to Antony
and Cleopatra, whose writings were a textbook for years to come,
is still an authority. A recent reprint is available, in English —
most of us are not as proficient in Latin as was the British school-
boy of an earlier generation.

Eleanour Sinclair Rohde felt that the *Grete Herbal*, a translation of the French *Le Grand Herbier*, printed in London in 1526
by Peter Treveris, was the first herbal ever printed in English.
I cannot resist an anecdote: at a meeting of supposedly knowl-
edgeable herb gardeners, someone spoke of '*Grete's Herbal*' with
awe and apparent authority, as one of the first of the group of
herbals of the Middle Ages! A reprint of Richard Banckes' herbal
was sponsored by the New York Botanical Garden in 1941, and
advertised as the first printed in English. Whichever of the two
can rightfully claim that distinction, they were not printed more
than a few months apart. Other popular reprints have been
Thomas Tusser's readable (and rhymed) *Five Hundred Points of
Good Husbandry* ('worn threadbare by the thumbs of men'),
John Evelyn's *Acetaria* which the Brooklyn Botanic Garden had

reprinted in 1937, Thomas Hill, Nicholas Monardes, Nicholas Culpeper and John Gerard. The last named is sometimes characterized leniently and appreciatively, as rogue — as was also Culpeper, for both made rather exaggerated statements. They were both popular, apparently digging out many facts for themselves even though arrant copyists, relying for the bulk of their descriptions and data, as well as illustrations, on earlier writers. However, we know that most of our books on herbs, today, proudly follow the same practice. And I will stand up for both Culpeper and Gerard, since having the common touch in their writing they are eminently readable as well as popular. An audience loves a speaker, a demonstrator who makes an occasional slip of the tongue — or of a carving knife!

Since few of the earliest herbals, Greek and Roman, are available except for study in the carefully guarded rare book rooms of libraries and museums, we cannot become too familiar with these manuscripts except in copies, so far be it from me to scorn digests of centuries-old writers. But we can with dilligence and searching find herbals of the Middle Ages, if not orginal editions at least in reprints, sometimes fine facsimiles.

John Gerard's *General History of Plants* has been reprinted in many editions. However much he quoted, with chapter and verse, he often engagingly let us know he was a true dirt gardener, with references to his own garden, with seed, with plants sometimes gathered from afar or given to him. He traced the course of their growth and cultivation, soundly and with helpful detail. He wryly commented on the use of rose hips (of the eglantine or sweetbrier rose) now proven to have enormous vitamin A content); "the fruit," he wrote, "when it is ripe, maketh most pleasant meats and banqueting dishes, as tarts and such-like, the making of which I commit to the cunning cook, and teeth to eat them in the rich man's mouth." Any herb gardener reading his quote from Clusius on the subject of rue would surely approach that herb with respect. I wish I had read that passage before my case of poisoning one hot week in July, from seeding rue! Clusius recorded: "a historie of a Dutch student . . . that went with him a-simpling, who putting some of it [rue] between his hat and his head to keep him the cooler, had by that means all his face presently in-

3 4 6 7 5 8 9 10

Œm. ad nat del et pinxt.   HÙMULUS LÙPULUS, Linn.

flamed and blistered wheresoever the sweate ranne down." It was found wise to eliminate rue entirely from the Children's Gardens at the Brooklyn Botanic Garden, for although the poisoning (which resembles ivy poisoning, with pain rather than itching) is seasonal, chances with groups of children could not be taken.

Gerard was tireless in tracing down plants and observing their virtues — and their faults, as well as botanical characteristics. He gives the impression, from his relating of the many qualities of plants, and experiences with them, of a courageous man — one who would "take on Hell with a bucket of water." For he often relates experiences, offering to help in an accident, effecting miraculous cures in poisonings, wounds and plagues. He recorded that the 'potato of Virginia' was a meat for pleasure, rolled in the embers and eaten with oil and vinegar and pepper, then quoted Bauhine: "that he heard the use of those roots was forbidden in Bourgondy for . . . the frequent use of them caused the leprosie." As for Jerusalem artichokes: "In Au 1617 I received two small roots thereof from Mr. Tranquevill of London, no bigger than hens' eggs, the one I planted and the other I gave to a friend; myn brought me a peck of roots wherewith I stored Hampshire." And of the common mallow: obviously indefatigable in tracing its places of growth: "it groweth very plentifully in the marshes both on the Kentish and Essex shore along the river, as Thames about Woolwich, Erith, Greenhyth, Gravesend, Tilbury, Lee, Colchester, Harwich and in most salt marshes about London: being planted in gardens it prospereth well and continueth long." He did get around — by horse or by foot, he saith not.

So, the British herbalists flourished in the 15th and 16th centuries then a gap, presently followed by a spate of doctors and medical students, also botanists. There were several women botanists who drew and painted plants exquisitely — Maria Sybilla Merion, Elizabeth Blackwell, and in 1846 Jane Louden.

A thoroughly scientific herbal was published in Philadelphia in 1848. Its author, Charles Frederick Millspaugh, a graduate of the N. Y. Homeopathic Medical College, practiced medicine for ten years before giving up active practice for devotion to botany and its application to medicine and economics. He taught Botany at the University of West Virginia and thereafter was curator of Botany at the Field Museum of Natural History in Chicago, taught at the University of Chicago and the Homeopathic Medical College. A study of his *American Medicinal Plants* affords an insight into the interest and enthusiasm which his exhibits, combined with his teaching, received. His passion for accuracy is notable — descriptive botanical details as well as his beautiful illustrations include each plant's history, habitat, parts used and their preparation for medicinal use, plus the chemical contents and physiological action... these comparable to the Virtues listed as such in the old herbals. In the case of Hops (*Humulus lupulus*), illustrated, the acid and essential oil content are analysed — Humulo-tannic, valerianic and lupulic acids, oil of humulus and resins, choline and trumethylamine — and he states that large doses of the oil may have dangerously serious results although in minute quantities there is a useful sedative effect, 'probably not narcotic.' There is also an extensive Bibliography of his sources of research. This just-yesterday's herbal is a clue to the great herbals of the past, and interest in it, a guide to our reading of those. We may realize that even with our up to the minute access to scientific research, our super-computerized methods, we may lose sight of the human element, and to turn to the past for such contact is a most rewarding experience, not at all to be ignored. When we use a modern paper tea-bag, for example, labelled 'Peppermint Tea' we expect it to contain the leaves of *Mentha piperita*, having absorbed into its growth the minerals of the soil in which it grew, the action of the air, the sun, the rain, the mists of early morning, the moonlight and starlight — until our eye is caught by the fine print, as the envelope is plunged into the boiling water —'artificial flavor'— has our science progressed?

Artificial flavor — that may be the phrase descriptive of many of the herb books published today — copies without a basic background of knowledge, sometimes even ignorance of correct nomenclature, and often no knowledge or experience in actual growing of the herbs included. Better that we turn to the past, the touch of an ancient good green thumb over the intervening years can often set us on the straight path. If we cannot in this hectic race for time experience the slow turn of the year, the growth of a leaf, the ripening of seed and fruit, the drying of our herbs, than we must borrow wisdom from those of the past who experienced it through necessity, through the lack of our short-cuts — and were the richer for it.

So sharpen your appetite with samples of those early herbalists, but go to the originals (never be satisfied with digests) — and be inspired to raise, to use, to appreciate herbs by those clear voices of the past. F. Dawtrey Drewitt in his *History and Romance of the Apothecaries' Garden, Chelsea,* observed with truth: "Each generation must inherit imperfect truths from earlier generations. These well-worn clothes it seems sometimes better to mend and use, than hurriedly to throw aside — we may feel chilly without them."

Herbals — Ancient and Modern

(Those starred are in the Brooklyn Botanic Garden Library)

340 B.C. Aristotle.

*350 B.C. Theophrastus — *Enquiry into Plants.* English transl. Putnam, 1928. Minor works on odors, weather signs, etc. Much quoted by later authors.

410 B.C. Plato.

*1st or 2nd Century A.D. Dioscorides — *De Materia Medica.* (Physician with the Roman army — material at first hand. For 1300 years a principal textbook.) Reprint: 1938.

130 A.D. Galen. Wrote over 400 works. "Lord and master of Medicine" for 1,500 years.

*78 A.D. Pliny the second. *Natural History.* 1st transl., Philomon Holland. Bostwick & Riley transl. London 1887-1900.

*500 A.D. Apuleius Barbatus. Few known original copies. One printed (from manuscript) at Rome in 1485, hand colored. A copy in the Huntington library.

800 A.D. Pythagoras. Charlemagne's list of herbs (60). Most known today.

900-950 A.D. Leech Book of Bald. For King Alfred.

1248 A.D. Ibn Baithar. Arabian director of school (pharmacy?) at Cairo.

*1470 A.D. Bartholomeus Anglicus — *De Proprietibus Rerum.* 17th book, Herbs — basis. English edition 1495.

*1485 — Peter Schoeffer — *Ortus Sanitatus.* Maintz 1725 facsimile. Woodcuts from this used in "Herbs from Mediaeval Households" (Metropolitan Museum). See *Modern Herbals.*

1510 Walafred Strabo. 1st ed. Vienna. The Abbot-founder of St. Gall, France, when he was 85! Reprint by Hunt Library, Pittsburgh, 1966.

1525 Richard Banckes — First herbal printed in English, London. *Reprint, 1941, New York Botanical Garden. This herbal copied mostly from early manuscripts of various authors. 20 editions testify to its popularity, probably because small and comparatively inexpensive.

1526 *The Grete Herball.* Printed in London by Peter Treveris. Transl. of the French "Le Grand Herbier." E. S. Rohde says: This is the first printed in English.

1528 William Turner — *Herbal.* *Reprint, 1877, E. D. Jackson.
—— Paracelsus, Switzerland) Both expound the doctrine of
—— Della Porta, Italy   ) signatures and astrology.

*1542 Fuchs — Herbal with fine woodcuts used by later herbalists. In many respects a "first" of early herbals. Fuchs succumbed to that "peculiar fury which comes from overmuch study."

1550 Anthony Askam — *Possibly an edition of Banckes' Herbal.

*Thomas Tusser — *A Hundred Points of Husbandry*
—— *Five Hundred Points of Good Husbandry*
These popular with countrymen and farmers — weather and country sayings recorded. Tusser was in turn schoolmaster, musician, poet, servingman and farmer — "skillful in all, thriving in none — whether he bought or sold, he lost!" (Rudyard Kipling, in a foreword to Tusser, ed. 1931.)

*1552 *Aztec Herbal* — Badianus manuscript. This found in the Vatican Library whither it had been taken from Mexico (New Spain) where it had been written in the College of Santa Cruz.

1562 William Bulleyn — *A Bulwark of Defense*

*1563 Thomas Hill — *The Profitable Art of Gardening*
Gardeners' Labyrinth (designs for mazes). Brooklyn Botanic Garden has 3rd edition.

1596 John Gerarde — *Catalogue Arborum* — only known copy of 1st ed. in British museum

*1597 —— *Herbal* or General History of Plants. ("Who would look dangerously up at planets who could look safely down at plants?")

*1633 —— Edward Johnson edition.

*1677 Nicholas Monardes — *Joyfull Newes Out of the Newe Found Worlde.* Botanic Garden has 1925 edition. First herbal of herbs of the Americas.

*1583 Rembertus Dodoen (Dodonaeus). Belgian botanist, professor at Leyden. 4th, 1619 edition trans. by Henry Lyte.

1599 Richard Gardiner — *Profitable Instructions for Kitchen Gardens*

1606 William Ram — *Little Dodoen* (Recipes)

*1629 John Parkinson — *Paradisi in Sole, Paradisi in Terrestris*

1649 Gervase Markham — *The English Housewife*. Household uses of herbs.

*1662 Nicholas Culpeper — *The English Physician* — Doctrine of Signatures, i.e., the influence of the planets on plants, and their uses in medicine. His attention turned to the planets as governing the affairs of men by the fact that the heiress with whom he was eloping was struck by lightning on her way to meet him.

*1656 William Coles — *The Art of Simpling* (Herbs as "simple remedies for simple ills")

*1658 John Evelyn — *The French Gardener*, and other gardening books

1699 — *Acetaria*, A book of salads — Reprint, 1937 by Woman's Auxiliary, B.B.G.

*1672 William Hughes — *The American Physician*

*1672 John Josselyn — *New England's Rarities Discovered*. Reprint 1865.

1725 Maria Sibilla Merion — Engravings of Plants
This begins women's entrance into the botanic book field: She visited Surinam in 1695. This collection of botanical drawings is labelled in Latin and French.

*1737 Elizabeth Blackwell — *A Curious Herball*. 2 vols. beautiful drawings, engraved on copper by Mrs. Blackwell, printed and colored by herself. She kept her husband out of debtors' prison by this work.

1744 Anonymous — *Adam's Luxury and Eve's Cooking*

*1756 Sir John Hill, M.D. *The British Herbal* (copies often colored)

1776 —— *Virtues of British Herbs*

*1800 J. C. Louden — *Encyclopedia of Plants*

1836 C. S. Rafinesque — *New Flora and Botany of North America*. Reprint 1946.

*1846 Mrs. Jane W. Louden — *The Ladies Country Companion*
        —— *Gardening for Ladies*

First American Book on Kitchen Gardening by John Randolph of Virginia published 1780.

Modern Herbals — 20th Century

Lady Rosalind Northcote, *The Book of Herbs*, 1903

*Agnes Arber, *Herbals, Their Origin and Evolution*, 1912

Eleanour S. Rohde, *Old English Herbals*, 1922

—— *The Story of the Garden*, 1932

—— *Garden of Herbs*, 1926

—— *Herbs and the Herb Garden*

—— *The Scented Garden*

—— *Gardens of Delight*

C. F. Leyel, *Magic of Herbs*, 1926

—— *The Truth About Herbs*, 1943
—— **Herbal Delights*
—— **Elixirs of Life*
—— *Cinquefoil*
—— **Compassionate Herbs*
—— *Gentle Art of Cookery* (Leyel and Hartley) (recipes)
*Maud Grieve, *Culinary Herbs and Condiments*, 1934 (recipes)
—— *A Modern Herbal*, 2 vols. 1931
*Frances Bardswell, *The Herb Garden*, 1930
Alice Morse Earle, **Old Time Gardens*, 1901 (Chapter on herbs)
—— *Sundials and Roses of Yesterday*, 1902 (Chapter on herbs)
—— *Home Life in Colonial Days* (Chapter on herbs)
Helen M. Fox, **Gardening with Herbs for Flavor and Fragrance*
—— *Gardening for Good Eating*
—— **The Years in my Herb Garden*
Henry Beston, *Herbs and the Earth*
Boulestin and Hill, *Herbs, Salads and Seasonings* (recipes)
Rosetta Clarkson, *Green Enchantment*
—— *Magic Gardens*
—— *Herbs, Their Culture and Use*
*Helen N. Webster, *Herbs, How to Grow Them and How to Use Them*, 1933
*Louise Mansfield, *An Artist's Herbal* (38 plates), 1937
*Margaret M. Freeman, *Herbs for the Mediaeval Household*, 1943
*Irene B. Hoffman, *Book of Herb Cookery*, 1940 (recipes)
Irma Mazza Goodrich, *Herbs for the Kitchen* (recipes)
Dorothy Hogner, *Herbs from the Garden to the Table*
*A. H. Graves, *Medicinal Plant Garden of the Brooklyn Botanic Garden*, 1943
*Van Brunt and Svenson, *Herb Garden of the Brooklyn Botanic Garden*, 1943
*PLANTS & GARDENS Handbook on Herbs, Brooklyn Botanic Garden, Summer 1958
Leonie de Sounin, *Magic in Herbs* (recipes)
*Edith Foster Farwell, *Have Fun With Herbs*, 1958 (recipes)
Herb Society of America, *A Primer for Herb Growing*
        300 Massachusetts Ave., Boston, Mass. 02115
Dawn Macleod, *A Book of Herbs*, London. Transatlantic Arts,
        565 5th Ave., New York City
Craig Claiborne, *An Herb and Spice Cook Book* (recipes)
Dione Lucas, *The Cordon Bleu Cook Book* (recipes)

Flowers and Perfume

GRACE CHESS ROBINSON

I have been asked to tell you something about perfumes in relation to flowers. I've used as references: "Natural Perfume Materials" by Naves and Mazuyer, translated from the French by
Edward Sagarin; "The Science and Art of Perfumery" by Edward
Sagarin; "The Romance of Perfumes" by Richard Le Gallienne;
"The Mystery and Lure of Perfumes" by C. J. S. Thompson; notes
from lectures at Columbia University by Mr. A. L. Van Ameringen,
and notes from a talk given in Washington by Mrs. Frances Chase
Hollis, help from Mr. Charles Buckie and from my personal experience acquired through my sixteen odd years as a perfumer.

The more one delves into this subject, the more intricate and
interesting it becomes. I can only give a few high-lights, and before going to the flower fields of Grasse and all over the world, I
must go back a few centuries.

The earliest records of a people using a scent date back 6,000
years to the Egyptian and Asiatic people, who used a strong, and
to some, an obnoxious scent — that of musk. Myrrh is probably
the earliest aromatic gum of which we have a record. In an Egyptian papyrus dated about 2000, B.C., records show how extremely

valuable aromatic perfumes were regarded in ancient times and how extensively they were used. Their value equalled that of the precious metals — gold and silver. The Egyptians were the first to do what we call "Express" oils, that is, squeezing the rinds of citrus fruits. They not only did this by hand but, according to their hieroglyphics they had crude distilling apparatus. The Egyptians, however, relied mainly on gums and resins, which they got by tapping trees or from trade with the Phoenicians. At the height of Egyptian splendor women bathed in perfumed water and men used sweet-scented unguents on their bodies. Cleopatra used scents lavishly.

Now we come to Greece, where we find the great figures of Grecian mythology, poets and scientists, who wore perfumes or sang of perfumes or made studies of the "Art of Perfumes." Homer said, referring to Juno, "Here first she bathes, and round her body pours soft oils of fragrance and ambrosial showers." The Greeks passed on their knowledge of the Art of Perfumes to the Romans, who, before the fall of the Empire, used them to excess. Both the Greeks and the Romans often used flowers steeped in wine for perfume. The perfumes used by the Romans were mostly solid and costly unguents, usually with a single fragrance like rose, narcissus, quince, or some other flower. Dry and powdered gums and resins were used in houses for perfuming the rooms, scattering them among their clothes, wall hangings and beds, or using them for incense. In fact, the word perfume comes from the Latin "per fumum" — by smoke. The Romans, too, used a small purple flower which they crushed in water and used in their baths; hence the flower we call Lavender, a name which comes from the Latin "to bathe."

The earliest known formula for perfume is that given in the "Book of Exodus." This perfume was made of dried substances; i.e., spices, frankincense and oils, such as galbanum and olibanum, all mixed together. After the fall of the Roman Empire and until the Renaissance, the development of perfumes — as in medicine and other sciences and arts, came from the Arabs and Persians. The Persians made great strides in development of distillation. From the Persians came the word "Attar" of Roses — meaning essence of roses.

The discovery of the use of alcohol in perfume dates from the 11th century. But the first product we know of made in the modern way, i.e., with alcohol, was in 1370 and was the famous "Hungary Water" made from a secret formula given Queen Elizabeth of Hungary by a hermit. This has a rosemary base. The Renaissance brought a flourishing perfume era — centering in Italy. It was Catherine de Medici who furthered the interest in perfumes in France when she married Henry II, taking with her her own private cosmetician and perfumer — one René. It was she who sponsored the cultivation of the French flowers for perfumes and so helped develop that industry in France which is still the greatest place on earth for flower essential oil. However, it was not until the latter part of the 18th century that the essential oil and flower industry began to thrive in Southern France. Owing to climatic reasons, Provence, in Southern France, became the logical place. In the early part of the 18th century, an Italian named Femmis, doing business in Cologne, Germany, made a new fragrance which became the sensation of the day, and is still going strong. A hundred years later, a descendant of Femmis named Farina made some modifications of the original "L'Eau Admirable," as it was originally called, and renamed it "Eau de Cologne." Its formula is built around Italian citrus fruits, i.e., neroli (or bitter orange blossoms), lemon, bergamot, lavender and rosemary. This was the beginning of the "mixed bouquet" in perfume, i.e., not entirely of one flower scent. Napoleon was said to have been extremely fond of "Eau de Cologne" and used it lavishly — always when washing pouring it over his neck and shoulders. He is said to have used sixty bottles a month.

It is perhaps not out of place here to say that we should realize that the art of perfume has coincided with the flourishing of all other arts when countries *were at their peak of civilization.* From Egypt, China, Greece, Persia, Rome, the Italians of the Renaissance, the English in the time of Queen Elizabeth, the French from the Crusades to the Revolution considered perfumes and perfumed products as necessary to gracious living as any of the other arts and they were held in as high value as gold and silver. So we come to modern times. Here in the United States, with our Puritan background, we have been somewhat afraid of sweet-smelling things, feeling that they were a sign of decadence and the effete, rather than what they are — a necessity for refinement and a high standard of living. We have neglected our sense of smell for so long. Try smelling — it's a new pleasure in store for you.

Now, for flowers in perfume, we must go to the most important place — Grasse, in Provence, in Southern France. This is the focal point of the flower fields of the world. There the essential oils of the inimitable jasmin, mimosa, tuberose, jonquil, rose, narcissus, hyacinth, violet (and violet leaves), carnation, lavender and gardenia are made. The best lavender, however, comes from Surrey, England. Then, from a little town called Réunion, on the island of Madagascar, we get geranium, ylang ylang, vetiver and other oils. Note: It is interesting to know that the best ylang ylang grows in the Philippines, altho it also grows in Thailand and Réunion in Madagascar. Java produces citronella, vetiver and particularly patchouly — which comes from a mint-like shrub and is the strongest scent in the vegetable kingdom. All these and many other essential oils are found not only in flowers but in trees, shrubs, herbs, lichens and roots. It has been said that every plant that has a scent has an oil; but due to the cost of extracting these oils, some have been found not worthwhile financially. This list includes lilac, sweet pea, lily of the valley, heliotrope and others. Sometimes the oils are found in the petals of flowers, this oil being the most valuable — as in rose, jasmin, mimosa, violet, etc., sometimes in both petals and leaves, as in violet and lavender. In others the oil is found in leaves and stems as in verbena and patchouly; in bark, as in cinnamon; in wood, as in sandal; in roots, as in vetiver and iris and angelica; in fruits, as in bergamot, lemon and orange; in pods, as in vanilla; in gums, as in frankincense, myrrh, storax and benzoin; and in seeds, as in bitter almond and tonka beans. On the outside of the tonka bean is a white crystalline substance which is brushed off, and this is the lovely Coumarin powder.

There are five major methods of extracting the essential oils. The least expensive and the oldest form is by distillation. Perhaps some of you have seen this done at Grasse. I won't go into the details of distillation but let us say that oil and water won't mix —

therefore, water, being heavier than oil, goes to the bottom of the still and is carefully drained off, leaving the precious oils. Rose, orange blossom and ylang ylang are some of those steam distilled. But most of the flowers are *not* steam distilled nowadays, but are done by a more expensive method called "enfleurage;" the flowers are picked in the fields in the morning before 10 o'clock, or in the late evening. They are brought to the near-by factories where, *within a few hours* they are placed, by hand, on layers of fat. These fats are made up primarily of highly refined lard from a certain breed of healthy hogs from Italy, and sometimes suet is used from a certain part of healthy bulls. Sometimes a mixture of these two fats is used. This fat is laid on about one quarter inch thick on both sides of a glass frame two or three feet long and the frame three inches deep. The petals of the flowers are placed on the fat and allowed to remain from 10 to 72 hours depending on the flowers. Tuberose stays 48 hours. Jasmin takes 24 hours. During this period the flowers continue to manufacture and exhale their perfume and the absorbent fat captures and holds the oils. The fat, then containing the flower oil, is heated slightly — or melted — and then frozen in a uniform waxy substance called "Pomade." These pomades used to be made directly into perfumes. In my ignorance, I used them once, as I like to try everything, but I found, as other and wiser ones had found, that they are too difficult to handle. It is much better to make an extraction from them with alcohol. In doing this, the alcohol is agitated in the pomade and the perfume oil is dissolved in the alcohol, finally passing completely from the fat. From these alcoholic washings there comes what is called "lavage de Pomade" or pomade washings, being alcoholic solutions of the flower oils which were obtained by enfleurage. The alcoholic solution, being removed, a pure flower oil is left. This removal of alcohol is done by a process known as "vacuum distillation," which avoids heating oils up to a temperature that would be harmful to its quality. When this process is finished and the pure flower oil remains, it is called "absolute of Pomade" and only the most perfect blossoms are used — particularly in jasmin and tuberose. The oil of tuberose is usually extracted in the dark as it is especially fragrant after sunset. The flower petals that have been picked and used in enfleurage are not thrown away for there are still waxy substances and other by-products left that have a decided perfume value. These exhausted flowers are subjected to extraction by solvents and are known as "chassis;" that is to say, if it is done with the exhausted jasmin petals, it is called "jasmin chassis."

The absolute of enfleurage strongly resembles the fragrance of living flowers but is not an exact duplication of it. Each house, or factory in Grasse has a different and very secret way of doing enfleurage and each particular brand has a special character all its own. In order to guard that typical note, the big producers grow their own flowers on plantations owned by the factory. In this way, from the fertilization of the plant, to the harvesting they can control the production of the flower and the oil.

I was horrified not many weeks ago to be told that when I sold my business two or three years ago, a so-called perfume chemist was brought in who was supposed to go over the formulae and, among other things, to state the source from whom we bought the various essential oils, etc. When he came to a certain oil, say Chypre, he wrote down "from any reliable firm." It had taken us fifteen years to find the source of each particular oil that best suited our formula — no matter how reliable another firm might be, no other would do. It seems to me any layman would know that much. There are, of course, small farmers and peasants growing flowers for the Grasse industry. They bring their flowers (in their broken-down horse-drawn wagons) to a community or co-operative factory. All the processes used are very involved and complicated as different perfume oil manufacturers use various terms for their products. The whole business is rooted in tradition, with methods originating centuries ago and its secrets passed down by word of mouth and guarded jealously within a family.

There is another method called "maceration" or "digestion." This means to soften. Maceration is different from enfleurage in that the fats are hot instead of cold and the flower petals are immersed in the fats. This method is used with certain flowers that wither quickly, but is not used extensively today — except for the French "Rose de Mai," mimosa and hyacinth.

Since 1890 a new system has been developed in getting the oil from flowers — i.e., by using solvents. By solvents is meant a substance in which another substance will dissolve; i.e., when flowers come in contact with a solvent the flower oil dissolves. In this process the flowers are placed in grills separated from each other and a giant apparatus known as an "extractor" rotates and the solvents flow past the flowers over and over again — somewhat like a percolator. When the solvents are removed or evaporated it leaves a concentrated oil known as "concrete" and this, then, must be purified. This concrete is extracted in many times its own weight in alcohol in an apparatus called a "batteuse." Usually ten are used at once which are called a "batterie." The alcoholic solution is frozen and the waxy substances come out of the solution. When these are removed there is left that wonderful and very expensive "absolute" — said by experts to be the truest reproduction of the natural flower oil that man can get. This is *not* an easy process and is very expensive.

There is another process known as "expression"—pressing parts of the plants—say peels of citrus fruits—until the oil is squeezed out. This is now done by mechanical pressure, or by hand. Sometimes both methods are used. Primitive methods of expression are still used in Sicily where they scrape the peels letting the oil escape and sponging it up and squeezing the oils out into some suitable container. In America hydraulic presses are used. Bergamot, a shrub with a small pear shaped fruit, is extracted by expression in southern Italy where it grows around Reggio; also in Sicily and in Brazil.

In Grasse during the season *70,000 pounds of orange blossoms a day* are carried to each of the fifty factories. There are 60,000 acres in and around Grasse given over to the cultivation of flowers. This acreage produces a yearly average of *2,640,000* pounds of roses, *3,300,000* pounds of orange blossoms, *2,200,000* pounds of jasmin, *2,200,000* pounds of tuberose. *110,000* pounds of roses *must* be disposed of in a day in Grasse. On a smaller scale carnations and violets are gathered at Nice and Cannes, and thyme round Nîmes.

Flowers and perfume couldn't exist long or hold their scent without what one author calls "the Perfumer's Zoo;" i.e., animal fixatives such as musk, civet, ambergris and castoreum.

These fixatives have been used for many centuries. We know that perfumes have existed for 6,000 years and probably centuries before that. Musk comes from the musk deer found in the Himalayas, Tibet and Northern China. This little deer is only about 20" high and lives anywhere from 7,000 to 15,000 feet high in the mountains. So it is very difficult and exhausting to hunt them in the almost inaccessible high mountains. It is said they love music and melody and are easily lured within shooting range by the hunter playing on the flute. The little sac holding the musk grains is associated with the sexual attraction between male and female. It is located somewhere below the abdomen and the little animal must be killed to get the sac. They are becoming extinct and there is an idea that if it would be possible to trap the animals, this musk sac could be released in some way without killing them. But so far, nothing has been done about it. It is the best of all fixatives and quite indispensable in every fine perfume.

The civet cat comes mostly from Abyssinia, and I have heard that Hailie Selassie is so fond of this scent that he rubs it on his hair and beard.

Ambergris is another very valuable perfume fixative and the most lasting of them all. This, as we all know, comes from the whale and is found floating in the ocean, or washed up on the shore almost anywhere at all. But usually it is found floating in the seas near the islands of Sumatra, Madagascar, and near the coasts of Brazil, America, China, and Japan. By itself it will keep its scent for centuries. There are authentic records that its odor has been detected after a period of 300 years. In a room in Hampton Court Palace there is an ambergris perfume said to have lingered for over a century — its fragrance is still perceptible. Some authorities say this substance of ambergris is thrown up by the whale and may be so indigestible as to eventually kill the whale. It is said to come from the great liking the whale has for a little fish called a squid. The squid have sharp beaks and are indigestible even for a whale. Ambergris is very light. It floats on the ocean. It looks somewhat like pumice, gray in color. It has a low melting point but not low enough to have the hot sun cause any disintegration while it is floating on the ocean. In fact, the best ambergris is considered to be that which has floated for years before discovery. A tincture (which is the dissolving of a product in alcohol) is made of this ambergris and it is extremely valuable. It makes certain types of perfume mellow and, of course, lasting, although in itself it has a rather sharp, dry, tart smell.

Now for the gums and resins that exude from trees and roots and plants and are later distilled. These include *Opoponax* grown mostly in Persia, Somaliland and on the shores of the Red Sea. It is said to be the Myrrh of Biblical times. This is one of the most important resins with which the Phoenicians carried on trade with the Egyptians and Arabians in antiquity.

Olibanum.   From trees growing in Southern Arabia, Somaliland and the hot and arid regions of East Africa. This is the *frankincense* of the Bible.

Benzoin.   From the bark of a certain species of Styrax tree grown in China, Thailand, French Indo-China.

Galbanum.   It has an aromatic, powerful and tenacious odor somewhat like fresh green peppers.

Balsam of Peru.   Does not come from Peru — but Central America — mostly San Salvador. It is obtained from bruising the bark of the tree.

Labdanum.   Exudes from shrubs like the Rock Rose of Southern Europe and of Crete, Cypress, Morocco and Corsica where the large flocks of sheep collect the resin on their fleece. It is regularly combed out by the shepherds. Labdanum is the nearest thing to ambergris that the vegetable world produces.

Storax.   Comes from Asia Minor.

All these resins and gums have remarkable fixative qualities. Their odor is, I think, refreshing and lovely, many smelling like vanilla.

I can't round out even this sketchy talk about "Flowers and Perfume" without a mention of the Aromatic Chemicals which are being used more and more in modern perfumery and are considered an indispensable complement to them. It is said that all great perfumes of today are a combination of (1) Absolutes — i.e., the natural flower scents produced by enfleurage or distillation or some other method, (2) Aromatic Chemicals, (3) Animal Fixatives and (4) the Gums and Resins.

The Aromatic Chemical angle of perfumery is only sixty years old. These chemicals are sometimes called Synthetics — but this is not always correct. They are mostly made from the by-products of various trees, plants and flowers. Take, for instance, vanillin, which smells like vanilla, is made from lignin, i.e., a sugar and alcohol found in the waste liquors of the paper factories. Indole is another Aromatic Chemical widely used in perfumes. It is taken from those "exhausted" flowers spoken of before. When you smell indole and then smell lilac, you can detect the indole in the lilac, in minute quantities of course. It is very ill-smelling, but perfumers must use it in lilac, lily of the valley and many other compounds. Heliotropin is another Aromatic Chemical found in lesser known essential oils and indispensable in compounding heliotrope.

Let us take violet. Very little real essential oil of violet is made today. The cost is prohibitive. So the Aromatic Chemical scientists took citral, which is extracted from lemon grass and has the odor of lemons. It was found by condensing this with acetone and treating the product with sulphuric acid, the odor of violets was produced. This is known as Ionone.

From the oil of turpentine come various chemicals to make Geraniol — for rose geranium, lilac, lily of the valley, etc. This Geraniol is isolated from citronella, the so-called mosquito oil.

In other words, the chemist, in carrying out his processes in making Aromatic Chemicals for perfumes, is employing the same substances that are found in plants, that is, nearly always. Some chemicals are made from coal tar products. The most valuable come from the complicated chemical substances found in abundance in the true essential oils. It is said by competent authorities that these Aromatic Chemicals have made the greatest contribution to the science of perfumery since alcohol. The center of aromatic chemistry is in Geneva, Switzerland.

I have tried to give you a little sketch of the intricacies of

"Flowers and Perfumes," to try and show you that perfumes aren't a haphazard, easy performance. Not at all like two experiences I had. A few years ago I was standing in the lab, at one of the tables talking to some of the women workers about a small piece of leather we were looking at. Whether we were discussing experimenting with perfuming it or to have boxes made for perfume bottles, I don't remember. While we were talking, a friend of mine came in and peered over our shoulders. She was a most intelligent woman, a graduate cum laude from Vassar. She saw this small piece of leather and said, "Oh, you're going to make leather perfume, aren't you?" Another time, in the late spring, we were drying quantities of peony petals and snapdragons for Pot-Pourri. They were spread out on any of the long tables that were available and all over the floor on newspapers in every vacant corner. A cosmetic buyer and his assistant from one of the big New York specialty shops came in with some other people. They were wandering around, as we allowed people to do if they were interested, watching the women doing their various jobs — when they came across the flowers drying. They became quite excited and said, "Oh, you're getting ready to do a perfume of these flowers, aren't you?" One would think a cosmetic buyer and others in his trade would know better than this.

No, perfumes aren't made by throwing a bit of leather into a pot of boiling water, or stewing up flower petals some way. Perfume is an art, a great creative art. It seems to me that the man who has created a great perfume (and in my very personal opinion, I know of only three, truly great perfumes — Lanvin's Arpège, Guerlain's L'Heure Bleue and Chanel's #5) should be known and recognized as any true artist is. I have had two men, both Frenchmen, tell me they created Chanel #5. No one seems to know definitely the name of the man who *did* create this fine perfume, or Lanvin's Arpège. We do know that the son of Guerlain, an outstanding perfumer, *did* create L'Heure Bleue.

When you take up a bottle of perfume you like, whether it be a dram or an ounce, the mere sight of it should make your imagination fly. Not only as one writer puts it, "The length and breadth of Time," but, to quote, "To follow its association is to survey all history and to trace its adventures would be to write the story of civilization."

When you open and smell that precious bottle of perfume you spent your good money for, just think what you can see in it. There is mystery in it; and in your imagination you can go *all over the world*. You can say to yourself, surely there's a bit of jasmin in it from Southern France. (I should say that almost every fine perfume has some jasmin in it.) That sweet smelling little yellow jonquil, roses perhaps from those great fields in Bulgaria, or another kind of rose from Persia or Northern Africa, or even from Egypt, where they are now making rose essential oil. There's musk in it surely, from the great mountains of the Himalayas, and gums from the hot arid countries, or from Greece, a little bit of civet from Abyssinia and ambergris that has floated around the seas for years and years, a touch of sandalwood from India. Some of these and perhaps many, many more are in that little bottle of perfume, for it takes from 25 to 125 different ingredients to make a perfectly rounded perfume. It holds in it something to give you exhilaration, a feeling of happiness and well-being. It fires your imagination and creates memories and pictures in your mind of far away, pleasant events; of the thought of all the celebrated women of history who have used sweet-smelling scents: Cleopatra, Helen of Troy, Elizabeth of England, Marie Antoinette, Mme. de Pompadour and countless others.

In that little bottle the great scientists from the beginning of time till now have captured *for you*, as Richard Le Gallienne has said, "the concentrated youth of flowers." To quote Le Gallienne again, "Nothing so swiftly creates an atmosphere of happiness as perfume." Rudyard Kipling has said that, "Scents are surer than sounds or sights to make your heart strings crack." Surely we know that when we are subjected to offensive odors we become irritable and impatient, while if we are in a pleasantly perfumed atmosphere, we become cheerful and bright. Two thousand years ago a slave said to a king, "I see, O Lord, that you are a happy man, you smell so costly."

THE 17th CENTURY STILL-ROOM

ADELINE P. COLE

> The knowledge of
> Stilling is one pretty feat
> The waters be wholesome
> The charges not greate.
> —*Tusser's " 500 Points of Good Husbandry,"* 1573.

THE good house-wife of the 17th century was expected to be very wise in the preparation and use of the herbs she grew; in large country houses a room was set apart for the lady of the manor to carry on these house-wifely arts: this room was called the still-room, and its story is almost hidden in the closely-woven warp of the domestic life of the period. To the 20th century such a room is a sort of mystery, as it has no counterpart in our life; the still-room was a sort of composite, partly a laboratory, a medicine closet, and somewhat a storeroom and pantry.

Its location was not fixed; we may pore over old plans, read into the domestic life of the people, yet fail to find that it had a definite place in the manor house, like the kitchen or dairy; it was there, a part of every country house, sometimes even on the second floor,[1] next the bedrooms; sometimes, as in the drawing of William Lawson,[2] in a tiny detached house. But in whatever place we find it, it was here that the lady of the manor directed her maids in the composition of the laborious recipes by which she produced the domestic remedies for her household, and the poor in her parish; here she dried the herbs for the flavors for the kitchen, and distilled the sweet waters, scents and toiletteries in which she delighted.

We get a very good picture of the activities in the still-room from the old still-room books, in which the cherished recipes were kept. Some of these books are preserved in MS. in the libraries in England, others are still in possession of descendants of the writers; fortu-

---

[1] Hawstead, Surrey.
[2] *A New Orchard and Garden* by W. Lawson, 1617.

nately, a few have been made more available by publication.[3]

The still-room book has a character all its own; it is more than a cook book, less than an herbal, but it contains the accumulated knowledge of the family of the virtues and preparation of the plants, which formed such an important part of the domestic economy of the day. How these 17th century women cherished these recipes from their friends! What joy to plain Elizabeth Wainwright to get the recipe for "Lady Allen's Water"; it reads like an herbal, with its list of thirty-three herbs to be steeped in white wine and brandy, and then distilled.

In addition to these MS. books, several contemporary works were printed "contayning the vertious knowledge . . . which ought to be in any compleat housewife, of what degree or calling soever."[4]

These also were collections of recipes from relatives and friends, mixed with the writer's own philosophy as to a woman's duties.

An early "Approved Book" was the *English House-Wife* of Gervase Markham; to begin with, Markham would have this ideal woman skilled in the preparation of medicines for the health of her household; then she must have knowledge of all sorts of herbs belonging to the kitchen, which skill she must get by her own labor and experience: "When our English house-wife is exact in these rules she shall then sort her mind to other secrets. Therefore first I would have her furnish herself with a good still for the distillation of sweet waters. . . . Then she shall know that the best waters for the smoothing the skin, and keeping the face delicate and amiable are those distilled from strawberries, flowers of lillies, etc." With this summary of the duties of an English house-wife, and his large collection of recipes, Gervase Markham gives a good index of the activities in the still-room of the 17th century.

---

[3] *A Proper Newe Booke of Cokery.* From a Ms. left to Corpus Christi College, Cambridge, by Archbishop of Canterbury.

Customs of Yardley Hastings.

Arcana Fairfaxiana. Facsimile of Mary Cholmeley Still-Room Book.

Plain Plantain. Madam Susanna Avery Ms. Still-Room Book.

[4] *Jewel House of Art and Nature* by Sir Hugh Platt.

Tusser's *500 Points of Good Husbandry.*

Country House-Wife's Garden by William Lawson, 1617.

English House-Wife by Gervase Markham, 1637.

HERBS FOR MY LADY'S TOILET

MRS. A. L. P. DENNIS
BERNEVAL LE GRAND, FRANCE

IN earlier days the herb bath was taken as a relief for "edgy" nerves and tired muscles, and surely we have plenty of both in these days. An old French book entitled *Mon Docteur* gives the following directions for this bath.

Leaves of Peppermint	60 grams
Leaves of Sage	60 "
Leaves of Rosemary	60 "
Leaves of Thyme	60 "
Flowers of Camomile	70 "

These are to be dried, sewed up in bags of cheesecloth, or fine linen, and a bag dropped into the bath water. *Mon Docteur* does not tell us how much to put into a bag, but I make them about three inches square and fill them as full as they will hold.

If one is not inclined to an herb bath, one can use an aromatic water as a rub-down after an ordinary bath. This is most useful after a swim in salt water, for it is very refreshing. For this, one uses:

Sage	60 grams
Melisse (Lemon balm)	60 "
Rosemary	30 "
Peppermint	30 "
Flowers of Lavender	30 "
Seed of Fennel	10 "
Cinnamon, broken fine	18 "

These leaves can be used either green or dried: the water is usually made when the fennel seeds are ripe. Put all these ingredients into a glass or stone jar and add alcohol at 90 per cent, 400 grams. Let stand for two weeks, corked tight, then filter and add 1,000 grams of pure water. It is really astonishing to see how this will bring up one's spirits after a tiresome day.

The Carmelite nuns used to make — perhaps they still do — an aromatic water which, if used as a rub-down before retiring, will relax one's muscles and, after a strenuous day of gardening, will help a good deal toward a comfortable night's sleep. For this Eau des Carmes, or Eau de Melisse, we should have the fresh green leaves of Melisse or Lemon Balm.

Leaves of Melisse	70 grams
Nutmeg—grated	30 "
The yellow part of lemon peel	60 "
Cinnamon, broken	15 "
Cloves—whole	15 "

Pound these well in a mortar or wooden bowl and add alcohol at 68 per cent, 1,000 grams. Let it stand eight days and filter. This is also excellent to rub gently on the forehead in case of headache.

Nowadays every woman seems bent on reducing her weight. Here is a simple remedy for this purpose, given in old herbal of 1585: " To make one slender take fennel seed and seethe it in water, a very good quantity, and wring out the juice thereof when it is sod, and drink it first and last, and it shall swage either him or her." This fennel tea is not disagreeable to take and it might help.

With the modern methods of treating the hair, with permanent waves and frequent hot oil shampoos, we are all looking for some remedy which will prevent us from losing what hair is left us. In *The Toilet of Flora,* under date of 1775, we find this: " Powder your hair with powdered parsley seed three nights every year and the hair will never fall off."

Here, then, are a few ways in which we can use some of the simple herbs which now grow in almost every garden. Of course there are creams and pomades and bleaching creams to be made of other herbs but their manufacture is a complicated business and we need not go into it now. These recipes call only for the ordinary herbs and are simple to make. Try these and see if they are not helpful.

"RESEMBLING A CITRON PILL"

By KAY BETTS

❖❖

ONE of the most refreshing of all garden fragrances is that of the lemon-scented plants. "Of a sweet smell, comming neerest to a Citron or Lemmon," is a phrase describing *Melissa officinalis* — lemon balm or sweet balm — by Parkinson in his *Theatrum Botanicum.* The 17th century apothecary of London continues in glowing terms to extol the "vertues of Baulme," whose flowers are "small and gaping, of a pale carnation color, almost white," and whose roots fasten themselves "strongly to the ground and endureth long, the leaves and stalkes dying downe yeerely."

Old herbals recommend the whole plant as medicinal. It contains a little tannin, gum, and a peculiar volatile oil, a pound of the plant yielding about four grains of oil. From an early period this essential oil has been employed for its redolence, especially in France, in the southern parts of which balm grows wild. It was believed to possess invigorating properties when taken internally, and formed one of the ingredients of the celebrated *Eau des Carmes,* so largely used as a cordial in the 17th century. History records that Charles V, when in the Monastery of St. Juste, used it daily in his bath and inhaled it on a handkerchief "to refresh and preserve his intellect."

For centuries the aromatic leaves have been used to brew a tasty tea for those suffering with feverish colds. Back in the 1st century, Dioscorides was confidently prescribing balm leaves to "assuage ye pains of ye goutie."

The generic name, *Melissa,* of this hardy perennial is synonymous with the Greek word for bee, perhaps in allusion to the shape of the flower, or to the sweetness of the plant. However, Parkinson tells us that it is "an hearbe wherein Bees do delight, both to have their Hives rubbed therewith, to keep them together, and for them to feed upon; and is a remedy against the stinging of them."

A variegated-leaved form, *Melissa officinalis aurea,* is also very fragrant and with its decidedly yellow-green splash of color is popularly used in borders. Undoubtedly the long list of soothing qualities attributed to this herb has warranted its recognition in the language of flowers as the emblem of sympathy.

Basil is listed as another favorite of bees, though the lemon variety seems to appear infrequently in garden dictionaries and encyclopedias. Parkinson is one of the earliest to identify this species as *Ocimum maximum Citratum*, and to describe it as having "a very sweet scent, resembling a Citron pill." Of its virtues he is lavish, emphasizing however that all basil varieties are valuable. The seeds were among the Cordial Spices named by Arabian authors "for the comforting of the heart in the trembling thereof and the expelling of Melancholy." Most of the old herbalists from Pliny down have kind words to say of this herb and its reviving smell. Aside from its early medicinal qualities, lemon basil now is enjoyed as a spicy accent in pot-pourri, scented bags and pillows, salad vinegars, and as a delectable dash to all tomato dishes.

From a gardener's standpoint the hardy little thyme shrubs and creepers rate high as year-round mats and borders "for use and for delight." Parkinson lists two lemon-scented species, *Serpillum citratum*, a lemon thyme somewhat like the wild kind, and a variegated form, *S. aureum sive vericolor*, "the Guilded or Embroidered Tyme." Performing admirably as a substitute for slices of true lemon, sprigs of our *T. citriodorus* add a subtle tang to hot or iced tea, sea foods, salads and fruit dishes. Happily, we may dry these tiny leaves and be assured that they will retain their spiciness, even (from our experience) over a period of several years.

Welcome emigrants from South Africa are the prolific Pelargoniums. Although they are known to have been introduced in the early 1700's, their nomenclature is still confusing. Pliny and Dioscorides were acquainted with two or three "sorts of Cranes bills or Crowfoot." Parkinson describes many more and distributes them into three ranks or orders according to the shape of their leaves. Apparently the citron-scented varieties will fall into the third rank, for their leaves are certainly "much cut in and jagged."

The modern gardener's chief source of delight in growing the lemon-scented varieties of Pelargoniums in particular is the lively interest which they stimulate in sachets and pot-pourri. During the last century, when an acquaintance with floral linguistics was considered "a graceful and elegant accomplishment," *P. Citriodorum* was interpreted by some dilettantes to express an unexpected meeting, and by the more sedate, tranquillity of mind.

Mentha citrata, if not so handsome as its woolly sister *M. rotundifolia,* is certainly one of the most fascinating of the Mint family. Its dark green leaves striped with lemon yellow have a distinctive citrus tang, which is most refreshing in iced tea. Culpeper recommends "the juice of the gentler tops" of this mint mixed with orange juice and a little sugar as a favorite conserve. He speaks of this plant as Orange Mint, as do many writers of our day. In several nursery catalogues it is listed as the Bergamot Mint, with flowers of reddish purple.

Bergamot Mint Oil, derived from *Mentha citrata,* strangely enough has a fragrance more like lavender than true bergamot. Furthermore, *citrata* is valued for a precious ingredient that endows Chartreuse with its exquisite, indefinable flavor. This famous liqueur dates from 1607, when the Carthusian monks came into possession of a formula calling for essences of herbs and flowers of the Dauphiné Valley, and commenced distilling it at their monastery in southeast France.

Long acclaimed the aristocrat of the lemon-like herbs, Lemon Verbena, *Lippia citriodora,* is native to Argentina and Chile. It is often identified with its older name of *Aloysia citriodora* or *Verbena triphylla.* The genus *Lippia* was given in honor of Auguste Lippi, an Italian naturalist and botanist, born in Paris in 1678. Although considered a shrub or small tree, growing from 10 to 20 feet high, *citriodora* is hardy only in warm localities but keeps its leaves the year round under greenhouse cultivation. The leaves retain their delicious odor when dried and add a clean freshness to the sweet scents of our finest pot-pourri. Genuine Verbena Oil is obtained from *L. citriodora,* cultivated so extensively in the south of France where most of the oil is distilled. It has long been used in *eau de Cologne* and perfumes, but more recently as a scent for bath salts.

Bailey's *Hortus* acquaints us with *Cymbopogon citratus,* which is the lemon-scented grass cultivated in our gardens, indigenous to the Old World and grown for oil from the herbage and roots and sometimes for ornament. Lemon-grass oil, distilled from *C. citratus,* is known also as Verbena Oil or Melissa Oil and is used in the manufacture of soaps and as a cheap perfume for hair oils and bath salts. For a reviving cup of tea, too, nothing is quite equal to a brew of lemon grass with perhaps a drip or two of honey on a slice of lemon rind for zest.

Eucalyptus citriodora is an immense, fast-growing tree with ornamental foliage, strongly scented of lemon. Indigenous to Australia, it was first introduced to our country about 1810. Eucalyptus are commonly called Gum Trees from the quantity of gum which exudes from the trunks; the thick, leathery leaves of most of the species give off balsamic odors supposed to increase the healthfulness of districts where they thrive. The lemon-scented oil distilled from *E. citriodora* is used medicinally, employed as a flavoring agent in dental preparations, and listed as an essential oil in perfumery.

Finally we come to *Pittosporum eugenioides,* known as the Lemonwood tree. This beautiful species native to New Zealand has pale green leaves which emit a lemonlike odor when bruised. In October the tree produces masses of yellowish green flowers, densely packed in several short terminal clusters whose heavy fragrance is honeyscented.

The Almighty must have been pleased with Lemon, which He created on the Third Day, to have repeatedly endowed so many plants with the refreshing scent, " resembling a Citron pill."

SCENTED GERANIUMS

By HELEN VAN PELT WILSON

Author of

Geraniums (Pelargoniums) For Windows and Gardens

PART I

History and Classification

THE scented geraniums, replete with charm, are ancient herbs of modern appeal to gardener and collector. Once there were two hundred and fifty of them. Today they may be assembled in only about seventy-five varieties and within six fairly well-defined classifications of Rose, Lemon, Fruit, Mint, Spice, and Pungent. From the African Cape they have come to us in divers ways and in the course of time their popularity has waxed and waned.

The heyday of the scenteds occurred early in the nineteenth century when it was discovered that *P. capitatum* would furnish an adulterant for the costly Attar of Rose, and great plantations were developed by the British in Kenya colony in Africa. These had to be extensive since it takes thirty-five ounces of leaves to produce two drachmas of the volatile, crystallizable oil. But the English grew the scenteds at home too in cottage windows, manor halls, and greenhouses. The geranium was never aware of class distinction!

The earlier general interest, however, did not last, perhaps because the scenteds were over hybridized and so vast a confusion of new varieties arose from the crossing of the various species that public interest was satiated. So carelessly multiplied were they, in fact, that no botanist has since been able completely to untangle and identify them. Although some species grown today exactly resemble the paintings in Robert Sweet's and H. C. Andrews' volumes—now more than a cen-

tury old—many bearing the same names show considerable
variation. Doubtless this is sometimes due to outright confusion and the substitution of unrecorded or self-hybrids for
originals but also, perhaps, to natural changes wrought in the
species themselves through three centuries of varying soils and
climates. As Helen H. Clark once remarked, "Collecting these
plants is like stumbling along a disused road with few sign-
posts left and those still standing often pointing in the wrong
direction."

Still, difficulties never deter a collector and today, as our
taste for things Victorian returns, our appreciation of the
scented geranium increases. These herbs of nostalgic memories
now seem just right with rosewood lady chairs, pedestal center
tables, and cabbage rose carpets, and their sentimental charms
increase when we discover they even have a language of their
own. The Oak-leaved geranium signifies True Friendship; the
Rose, Preference; the Nutmeg, Expected and the Lemon, Unexpected Meeting!

In collecting them within the six classifications the odor of
the slightly bruised or fingered leaf usually gives the clue to
variety, although when sunshine is strong and the day hot,
volatile oils may be automatically released to enliven the air
with sharp herbal scents. More often, unless the foliage is
touched, it yields no scent, so if you would identify unknowns
you must touch each one and then wash your hands before going to the next. Otherwise your fingers themselves soon emit
the pleasantly combined fragrance of a spicy bowl of potpourri
and you cannot qualify strawberry and mint from apple or
pine.

Even then your nose won't always know. One day Clorinda
leaves may bring you the scent of lemon. At another time you
will describe it as nutmeg. Other enthusiasts may insist this
aroma resembles eucalyptus or pepper. Rollison's Unique, classified as peppery, suggests only mint to me. Uncertainty is

partly due to varying conditions of perception but also to the degree of oil released. A plant may emit one perfume from a lightly bruised leaf, another from a crushed one. Weather and time of day have an effect, too, and also the inherent strength of perfume in different specimens of the same plant and at different stages of growth. In fact, the scent of geranium leaves isn't a subject for logical argument at all, only a cause of delight.

The ROSE-SCENTED kinds, today numbering over twenty-five varieties, never really disappeared. The leaves of this group are usually broader than long and vary in the cutting of the foliage from the finest ferny *P. filicifolium* and threadlike *P. denticulatum,* to the large, scalloped *P. capitatum.* The true rose geranium is probably *P. graveolens* and the quality of its fragrance is unmistakably rose. If in one plant you would have quality of flower, interesting leaf form, and intriguing fragrance, do discover among these the variety, Red-Flowered Rose with its cerise flower, silvery Grey Lady Plymouth, or white-streaked Snowflake.

The LEMON-SCENTED geraniums include the tiny-leaved *crispum* varieties which resemble miniature upright yew trees. *P. crispum minor* is the finger bowl geranium. *P. limoneum* sometimes called citronella-scented, the scarcely fragrant variety Lady Mary, Rober's Lemon Rose, *P. citriodorum,* Prince of Orange, and *P. melissimum* also known as Lemon Balm, are interesting varieties.

The FRUIT-SCENTED geraniums offer an unbelievably wide variety of more or less definitely distinguishable leaf odors. Orange, lime, strawberry, apricot, and apple are but a few of them. Nut odors of cocoanut, almond, and filbert are also apparent. *P. scabrum* which is doubtfully apricot but beautifully rose-flowered, *P. nervosum* with an excellent lime aroma and an attractive lavender flower, and the apple-scented *P. ador-*

SCENTED-LEAVED FORMS
Courtesy of the Author and Publishers

atissimum, with its light green scalloped leaf of velvety texture, will delight the collector of scenteds.

The MINT-SCENTED geraniums, so long dear to many of us, include that old and handsome favorite *P. tomentosum* with its large downy leaf and horizontal manner of growth. Then there is *P. denticulatum* and *P. denticulatum tomentosum,* the pungent peppermint with its penetrating minty scent. This bears a profusion of small white flowers, carmine-brushed.

The SPICE-SCENTED varieties have "flat, soft leaves, thin and silky, mainly round in shape" and finely toothed. These include the Nutmeg, *P. fragrans,* the Ginger, *P. torento,* and one of the most handsome of all geraniums, Rollison's Unique. This produces cerise flowers of true magnificence to adorn a greenhouse wall or cover a stalwart trellis thrust into the back of a pot, for Rollison's Unique has a definite penchant for climbing. Its foliage is considered by many to be pepper-scented, thus requiring that it be included here to the special glory of this spicy class.

The PUNGENT-SCENTED geraniums, with strong, almost rank, growth and heavy-textured leaves, some will declare have more smell than scent since a number of these emit a heavy oily odor. Others are pleasant and aromatic. Here belong the *quercifolium* or Oak-leaved varieties, the gawky though brilliant Old Scarlet Unique, the bright red *P. ignescens,* Mrs. Taylor, *P. blandfordianum,* and *P. abrotanifolium.* Handsomest of all is the stunning, bright rose Clorinda with blossoms to rival the best of the garden zonals. *P. viscosum* in this class is also noteworthy for its contrasting foliage of finer texture, the variety Pheasant's Foot being named for the resemblance of its leaf to the bird's footprint in the snow.

Grown and loved by so many ardent gardeners for so many years the appealing scenteds have inherited many common names. Although these are highly descriptive and often amusing, they are confusing to those of us who would prefer to mean what we say when we call one of the scenteds by name.

Part II
Culture and Use

These sweet geraniums with their mimicry of scents are easy enough to grow. Those of unimportant flowering, like the *crispum* and *graveolens* varieties, do well enough in any light place. Such blossoming favorites as Mrs. Taylor and Clorinda require sunshine.

Good drainage in pot or garden is essential for all with a soil mixture somewhat lighter than that of the large-flowering zonals. Three parts loam, one part coarse sand, and one part leafmold, or one-half part leafmold and one-half part peatmoss is a mixture which has given excellent results. Bone meal is added in the usual proportions. Roots are better slightly pot-bound to promote compact growth and also conserve space so that there will always be room for that indispensable one more variety every lover of geraniums is forever discovering.

In their South African home these scented-leaved plants grow into handsome treelike shrubs of year-round beauty. Some reach ten feet, others form dwarf and spreading shrubs. In sections of California where evergreen growth is also possible, scented varieties planted directly in the soil soon reach three or four feet. To keep them in bounds, particularly if they are part of a collection, pot culture is better than bedding, with renewal of the soil, so far as it is possible, taking the place of shifting to larger quarters. And in this blessed climate they produce their gay little blooms all through the year.

In cooler sections, like New England, the scenteds spend their winters as pot plants in greenhouses or on the shelves of spacious windows gardens. Unless there is plenty of room, however, large specimens must constantly be discarded and spring cuttings grown on each summer for next year's enjoyment. Mature plants, according to variety, flower freely from March until October, and then indoors sporadically according to the degree of sunshine the season affords.

Outdoors, large plants have many decorative uses. Selected according to type, they are attractive on stoop, terrace, and porch, or placed emphatically about a patio. They also make interesting standards.

Whenever roots are confined, special attention must be given to watering. In clay pots evaporation is rapid. If these are set in jardinieres or if glazed pots are used, less water is needed. In any case soil should dry out, *though only a little,* between each thorough soaking and water should never be allowed to collect in saucer or jardiniere. Such neglect will promptly kill the plants.

Imaginative collectors have used scented geraniums in a number of different ways. They are attractive planted in white, green, or red tubs for accent on each side of an entrance, at the end of a walk, or in contrasting groups beside a greenhouse or around the garden. They are suited to rock gardens and also to window boxes.

At Village Hill in Williamsburg, Massachusetts, Dorcas Brigham fills ancient black kettles supported on tripods with luxuriant plants of Prostrate Oak and *P. tomentosum.* One of these stands at the top of a little flight of stone steps which leads to the Scented Geranium Terrace. This entire triangular area, with its southeastern exposure, measures only about ten by thirty feet but here are displayed some seventy-five varieties of scenteds at their most interesting, eastern best. On one side of a wide barn door at the back is a bed emphasizing *quercifolium.* Here contrasting values of plant growth and color are easily observed. On the other side is a section devoted mainly to rose types, while the long border at the edge of the dry wall, over which the rambling Beauty and Mrs. Taylor may fall, includes the others—mint, spice, and fruit. On a warm summer morning this is, indeed, a pleasant spot for the aroma here is tantalizing and pleasing, evoking memories and increasing enthusiasm for geraniums.

How to Grow Plants for Cuttings
Courtesy of the Author and Publishers

A sunny pathway edged with rose and mint varieties also affords the passerby who lightly brushes the plants or crushes a leaf as he steps along, a delightfully tonic aroma. A bit of Lemon Balm, a branch of almond Pretty Polly, or a sprig of spice from *crispum* "tucked into the belt, through the button-hole, or carried in the hand on a warm day enlivens and refreshes one amazingly," as that connoisseur of fragrance, Louise Beebe Wilder, once observed.

And then there is the fragrance of the dried foliage in winter. Who, indeed, is not refreshed by a whiff of geranium pot-pourri? The leaves of the heaviest scented of the lemon rose (*graveolens*) and lemon varieties (*limoneum* and *crispum*) with a small amount of mint (*tomentosum*) combined with some fixative agent like orris root (one ounce to one quart of dried leaves) make a delectable potpourri. In winter, every time the jar is uncovered a pungent spicy smell pervades the room, reminiscent of the beauty of scented plants in the sunny summer garden.

The possibilities of geraniums for flavoring are also fun to explore. For iced tea I have made "geranium ice cubes" by freezing sprigs of the fine-leaved lemon or pieces of mint geranium leaves in the ice tray. If the tray is divided into oblong sections, these form the prettiest cubes, particularly when they are filled only one inch deep.

A simple syrup can also be made for iced tea with one cup sugar and one cup water combined with a handful of mint, lemon, or lime geranium leaves first crushed in the bottom of a saucepan. This gives a marvelous flavor to the tea and makes sugar go farther too. A fruit cup prepared ahead of mealtime and left to stand with crushed mint geranium has a fresh and delectable taste. Geranium Crystals, made of frosted whole leaves of lemon geranium or fragments of rose or mint, are a pleasant substitution for sugar cubes in hot tea and lovely too for decorating an iced birthday cake!

It seems, indeed, that there is no end to the possibilities of these appealing scented herbs. Horticulturally, however, to select and use to advantage,

> ". . . genteel Geranium,
> With a leaf for all that come,"

it helps to know the type of growth of each kind and the distinctive qualities each offers. Below are some broad classifications made for your guidance.

Finest Flowering Scenteds

P., Brilliant, deep pink

P., Capri, crimson

P. *citriodorum,* Prince of Orange, purple

P., Clorinda, cerise

P. *graveolens,* Red-flowered Rose, rose

P. *ignescens,* Mrs. Taylor, scarlet

P. *limoneum,* Lady Mary, magenta

P., Pretty Polly (when it blooms)

P. *quercifolium,* Fair Ellen, lavender

P. *rapaceum,* Mrs. Kingsbury, cerise

P. *scarboroviae,* Countess of Scarborough, bright rose

P., Shrubland Rose, Tyrian rose

Variegated-leaved Scenteds

P. *crispum variegatum,* Variegated Prince Rupert

P. *graveolens,* Grey Lady Plymouth

P. *grossularioides,* Gooseberry-leaved

P. *odoratissimum variegatum,* Variegated Apple

P., Round-leaf Rose variegated, Snowflake

Tallest Scenteds

P. *acerifolium*

P. *graveolens* group, Rose

P. *melissimum,* Lemon Balm

P. *quercifolium,* Oak

Rambling or Prostrate Scenteds

P. *fragrans,* Nutmeg
P., Godfrey's Pride
P. *parviflorum,* Cocoanut
P., Prostrate Oak
P. *quercifolium,* Beauty
P., Rollison's Unique
P., Skelton's Unique
P. *tomentosum,* Peppermint
P. *tomentosum* x *graveolens,* Joy Lucille

Compact Scenteds

P. *citriodorum,* Prince of Orange
P., Clorinda
P. *crispum,* Finger Bowl
P. *Crispum minor*
P. *crispum,* Prince Rupert
P. *crispum variegatum,* Variegated Prince Rupert
P. *graveolens,* Lady Plymouth
P. *grossularioides,* Gooseberry
P. *limoneum,* Lady Mary
P. *odoratissimum,* Apple
P., Red-flowered Rose
P. *scarboroviae,* Countess of Scarborough. Strawberry
P., Shottesham Pet, Filbert
P. *terebinthinaceum,* Little Gem

OUR OLDEST GARDEN ROSES

By EDWIN DeT. BECHTEL

IN attempting to search the records for our oldest garden roses, we find that romantic rose enthusiasts make generous assumptions, that experts have confusing differences of opinion and that dependable facts are scarce and remote. But, as we proceed, the facts as they reveal their meaning surprise and convince us, the conjectures and hypotheses sometimes persuade us, and even dogmatic arguments serve to warn us to avoid diverting by-paths. Thus we are lured and rewarded on our way.

I.

Of course, one cannot follow the rose back to its origin. Rose fossils which are more than 30,000,000 years old show the leaves and stems of a prehistoric rose, which may have begun its life cycle millions of years before the fossils. But we regret that, however fundamental geologic facts are, they cannot help us in our horticultural search.

The first record of a rose with an important meaning for us, so far as we know, is a Minoan fresco dating from the ancient civilization of Crete, the land of the Minotaur. It is a wall painting, one of many wall-frescoes of Minoan plants and animals. It was discovered in the excavations of the palace of King Minos at Knossos in Crete by the English archaeologist, Sir Arthur Evans, early in the present century. Minoan art and culture, on the basis of his archaeological discoveries, antedate the civilization of Mycenae and, of course, of Troy. The wall-frescoes of Knossos were nearly contemporaneous with the reigns of two great Egyptian sovereigns of the 18th dynasty: Queen Hatshepsut, who sent her vessels to the land of Punt (perhaps Abyssinia) for plants and myrrh trees for her palace gardens; and King Thutmosis III, who brought back plants from Asia Minor on returning from his military conquests. Paintings of the expedition to Punt still remain fairly well preserved on walls of Queen Hatshepsut's palace west of the Nile opposite Luxor. And the Syrian plants of Thutmosis III may be seen today carved on the walls of an inner sanctuary of the great Temple of Karnak. As no rose was included among these plants, this omission may mean that roses were not regarded as foreign and they may have been domesticated in Egypt from Asiatic sources.

Pottery made in Crete and found in Egypt and in Asia Minor, and Egyptian and Mesopotamian artifacts found at Knossos tend to prove that the seafaring Cretan-Minoans visited and traded with Egypt and Asia Minor. Adventuring traders from the countries to the south and east also touched the shores of ancient Crete, which was on the highway to the mainland of Greece. Plants as well as wares were brought to Crete, and among the plants were lilies and papyrus and probably roses.

The wall-fresco of the rose of the "House of Frescoes" at Knossos is puzzling; but the fresco artists, although they painted birds and animals native to Crete naturalistically, often used flowers and plants decoratively and conventionally. Nevertheless, rose experts deduce that the fresco represents a rose foreign to Crete, and some of them believe that it may be a variety of the Damask. Or, the artist may have seen a form of Gallica. If the Minoan rose is foreign, it may have been introduced from Asia Minor by way of the intermediate islands of Cyprus and Rhodes. On the island of Rhodes are archaeological remains of this later Minoan period. And, of course, the name Rhodes (Rhōdos) was derived from the Greek word for rose which is Rhōdon. For many centuries, the Rhodians stamped a rose symbolically on their coins; but unfortunately this symbol is insufficient for identification.

On the fall of the Minoan Kingdom in 1400 B.C., about a century after the date of the wall-fresco of the rose of Knossos, Mycenaean conquerors and colonists and their successors continued to spread plants and the knowledge of plants, as well as the general culture of the Minoan-Mycenaeans, throughout the Mediterranean and its shores. Roses were cherished, but in Greek literature there are few rose descriptions to supplement the countless rose metaphors. *Rodo-daktûlos,* rosy-fingered, is Homer's description of the dawn in the Odyssey. The lyrics of Anacreon, the bucolics of Theocritus, and Greek idyllic and pastoral poetry in general glorified the rose as the queen of flowers, the most lovely and most fragrant gift of the gods to man and as the supreme delight of the muses. But figures of speech do not aid in identification. Such references are as sadly inadequate as are the typical rose descriptions of the early English and continental herbalists.

Herodotus, the inveterate recorder of both fact and rumor, in his Book VII, about 450 B.C., mentions the gardens of Midas in Macedonia where very fragrant wild flowers grew "each one having sixty leaves." This partial description might warrant a conjecture that this rose was a variety of the European wild rose, *Rosa canina,* and perhaps its natural hybrid, the *Rosa alba.*—Theophrastus, a Platonist and a practical botanist, says, in his Book VI, that his roses differed in the numbers of their petals; that some had five petals, and others as many as a hundred. He also observed that roses varied in color from pink to white.

If one searches the Bible for rose references, one finds that such references as there are in the King James version of the Old Testament do not help us to identify the roses of Palestine. The use of the word "rose" in Isaiah Chap. 35, v. 1 and in the Song of Solomon Chap. 2, v. 1 appears to be an error of the translators, as the flowers referred to were very likely the

Narcissus tazetta and the *Nerium oleander*. However, the "rose" of the Apochryphal books, II Esdras Chap. 12, v. 19 and Wisdom of Solomon Chap. 2, v. 8, may be a true rose—the *Rosa phoenicia*. This rose is allied to the *Rosa moschata,* and is one of the wild roses of Asia Minor.

II.

In the literature of the Roman Empire there are many general references to roses and to rose gardens and the cultivation of roses. No flower was more sought, appreciated or praised. The Romans not only cultivated and developed roses, they forced their bloom by ingenious methods of horticulture. They also imported out of season winter roses from the milder climates of Carthage and Egypt. Their cultivated roses, of course, originally came from the same source as their art and their civilization, either directly from Greece or through Greek colonists in Italy.

About 600 B.C., Poseidonia was colonized by the Greeks. It was on the edge of what is now the Gulf of Salerno. It became the Latin city of Paestum about 270 B. C. (After the fall of the Roman Empire, the Silarius silted up and changed the fertile land to a miasmal plain, the deserted site today of the ruins of the three important Greek temples of the sixth and fifth centuries B. C.) Here in the time of Vergil were the gardens which he described in his Georgics (IV, 115-119) as *"biferique rosaria Paesti,"* the rose gardens of "twice blooming Paestum," where the remontant roses grew which after flowering in June also bloomed in September. Other Latin poets referred to the fragrant "rosaria Paesti," including Ovid (Met. XV, 708); Martial (IV, 41); Propertius (IV, v, 61), etc. These unusual repeating roses demonstrate the success of the rose growers of southern Italy in the Augustan age. Fortunately roses in Pompeian frescoes help to determine what the *bifera Paestum* rose was: it appears to have been a variety of the *Rosa damascena,* or was closely related to that rose. This conclusion is also supported by the rose list of Pliny the Elder in his Natural History. His list is contemporaneous with Pompeii as Pliny was killed in the eruption of Vesuvius which destroyed that city. Pliny's rose of Cyrinae, a Damask, appears to be the rose of Pompeii and the twice blooming rose of Paestum. Pliny also mentions another Damask, the Carthage rose, the imported rose of the winter season. A many-petalled rose with long, thorny branches was probably a Canina hybrid—perhaps a double Alba. He speaks of several many-petalled or hundred-petalled roses. We cannot be certain that any of them were the Centifolia, because of the controversy as to its origin and the belief of some botanists and horticulturists that it was not in existence before the 16th century, although some rose classifications list it as growing wild as a very double rose in the Caucasus.

Pliny also mentions two other roses: the Praeneste rose which flowered very late, and the Miletus rose, also flowering late and of a brilliant red. These roses were of the Gallica species which will take an important place among the roses mentioned in this article. For we are about to mention an item of evidence as to an ancient rose which should be more convincing than a word description or even a painting.

In the excavation of an Egyptian tomb near Haura or Hawara in the district of the Faiyûm in Egypt in 1888 (referred to in the British National Rose Society Annual for 1930), a funeral wreath of withered roses was found. It had survived the long lapse of about seventeen hundred years. Its discovery was more than poignant; it called for scientific verification. After being sent to Kew Gardens, portions of the wreath were forwarded to M. Crepin, the distinguished Belgian expert on rose classification, for his opinion. He decided that the rose was of a single rose species not native to Egypt, that it was a rose brought to

Egypt from Asia Minor, and that it was a member of the rose classification section of *Gallicae*. It would thus be a near relative of the Gallica and might be the *Rosa sancta*—the Abyssinian or Richard rose which may have been introduced into Egypt and Abyssinia by wandering eremites of the early Christian church.

III.

We know little about roses between the period of the Roman Empire and the Early Renaissance. The Benedictine Monasteries became the refuge of plants and shrubs as well as of learning. There in the physic gardens behind their mud or stone walls near the inevitable mint-pool and bee-skep was a rose bush. It was cherished by the monks as by all herbalists for its perfume and for medicinal virtues of its petals, its leaves and its haws.

Even before the year 1000 A. D., however, the utilitarian physic garden tended to encourage the culture of flowers for their own sake, and *le jardin d'agrément* of the seigneur began to flourish.—Radagonde, the wife of Clothaire I, had her garden at Poitiers and Venantius Fortunatus celebrated her roses in verse in the manner of Ovid.—Charlemagne in his capitulary published in 812 when he was building his palaces at Aix-la-Chapelle and at Ingelheim commanded that his domains be adorned with parks and gardens. He gave careful instructions for the planting of flowers and herbs, beginning with lilies and roses at the top of the list. Charlemagne's scholar and the founder of his schools for the Franks, the Englishman Alcuin, was devoted to his abbey-garden at Tours "where white lilies grew among small red roses." And four hundred years later, the great Dominican scholar, Albertus Magnus, spoke of the monastery gardens where flowers grew "for their beauty and fragrance as well as to adorn the altars on Saints' days." Thus herbalists became lovers of flowers.

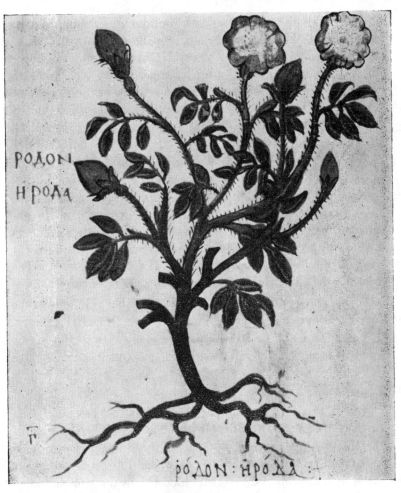

ΡΟΔΟΝ
Η ΡΟΔΑ

ρόΔΟΝ : ΗΡΟΔΑ :

THE GALLICA ROSE
From the Dioscorides Manuscript
in the Pierpont Morgan Library, New York
Courtesy of the Pierpont Morgan Library

During all these centuries and continuing through the later middle ages, the renaissance and into the seventeenth century, the writings of Pedanius Dioscorides were of great authority to all herbalists. They adopted his superstitions with his facts, many of which came from the ancient Greek herbalists. Dioscorides was born a Greek in Asia Minor in the first century A. D., went to Rome and became a doctor in the army of Nero. He wrote *De materia medica libri quinque* which included a herbal and supplemental disquisitions on natural history, materia medica, poisons, antidotes, etc.

Among the copies of the works of Dioscorides covering the herbal and the supplemental disquisitions, there are two Byzantine manuscripts in Greek which are of the greatest value in identifying a rose that was undoubtedly cultivated between the years of the later Roman Empire and the year 900 A. D. The evidence contained in these two manuscripts is astounding.

One of these manuscripts, the earlier, is what is known as the Vienna Codex and is now in the Austrian Imperial Library. It dates from 512 A. D., was illustrated by a Byzantine scribe and was made for presentation to Juliana Amicia, the daughter of Amicius Olybius. He was one of the last of the puppet Roman emperors.

The other and later manuscript or Codex was probably made in the Palace at Constantinople about 890 A. D. It is now in the Morgan Library, and is one of its very valuable possessions. The manuscript has 360 pages, of which 199 pages are given to the herbal proper and seven additional sections to the other supplemental subjects. Illustrating the manuscript are many drawings of plants and flowers, animals, fishes, insects, etc. At page 130 is a colored drawing of a *Rhōdon,* a rose bush. The roots and stems, leaves and prickles, buds and blossoms, and the general character of the rose are well represented. The accompanying Greek text does not describe the rose but recites

the therapeutic value of its leaves and petals. In the words of
the translation of John Goodyer (1655), in the edition of
Robert T. Gunther, published by the Oxford Press in 1934:
"The straining of drye roses sod in wine is good for the head-
ach, for the eyes, the eares, ye gummes," . . . and "without
straining, being bruised and sod . . . . they are good for . . .
inflammations," etc.—However, the drawing needs no explanatory text. It speaks clearly for itself: the rose is undoubtedly
a pink Gallica.

An examination of the Vienna Codex has not been possible
for this article. However, in the Gunther edition of Goodyer's
translation, drawings of the illustrations in the Vienna Codex
have been reproduced in black and white. The drawing of the
illustration of the *Rhōdon,* the rose bush, when placed side by
side with the photograph of the rose bush of the Morgan Library
Codex (which illustrates this article), shows such an extraordinary similarity that this conclusion would seem to follow: either
the rose of the Morgan Library Codex was copied directly or
from a copy of the rose illustration in the Vienna Codex; or
both drawings were made from the same original. And the fact
that we find the same rose in manuscripts dating from the 6th
and the 10th centuries A. D. proves that the Gallica rose was
an ancient rose well known for many centuries.

IV.

As the *Rosa gallica* appears to have been in cultivation at any
rate from the first century to the tenth century A. D., it is not
surprising to find it used often in conventional form in the
decoration of English and western European cathedrals. It
became the rose of *Le Roman de la Rose* (1230). The Agricul-
tura of Crescentius (1307) mentions it. He describes red
Gallicas and white Albas. Gallicas are among the few roses
in early Italian paintings. They are not uncommon in the
paintings of the renaissance. The rose of Botticelli's Primavera
is a Gallica.

The facts as to the hybrid double-white Alba are parallel. Albertus Magnus in the 13th century speaks of its cultivation and its development from five into fifty or sixty petals. The Albas also appear in early Italian paintings of Giotto and the early Sienese school. They decorate the Rose Arbor of Luini and are the roses in Botticelli's Birth of Venus in the 15th century.

For the period of the later Middle Ages and the renaissance, some of the English herbalists should also be consulted. In his *De Proprietatibus Rerum,* the thirteenth century Franciscan Bartholomaeus Anglicus contrasts a single wild rose with a double variety "entirely red or entirely white" of a "wonder good smell." This rose was probably a double Alba. William Turner, the first English botanist and the first English writer on herbs and plants who described only what he saw or knew about, notes in his 16th century herbal that Dioscorides referred to only one rose. Turner says that there are "divers other kinds"—"Damask Roses, Incarnation Roses, Musk Roses and certain other kinds." The Incarnation Rose was probably the double white Alba tinged with pink. It is probable that ancestral genes of the Musk roses were present in some of the forms of the ancient Damasks we have mentioned.

Another scientific English herbalist is John Parkinson, whose comments on roses are more valuable than the descriptions in other contemporary herbals. In Parkinson's *Paradisus* (1629), he says that "the great variety of roses is much to be admired being more than is to be seen in any other shrubby plant that I know both for colour, form and smell." He says he had "30 sorts notably different from the other." Among them were the Alba, the Gallica, the Damask and the Damask two-colored York and Lancaster rose, the Frankfort, the Musk, the Eglantine, the Evergreen, etc. He also includes two Centifolias, the *Centifolia Batavica incarnata* ("deep blush, like the Damask, with not as good a scent") and the red *Batavica Centifolia rubra.* But for fear of falling into error, Parkinson says that he does not undertake "to proportion them (the roses) unto the names set down by Theophrastus, Pliny and the rest of ancient Authors." In his *Theatrum Botanicum* (1640), Parkinson includes "all the rest of the roses," mentioning the Canina, the Briar, the Burnet or Rosa spinossima, etc. He then reviews Pliny's list and concludes that the Praeneste rose may have been a Damask (?) and that the Milesian rose is the Rose de Provins—that is the *Rosa gallica officinalis,* the double Gallica.

Thus the cultivated roses which have become prominent during our search through many centuries are among the roses on Parkinson's list, but the English and continental native roses which he lists do not come within the scope of this article. However, he also refers to the Centifolias which have not as yet found admission into the class of our oldest garden roses.

As to the Centifolias, Thory, who wrote the text of Redoute's *Les Roses,* stated his doubts as to whether the Centifolias were known before the 16th century. Thory (1824) and later Déséglise (1877) both quote Roessig's statement in his economic and botanical description of roses (1800-1817) that the *Rosa canina* is the true ancestor of the Centifolia and that its cultivation was begun in England by John Gerard in 1596. Déséglise raises the question whether the Centifolia should not be grouped under the *Gallicae;* and concludes that we do not really know where the Centifolias originated.

Bunyard admits that the Centifolia is "difficult to establish in the Mediterranean or even in Renaissance days"; and this difficulty applies to all of western Europe. Clusius, the botanist, mentions the Centifolia in his *Horti Germaniae,* which was published in 1583, and it actually appeared in Holland towards the end of the 16th century. Jan Breughel Seeghers and Van Huysum painted this rose. Gerard, who apparently cultivated it in his garden in 1596, undoubtedly obtained it from Dutch sources. I have come upon no proof that the Centifolias are

earlier than Clusius. Distinguished botanists and rose special-
ists today believe that we should regard them as Dutch deriva-
tions about 400 years old.

We have found no definite evidence as to the age of the
Persian or Chinese roses, but undoubtedly the *Rosa foetida* and
the varieties of the Persian yellow rose, as well as the Chinese
roses, the *Rosa odorata* and its related species and subspecies
Chinese roses, are very ancient. However, their influence on
western rose culture is recent, for the West has known the
Persian roses only since the 16th century; and the Chinese roses
were brought to Europe beginning in the 17th century. These
roses have, of course, had a completely transforming influence
on our existing rose varieties.

But as ancient garden roses, the forms of the Damask and
the Alba and the flirtatious gypsy Gallica are paramount his-
torically; and we must add the caution that intelligent rose
classification and also the recognition of rose varieties and the
culture of rose gardens as we know them today are modern developments that followed Josephine and her Malmaison *roseraie*.

SPICE CARAVANS

By FOSTER STEARNS

ALL who know the ancient city of Stamboul have visited the Missir Charshi—the Egyptian Market, generally known to Europeans as "the Spice Bazaar." Few now living can remember it as it was in its glory. The earthquake that half-destroyed it occurred more than half a century ago; and since then the quilt-makers and upholsterers have moved in and dimmed its fragrance with their stuffy wares. Enough of the old spice trade still remains, however, to give character to the ancient vaults, and to kindle the imagination with all the romance that clings about the phrase "odours of Araby." And in all the cities on the hither fringe of Asia, the trade in spices has had its honoured place. The part that "Araby" played in the trade, however, is an interesting instance of early business propaganda, since practically no spice-bearing plants are native to the Arabian peninsula.

It is hard for us, in these days when there are few unexplored regions left on the globe, and modern transportation brings all the world's products to our doors, to realize either the great value that our forefathers set on spices, or the romance that shrouded what was for them the mystery of their origin. This mystery was the product of ignorance; but it was unquestionably fostered by the Arabs, whose geographical location made them the natural middlemen through whom this trade passed, and who were reluctant to see it slip from their grasp. Arabia, as has been said, produced no spices, but brought them from the unknown lands beyond—pepper from India, cinnamon and nutmeg from the Moluccas or Spice Islands, ginger from China —and delivered them at the ports of the Mediterranean. And

ARMES
OF THE
GROCERS.

God Grant Grace

COAT OF ARMS OF THE GUILD OF PEPPERERS
later called the Grocers, or sellers *en gros*, granted in 1180.
A shield bearing six cloves and the crest a camel, showing
the association with the caravan trade in spices.

Drawn by Marjorie Rowell Sturm

in all this commerce, the camel and the caravan were essential features.

How far back into the origins of humanity this trans-Asian trade goes, no man can say. When in the Middle Ages, travellers like Marco Polo penetrated to the Flowery Kingdom, it was with a sense of having entered unknown lands. And yet Sir Gilbert Murray, in his book "The Rise of the Greek Epic," tells of a piece of white nephrite, or jade, found in one of the earliest of the six cities that overlie one another on the site of Troy, and points out what it implies as to commerce between China and the Mediterranean world, long before the era of recorded history.

The story of Joseph and his brethren is (or should be) familiar to all; but it takes on a new interest as constituting one of the earliest references to this commerce; and it is to be noted that the object of the trade here was, not precious stones, or silks, or other manufactured wares, but spices. The story is told in the 37th chapter of Genesis:

> "And they took him and cast him into a pit . . . And they
> sat down to eat bread; and they lifted up their eyes and
> looked, and behold, a company of Ishmeelites came from
> Gilead with their camels bearing spicery and balm and
> myrrh, going to carry it down to Egypt . . . Then there
> passed by Midianites merchantmen; and they drew up and
> lifted Joseph out of the pit, and sold Joseph to the
> Ishmeelites for twenty pieces of silver; and they brought
> Joseph into Egypt."

There is our first description in literature of a caravan; and down to the present day the bells of the camel-trains have been sounding over that same route across the Syrian desert.

Probably no human organization has changed less than the caravan. It is only in our day that the motor, on the ground or in the air, is providing it with competition; and if these features of what we are pleased to call "civilization" were to vanish from the earth, no doubt the strings of laden camels would still plod across the stony wastes that lie between the Persian Gulf and the Mediterranean. The name of "Caravan Cities" has been given to the ancient towns like Palmyra whose ruins alone remain to tell us of the trade that once made them great. "As soon as the earliest civilizations known to us were born in the deltas of the Tigris, the Euphrates, and the Nile, . . . caravans from all parts began to journey toward Babylonia and Egypt. First came the nearer neighbors: the Arabs of the desert and the dwellers in the Iranian hills. Strings of camels followed in their tracks, shaggy two-humped beasts, the northern brethren of the single-humped dromedaries of Arabia, bringing goods from the mountains of Iran. These . . . caravans were laden with the goods which Babylonia and Egypt lacked . . . They carried *inter alia* scents and cosmetics ever dear to the Oriental, or spices for use in cookery."*

We have little information as to the organization and equipment of these early caravans; it is not until European travellers, beginning with the Dutchman Hugo van Linschoten, in the fifteen-hundreds, began to use them in their journeys that detailed description became available. But the camel has not changed from the beast represented in the Assyrian bas-beliefs, the desert remains the same; doubtless if we could check up the merchandise bound with brightly striped woven bands upon the towering beasts, we should find many of the same items: long pepper, turbinth, cloves, cardamoms, nutmeg and mace from India, indigo, rhubarb, various roots and "the best sincerest musk" from China, and later, Mocha coffee from the Persian Gulf, tobacco from Iran and rose-water distilled at Basra. A description of even comparatively modern procedure has a timeless sort of accuracy as a picture of any period.

While caravans traveled many routes, and their camels may

---

*Rostovtzeff: Caravan Cities, Oxford, 1932, p. 6.

still be seen today in what is, after all, the European city of Istanbul, the two great areas covered were between points on the Mesopotamian rivers, from Bagdad to Basra, westward to Aleppo and Damascus, and the pilgrimage routes from the latter cities southward to Medina and Mecca. It is of the latter that Doughty draws so intimate a picture in his great classic, "Travels in Arabia Desert," but we are more concerned with the former.

In the first place, a caravan was a great cooperative undertaking. Merchants and other travellers owned or hired their own camels; and then they banded together for mutual protection and assistance in the journey, much like war-time convoys in the Atlantic. The camels (than which no more intractable and uncooperative beast has ever been subdued to the service of man) were fastened together, tail to head, in strings of fifty, more or less, the leader of a string being gaily decorated with brightly coloured worsteds and beads. Sometimes one of these strings would travel alone; more usually a group of them would go together, sometimes to the number of several thousand beasts. As there were no roads, but only a general track, the strings might at times spread out over a considerable area; when all in line, the caravan might extend to a mile or so in length.

The expedition was in charge of a leader who was selected by the travellers and paid for his services. He was captain, but not supercargo—he acted, that is, as a sort of manager but had nothing to do with the business side, the individual merchants doing their own bargaining when and where they saw fit. To avoid the burning heat of mid-day, the caravan usually made two marches daily; it got started before dawn, say at 3 or 4 o'clock, and marched till 10 in the forenoon, then again it was on the move from 2 or 3 o'clock until 6 or 8 in the evening, when camp was made for the night and the principal meal cooked and eaten. This means a total of 10 to 12 hours on the road; but as the pace of a laden camel is not much better than

2 miles per hour, the distance covered was not much more than 23 to 28 miles per day. If the company agreed, a halt of several days might be made in a favorable spot, so that the total journey would run into weeks and even months.

Of course many of the more prosperous travellers were mounted on horses, and they might ride ahead to enjoy the hospitality of friends in some village, or detour at their will. A most interesting feature of caravaning which goes back to the earliest times was the use of homing pigeons to report the progress and the continued safety of the expedition. Relay posts for the birds were provided on an average of every fifty miles on some routes, so that the travellers were never long out of touch.

Mrs. Christina Phelps Grant, in her fascinating book, "The Syrian Desert; Caravans, Travel and Exploration" (London, 1937), has gathered together far more of detail than can be even hinted at here. All that this brief paper attempts to do is to suggest some of the picturesque features that surround travel in the mysterious desert with its drifting sand and tracks so often erased, and that will still be read of with fascination

> "When those long caravans that cross the plain
> With dauntless feet and sound of silver bells
> Put forth no more for glory or for gain,
> Take no more solace from the palm-girt wells."

Nor is it complete as a story of the ways by which the spices of the East reached the countries of Europe and the Mediterranean basin. The whole subject of the ancient trade-routes of the world is one that has not yet had its due share of attention from our budding Ph.D.'s. Water-transport, from India to Basra in the Persian Gulf, and to the ports of the Red Sea, and the connection of this with the caravan routes, must also be treated of to make the picture complete.

In fact, much of the history of geographical discovery in the later Middle Ages is bound up in the battle for trade-routes—and not least, the routes of the spice trade. Reference has been made to the jealousy with which the secrets of the sources of their supply were guarded by the Arabs. It was no mere scientific enthusiasm, but a wish to circumvent the Arabian land routes and reach the realms of spice, that led the Portuguese navigators to push further and further down the west coast of Africa, until at last Vasco da Gama rounded the Cape of Good Hope, and a sea-route to the spice markets of India and all the East lay open to their trade. The caravan trade never ceased, but it had been effectually by-passed; and pepper and the other spices became a source of wealth and rivalry to the great seafaring peoples of the Atlantic. The Portuguese were succeeded by the Dutch and they in turn by the English, as leaders in this rivalry and wealth; and at the beginning of the 19th century our own Salem merchants for a time played an important part in the pepper-trade. But that is another story, with a romance of its own. Enough for the moment to set our dreams a-roving with those

"Who take the golden road to Samarkand."

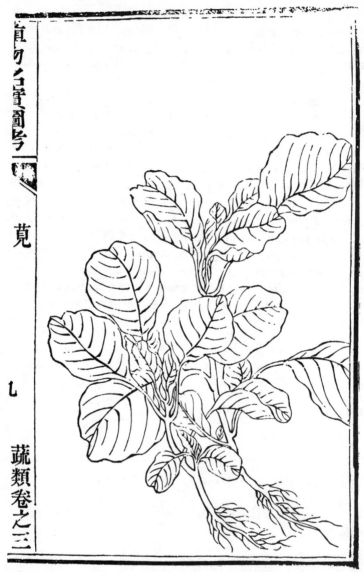

Fig. 1. The *vegetable shien*, photo by F. White from a Chinese woodcut loaned through the courtesy of the Chinese Library, Harvard Yenching Institute.

SHIEN—SOME NOTEWORTHY EDIBLE HERBS OF CHINA

By SHIU-YING HU

I

A friend, majoring in English, whose mind was filled with
lines, facts and emotions of English poetry, came to my apart-
ment recently. Her attention was caught by the Collection of
Three Hundred Poems of the Tang Dynasty on my bookshelf.
After exchanging ideas concerning the art and the beauty of
oriental and occidental poetry, we came to the conclusion that
both are exquisite and beautiful and further that the grand
period in the development of Chinese poetry came five hundred
years before the beginning of English literature. It is true that
both in the practical arts of living such as agriculture and
cookery and in certain more aesthetic phases of living like poetry and ethics, China has advanced rapidly and far. She has
a great deal to offer to the world. May the following record
about the empirical Chinese usage of certain plants not only
add some knowledge to the botanic world but may it also
catch the attention of some so that further investigations on
the what of the plant and why of the practices may be cleared
up and that a wider application may be made for the benefit of
mankind.

Shien in Chinese is very widely used in the sense of a generic
name. It is mentioned in literature dating as far back as
2750 B. C. In those passages concerning *shien* six different
kinds of plants are involved. They are the *white shien,* the *red
shien,* the *variegated shien,* the *manly shien,* the *wild shien* and
the *horse-tooth shien.* They are all common annual herbs with
small circumscissile capsules and shiny, usually black, seeds.

313

The first three are cultivated varieties of *Amaranthus tricolor* Linn. (Fig. 1.). They are planted in vegetable gardens and the young shoots are used as greens in the growing season. They are harvested before the flowers appear. The fourth one is *Amaranthus caudatus* Linn. (Fig. 2.). It is cultivated as a supplementary crop in corn or cotton fields to fill in the spaces where young plants may have been destroyed by insects or along the margin of the field so that a fuller utilization of the land is made. The plant often grows to a man's height and is thus called *"manly shien."* Though the young shoots of this plant are used as a green vegetable, the plant is usually left to mature. It is cultivated chiefly for its large leaves, massive fruiting panicles and numerous seeds. The fifth kind is *Amaranthus viridis* Linn. This species is never cultivated. As a common weed, the young shoots are sometimes collected and used as greens. The whole plant is also gathered and used as fodder for domesticated animals. The sixth or last kind is the common purslane—*Portulaca oleracea* Linn. (Fig. 3.). It is cosmopolitan and abundant. The fleshy cuneate leaf with its truncate apex resembles the front tooth of a horse in shape and size. Thus it is called *"horse-tooth shien."* The fleshy succulent shoots are used either fresh or dried as a vegetable. The whole plant is usually collected and is also used as a feed for fattening pigs. Its medicinal application is more significant.

II

1. *shien* as a vegetable: As a green vegetable, *shien* is known as *shien-tsai* ("tsai" means vegetable). On New Year's day, 1947, I saw Mrs. F. G. Dies in Michigan. She was once a missionary in China and returned twenty-five years ago. Knowing that I am a botanist, she asked, "Can you get me some *shien-tsai* seeds?" and she added, "The thing that I missed most in Chinese dishes is *shien-tsai*. It is the most tender and delicious vegetable that I have ever had. I wonder why it could not be introduced into this country?"

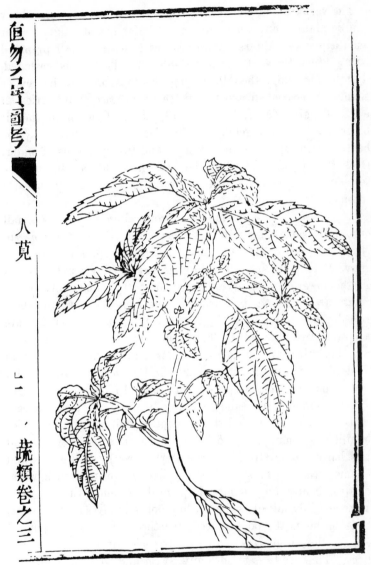

植物名實圖考

人莧

二一

蔬類卷之三

Fig. 2. The *candy-making shien*, photo by F. White from a Chinese woodcut loaned through the courtesy of the Chinese Library, Harvard Yenching Institute.

The varieties cultivated for greens are all fast growers. They can be planted any time between late March and August. For such a purpose, the seeds are broadcast in small well prepared beds. When the seedlings have 6-8 leaves, they can be gathered, first by thinning, then by taking the tops only. The tender shoots are cooked in a pan with the same ease as one fries an egg. To give flavor, brown small pieces of onion in the oil before adding the vegetable. After the leaves are wilted by the heat, add one spoonful of soy sauce and two spoonfuls of water. Cook the vegetable until tender and then add salt to suit the taste. It is a favorite dish all over China, especially in early summer.

2. *Shien* as a supplementary crop: *Manly shien* is a tall herb. Its shoots are not as tender as are those of *shien-tsai*. It is always cultivated as a supplementary crop, and the plants grow on to maturity. The crop is harvested when the leaves on the lower two thirds of the stem turn yellow. After the plants are gathered and dried in the sun, they are threshed. The dry leaves, parts of the panicles and smaller branches are separated from the seeds. The former are used as feed for pigs and the latter, known as *tien-shu-tze* (millet from heaven) in West China is used in candy making. For this purpose, the dry seed is popped in a deep hot cauldron. In China cane sugar is not common. In candy making, maltose, a sugar concentrated from a solution of the fermented grain of glutinous rice or millet is commonly used in place of cane sugar. When cold it is hard and brittle like ice but when warmed, it melts and becomes sticky. This sweet sticky base is kneaded in a warm cauldron containing the already popped seed until the materials are thoroughly mixed. The maltose not only gives a sweet taste, it also cements the popped seeds together. A dough of popped seeds is thus prepared. When it is cooled it is cut into thin slices. This candy is crisp, puffy, sweet and well flavored. On the Chinese New Year's Eve, in every farm house quantities of such candy are made. It is truly delicious.

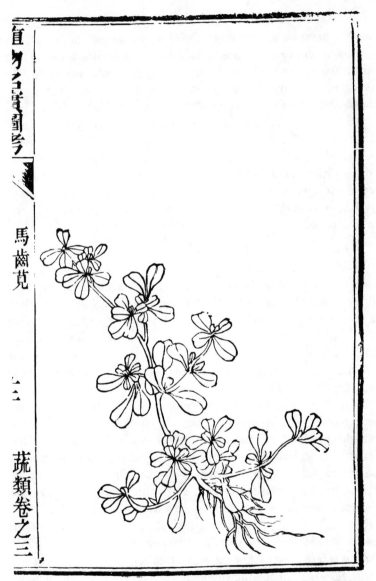

Fig. 3. The *horse-tooth shien*, photo by F. White from a Chinese
woodcut loaned through the courtesy of the Chinese Library,
Harvard Yenching Institute.

3. *Shien* as a drug: It is a well known fact that more than ninety percent of the total Chinese population never have a chance of consulting a trained doctor in their life time. Their ailments are treated by the use of wild plants as drugs. In cases of bacillary dysentery, the juice of the succulent *horse-tooth shien* (the common purslane) is squeezed out. It is mixed with boiling water and sugar and taken internally. It is said to be very effective. During the war, when China was completely blockaded and very few drugs could be imported, the juice of this common weed was administered even by some medical doctors for dysentery. Just what antibiotics it may contain, is still a problem to be solved. This plant is incidentally one of the commonest garden weeds in the United States.

III

The soy bean as a food rich in protein and minerals, the tea as a beverage found in every household, and the ephedrine as a drug in most remedies for the common cold are some of the best known gifts that China has given the world. They have touched and enriched the lives of people of practically every nationality and language. These plus all that we know about the Chinese art of living are not all that China has to offer. There are, in Chinese gardens, fields, kitchens and drug shops, many hidden treasures that the Chinese people have found to be efficacious through empiricism, the old trial and error methods which have been practiced for ages in that ancient land. They need to be enlightened by and weighed on the scales of modern science. All peoples in order to be benefited by such art of living, need an open-mindedness and willingness to acknowledge, to try, to imbibe and to develop such art of living. This is just what might be done concerning *shien*. The introduction of the *vegetable shien* into gardens for use as a pot herb, the use of the *candy-making shien* and an investigation of the juice of the *drug-forming shien*—the common purslane—would undoubtedly enrich the lives of many in the new world.

WREATHS AND GARLANDS

THERESA CUNNINGHAM

THE making of wreaths, garlands and chaplets is an ancient custom symbolizing many phases of life, the uses of which can be traced back to 1000 B. C. in Egypt. References to wreaths and garlands can be found in all nations of antiquity, Chinese, Medes, Persians, Chaldeans, Hebrews and many others. Wreaths of flowers were used on occasions of sacrifice, to convey honors, and in garlands as table decorations, the latter being considered a fine art by the early Egyptians. They were of such importance to these people that when the Court traveled it was as necessary for the servants to procure wreaths for adornment as loaves of bread for food. Love of flowers was a strong characteristic of these people.

Stepping several centuries forward, we read in Homer's Iliad the description of the shield of Achilles as decorated with pictures of dancing women wearing beautiful crowns of leaves and gold. In 600 B. C., Cato, in his treatise on gardens, says, " They should be planted and enriched with such herbs as might bring forth flowers for coronets and garlands." And Josephus has recorded the use of crowns of flowers in the time of Moses.

The ancient Hebrews acquired their love of floral ornament from the Persians, and the Greeks carried the taste home from the Eastern wars to the various Athenian cities, and thence to Rome. This later became the center of a floral cult so widespread that the Government was obliged to keep it under strict supervision. The Temple of Bona Dea, where their celebrations took place, was also a kind of herbarium where women dispensed herbs. The date of this temple is not known, but that of the Goddess Flora was built in 238 B. C.

From this time through the first centuries of Christianity the making of wreaths, garlands and chaplets became a great art requiring considerable mythological knowledge, and care was taken to apply the correct significance to each. The honors which they conveyed

319

GOLD BAY WREATH — Modern

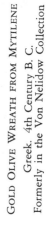

GOLD OLIVE WREATH FROM MYTILENE

Greek. 4th Century B. C.
Formerly in the Von Nelidow Collection

were eagerly sought. Warriors fought for the civic crown of oak leaves; * poets coveted the chaplet of ivy and statesmen their laurels; Cæsar's crown was of Alexandrian laurel,† the better to conceal his embarrassing baldness by its fuller leafage. As an added distinction to the honors of these crowns, laymen were required on penalty of arrest to go bareheaded except on specified occasions. When the Roman legions returned from the wars, their generals wore the most coveted of military honors, the " Crown Obsidional " made from the grasses, reeds and wild flowers gathered from the battlefields: this crown was bestowed by the grateful soldiers on their victorious leaders.

At the height of Roman civilization these floral decorations became not only a matter of taste, but of fashion, and there was great rivalry as to their beauty and cost. In Athens a quarter of the market place was devoted to the trade and called the " Wreath market."

The base of the Roman wreath was strips of linden bark, into which they wove the flowers. These wreaths, garlands and chaplets had five definite uses: sacrificial, honorary, nuptial, convivial, and for festival. Henbane, vervain and rue for the priests and the altars; oak, olive, pine, parsley, palm, poplar and laurel for the victors; myrtle, rosemary, hawthorn and orange blossoms for the bride; daffodils and poppies for funeral wreaths, and for festivity, roses and the fragrant wild thyme. Public buildings and private homes were decked with garlands; chaplets were for personal adornment. Honorary chaplets were the prizes in the great games — the Olympian crown was of wild olive; the Pythian of laurel or palm; the Nemean of parsley; the Isthmian of pine. At the Palestra where the young men were trained as athletes the prizes were poplar wreaths, associated with Hercules.

For several centuries after Christ, lavish use of floral ornament continued among the Greeks and Romans, until the counsellors of the Christian Church decreed this practice a pagan manifestation and

---

* Montesquier claims that it was with two or three hundred oak leaves that Rome conquered the world.

† Alexandrian laurel. *Ruscus racemosus.* " Though the stalks are flexible enough to wreath easily, and the leaves resemble those on ancient busts, yet the fruit being terminal does not agree nearly so well with the fruit represented on the crowns on these busts as that of the *Laurus nobilis.*" — *Arboretum et Fruticetum Britannicum*, J. C. Loudon, Vol. 4.

FRAGON À GRAPPES

RUSCUS RACEMOSUS
Alexandrian Laurel

forbade the hanging of garlands and their uses for personal adornment. Thus the extravagance heretofore displayed decreased, never
again to attain such magnificence. However, the early Christians
soon realized the importance of giving the traditional festivals, so
dear to pagan hearts, a Christian significance, and by a slow transition
the flowers changed their symbolism to suit the legends of the saints.
Lilies, sacred to Venus, were now dedicated to the Virgin; daffodils
and vinca came to signify purity and virginity instead of the short-
ness of life as in the time of Horace.

Five hundred years after the foundation of Rome, the cult of
Flora spread to England in the form of May Day celebrations, and
decoration for festive occasions again took the form of wreaths.

Flowers were felt to be an emblem of beauty, and their quick
fading made it natural to use them as tributes to the dead. In fifteenth century England it was the custom to have girls carry garlands composed of sweet scented herbs and flowers to be hung on
the inner walls of the church, in memory of the deceased. By 1707
this practice was carried to such an extreme that the walls were
dusty with dried garlands, so again after twelve centuries we find
the church forbidding their use.

These floral forms during the later centuries have in turn been
adapted to the beliefs and customs of the period. In the nineteenth
century we find many ceremonies where wreaths and garlands play
an essential part. Whatever its beliefs and customs, the human race
has kept alive an inherent love for floral decoration as an expression
of its strongest emotions.

" Ladies in a Garden, Making Garlands "
From an early 14th Century MS. British Museum

A CATALOGUE OF SELECTED DOVER BOOKS
IN ALL FIELDS OF INTEREST

A CATALOGUE OF SELECTED DOVER BOOKS
IN ALL FIELDS OF INTEREST

LEATHER TOOLING AND CARVING, Chris H. Groneman. One of few books concentrating on tooling and carving, with complete instructions and grid designs for 39 projects ranging from bookmarks to bags. 148 illustrations. 111pp. 7⅞ x 10.
23061-9 Pa. $2.50

THE CODEX NUTTALL, A PICTURE MANUSCRIPT FROM ANCIENT MEXICO, as first edited by Zelia Nuttall. Only inexpensive edition, in full color, of a pre-Columbian Mexican (Mixtec) book. 88 color plates show kings, gods, heroes, temples, sacrifices. New explanatory, historical introduction by Arthur G. Miller. 96pp. 11⅜ x 8½.
23168-2 Pa. $7.50

AMERICAN PRIMITIVE PAINTING, Jean Lipman. Classic collection of an enduring American tradition. 109 plates, 8 in full color—portraits, landscapes, Biblical and historical scenes, etc., showing family groups, farm life, and so on. 80pp. of lucid text. 8⅜ x 11¼.
22815-0 Pa. $4.00

WILL BRADLEY: HIS GRAPHIC ART, edited by Clarence P. Hornung. Striking collection of work by foremost practitioner of Art Nouveau in America: posters, cover designs, sample pages, advertisements, other illustrations. 97 plates, including 8 in full color and 19 in two colors. 97pp. 9⅜ x 12¼.
20701-3 Pa. $4.00
22120-2 Clothbd. $10.00

THE UNDERGROUND SKETCHBOOK OF JAN FAUST, Jan Faust. 101 bitter, horrifying, black-humorous, penetrating sketches on sex, war, greed, various liberations, etc. Sometimes sexual, but not pornographic. Not for prudish. 101pp. 6½ x 9¼.
22740-5 Pa. $1.50

THE GIBSON GIRL AND HER AMERICA, Charles Dana Gibson. 155 finest drawings of effervescent world of 1900-1910: the Gibson Girl and her loves, amusements, adventures, Mr. Pipp, etc. Selected by E. Gillon; introduction by Henry Pitz. 144pp. 8¼ x 11⅜.
21986-0 Pa. $3.50

STAINED GLASS CRAFT, J.A.F. Divine, G. Blachford. One of the very few books that tell the beginner exactly what he needs to know: planning cuts, making shapes, avoiding design weaknesses, fitting glass, etc. 93 illustrations. 115pp.
22812-6 Pa. $1.50

150 MASTERPIECES OF DRAWING, edited by Anthony Toney. 150 plates, early 15th century to end of 18th century; Rembrandt, Michelangelo, Dürer, Fragonard, Watteau, Wouwerman, many others. 150pp. 8⅜ x 11¼.   21032-4 Pa. $3.50

THE GOLDEN AGE OF THE POSTER, Hayward and Blanche Cirker. 70 extraordinary posters in full colors, from Maîtres de l'Affiche, Mucha, Lautrec, Bradley, Cheret, Beardsley, many others. 9⅜ x 12¼.   22753-7 Pa. $4.95
21718-3 Clothbd. $7.95

SIMPLICISSIMUS, selection, translations and text by Stanley Appelbaum. 180 satirical drawings, 16 in full color, from the famous German weekly magazine in the years 1896 to 1926. 24 artists included: Grosz, Kley, Pascin, Kubin, Kollwitz, plus Heine, Thöny, Bruno Paul, others. 172pp. 8½ x 12¼.   23098-8 Pa. $5.00
23099-6 Clothbd. $10.00

THE EARLY WORK OF AUBREY BEARDSLEY, Aubrey Beardsley. 157 plates, 2 in color: Manon Lescaut, Madame Bovary, Morte d'Arthur, Salome, other. Introduction by H. Marillier. 175pp. 8½ x 11.   21816-3 Pa. $3.50

THE LATER WORK OF AUBREY BEARDSLEY, Aubrey Beardsley. Exotic masterpieces of full maturity: Venus and Tannhäuser, Lysistrata, Rape of the Lock, Volpone, Savoy material, etc. 174 plates, 2 in color. 176pp. 8½ x 11. 21817-1 Pa. $3.75

DRAWINGS OF WILLIAM BLAKE, William Blake. 92 plates from Book of Job, Divine Comedy, Paradise Lost, visionary heads, mythological figures, Laocoön, etc. Selection, introduction, commentary by Sir Geoffrey Keynes. 178pp. 8½ x 11.
22303-5 Pa. $3.50

LONDON: A PILGRIMAGE, Gustave Doré, Blanchard Jerrold. Squalor, riches, misery, beauty of mid-Victorian metropolis; 55 wonderful plates, 125 other illustrations, full social, cultural text by Jerrold. 191pp. of text. 8⅛ x 11.
22306-X Pa. $5.00

THE COMPLETE WOODCUTS OF ALBRECHT DÜRER, edited by Dr. W. Kurth. 346 in all: Old Testament, St. Jerome, Passion, Life of Virgin, Apocalypse, many others. Introduction by Campbell Dodgson. 285pp. 8½ x 12¼.   21097-9 Pa. $6.00

THE DISASTERS OF WAR, Francisco Goya. 83 etchings record horrors of Napoleonic wars in Spain and war in general. Reprint of 1st edition, plus 3 additional plates. Introduction by Philip Hofer. 97pp. 9⅜ x 8¼.   21872-4 Pa. $2.50

ENGRAVINGS OF HOGARTH, William Hogarth. 101 of Hogarth's greatest works: Rake's Progress, Harlot's Progress, Illustrations for Hudibras, Midnight Modern Conversation, Before and After, Beer Street and Gin Lane, many more. Full commentary. 256pp. 11 x 14.   22479-1 Pa. $6.00
23023-6 Clothbd. $13.50

PRIMITIVE ART, Franz Boas. Great anthropologist on ceramics, textiles, wood, stone, metal, etc.; patterns, technology, symbols, styles. All areas, but fullest on Northwest Coast Indians. 350 illustrations. 378pp.   20025-6 Pa. $3.50

DECORATIVE ALPHABETS AND INITIALS, edited by Alexander Nesbitt. 91 complete alphabets (medieval to modern), 3924 decorative initials, including Victorian novelty and Art Nouveau. 192pp. 7¾ x 10¾. 20544-4 Pa. $3.50

CALLIGRAPHY, Arthur Baker. Over 100 original alphabets from the hand of our greatest living calligrapher: simple, bold, fine-line, richly ornamented, etc. —all strikingly original and different, a fusion of many influences and styles. 155pp. 11⅜ x 8¼. 22895-9 Pa. $4.00

MONOGRAMS AND ALPHABETIC DEVICES, edited by Hayward and Blanche Cirker. Over 2500 combinations, names, crests in very varied styles: script engraving, ornate Victorian, simple Roman, and many others. 226pp. 8⅛ x 11. 22330-2 Pa. $4.00

THE BOOK OF SIGNS, Rudolf Koch. Famed German type designer renders 493 symbols: religious, alchemical, imperial, runes, property marks, etc. Timeless. 104pp. 6⅛ x 9¼. 20162-7 Pa. $1.50

200 DECORATIVE TITLE PAGES, edited by Alexander Nesbitt. 1478 to late 1920's. Baskerville, Dürer, Beardsley, W. Morris, Pyle, many others in most varied techniques. For posters, programs, other uses. 222pp. 8⅜ x 11¼. 21264-5 Pa. $3.50

DICTIONARY OF AMERICAN PORTRAITS, edited by Hayward and Blanche Cirker. 4000 important Americans, earliest times to 1905, mostly in clear line. Politicians, writers, soldiers, scientists, inventors, industrialists, Indians, Blacks, women, outlaws, etc. Identificatory information. 756pp. 9¼ x 12¾. 21823-6 Clothbd. $30.00

ART FORMS IN NATURE, Ernst Haeckel. Multitude of strangely beautiful natural forms: Radiolaria, Foraminifera, jellyfishes, fungi, turtles, bats, etc. All 100 plates of the 19th century evolutionist's Kunstformen der Natur (1904). 100pp. 9⅜ x 12¼. 22987-4 Pa. $4.00

DECOUPAGE: THE BIG PICTURE SOURCEBOOK, Eleanor Rawlings. Make hundreds of beautiful objects, over 550 florals, animals, letters, shells, period costumes, frames, etc. selected by foremost practitioner. Printed on one side of page. 8 color plates. Instructions. 176pp. 9³⁄₁₆ x 12¼. 23182-8 Pa. $5.00

AMERICAN FOLK DECORATION, Jean Lipman, Eve Meulendyke. Thorough coverage of all aspects of wood, tin, leather, paper, cloth decoration — scapes, humans, trees, flowers, geometrics — and how to make them. Full instructions. 233 illustrations, 5 in color. 163pp. 8⅜ x 11¼. 22217-9 Pa. $3.95

WHITTLING AND WOODCARVING, E.J. Tangerman. Best book on market; clear, full. If you can cut a potato, you can carve toys, puzzles, chains, caricatures, masks, patterns, frames, decorate surfaces, etc. Also covers serious wood sculpture. Over 200 photos. 293pp. 20965-2 Pa. $2.50

EGYPTIAN MAGIC, E.A. Wallis Budge. Foremost Egyptologist, curator at British Museum, on charms, curses, amulets, doll magic, transformations, control of demons, deific appearances, feats of great magicians. Many texts cited. 19 illustrations. 234pp. USO 22681-6 Pa. $2.50

THE LEYDEN PAPYRUS: AN EGYPTIAN MAGICAL BOOK, edited by F. Ll. Griffith, Herbert Thompson. Egyptian sorcerer's manual contains scores of spells: sex magic of various sorts, occult information, evoking visions, removing evil magic, etc. Transliteration faces translation. 207pp. 22994-7 Pa. $2.50

THE MALLEUS MALEFICARUM OF KRAMER AND SPRENGER, translated, edited by Montague Summers. Full text of most important witchhunter's "Bible," used by both Catholics and Protestants. Theory of witches, manifestations, remedies, etc. Indispensable to serious student. 278pp. 6⅝ x 10. USO 22802-9 Pa. $3.95

LOST CONTINENTS, L. Sprague de Camp. Great science-fiction author, finest, fullest study: Atlantis, Lemuria, Mu, Hyperborea, etc. Lost Tribes, Irish in pre-Columbian America, root races; in history, literature, art, occultism. Necessary to everyone concerned with theme. 17 illustrations. 348pp. 22668-9 Pa. $3.50

THE COMPLETE BOOKS OF CHARLES FORT, Charles Fort. Book of the Damned, Lo!, Wild Talents, New Lands. Greatest compilation of data: celestial appearances, flying saucers, falls of frogs, strange disappearances, inexplicable data not recognized by science. Inexhaustible, painstakingly documented. Do not confuse with modern charlatanry. Introduction by Damon Knight. Total of 1126pp.
23094-5 Clothbd. $15.00

FADS AND FALLACIES IN THE NAME OF SCIENCE, Martin Gardner. Fair, witty appraisal of cranks and quacks of science: Atlantis, Lemuria, flat earth, Velikovsky, orgone energy, Bridey Murphy, medical fads, etc. 373pp. 20394-8 Pa. $3.00

HOAXES, Curtis D. MacDougall. Unbelievably rich account of great hoaxes: Locke's moon hoax, Shakespearean forgeries, Loch Ness monster, Disumbrationist school of art, dozens more; also psychology of hoaxing. 54 illustrations. 338pp. 20465-0 Pa. $3.50

THE GENTLE ART OF MAKING ENEMIES, James A.M. Whistler. Greatest wit of his day deflates Wilde, Ruskin, Swinburne; strikes back at inane critics, exhibitions. Highly readable classic of impressionist revolution by great painter. Introduction by Alfred Werner. 334pp. 21875-9 Pa. $4.00

THE BOOK OF TEA, Kakuzo Okakura. Minor classic of the Orient: entertaining, charming explanation, interpretation of traditional Japanese culture in terms of tea ceremony. Edited by E.F. Bleiler. Total of 94pp. 20070-1 Pa. $1.25